PANNE

A GUIDE FOR

PANNENBERG:
A GUIDE FOR THE PERPLEXED

TIMOTHY BRADSHAW

t &t clark

Published by T&T Clark International

A Continuum Imprint

The Tower Building	80 Maiden Lane
11 York Road	Suite 704
London	New York
SE1 7NX	NY 10038

www.continuumbooks.com

British Library Cataloguing-in-Publication Data
A catalogue record for this book is available from the British Library

ISBN: HB: 978-0-567-03255-3
PB: 978-0-567-03256-0

Typeset by Newgen Imaging Systems Pvt Ltd, Chennai, India
Printed and bound in Great Britain by CPI Antony Rowe, Chippenham, Wiltshire

CONTENTS

FOREWORD

Dr Bradshaw offers us a thorough, lucid and reliable guide to the theology of Wolfhart Pannenberg, in a way that should surely bring illumination to the perplexed reader. He patiently builds up the whole picture of Pannenberg's thought by way of a close reading of texts, beginning from Pannenberg's early work on revelation as history, through his magisterial work on Christology, to his mature account of Trinity, concluding with a final vision of human destiny in resurrection from the dead. Bradshaw's method in the 'story' of the book echoes Pannenberg's own theory of knowledge, that new horizons of understanding open up as history proceeds and new insights arrive from the future, that past events take on new meaning as more of history unfolds, and that only from the end or the 'whole' can the path of history be properly understood. It is the remarkable achievement of this guide to have a similar forward momentum that carries the reader on to the end. Bradshaw is taking the reader on a journey of understanding through careful exposition which is widely accessible and only occasionally technical.

This developmental approach seems to reflect the spirit of Hegel, whom Bradshaw argues is in fact the constant companion of Pannenberg. An original feature of this guide is the way Bradshaw exposes a much greater debt to Hegel in Pannenberg than is usually recognized, while judiciously pointing out his differences from the earlier thinker. With regard to Trinity, for example, Bradshaw shows how Pannenberg adopts Hegel's vision of reciprocal self-distinction of the persons, while avoiding his absolute subjectivity. He also shows how Pannenberg is strongly influenced by a Hegelian account of divine self-revelation through the processes of history, while at the same time insisting on the freedom of God as the God of the future. As Bradshaw aptly puts it, Pannenberg wants to 'out-Hegel Hegel'.

In showing how Pannenberg thus evades any neat labelling, Bradshaw also situates him in relation to such diverse thinkers as Barth, Schleiermacher, Jacques Derrida and the feminist writer bell hooks.

Notably, Bradshaw shows successfully that Pannenberg conforms neither to Enlightenment nor postmodern expectations. On the one hand, theology cannot base itself on assertions which are not subject to critical questioning by reason. But on the other hand revelation is also basic to theology, and there can be no 'God-free zone' in either history or science. While postmodernist thinkers might regard Pannenberg as an unreformed Enlightenment thinker, he insists on the provisionality of all theology until the end, and the openness of history to expanding meaning and all things new. It is an irony, Bradshaw thinks, that this openness to the future seems to be somewhat suppressed by Pannenberg's stress on simultaneity of time in the eschatological destiny of human beings. Nevertheless, Pannenberg emerges from this engaging and perceptive review as a thinker shaped by German idealism, but one who supplants the model of mind with relations of mutual love at the heart of reality in which we are invited to participate for ever.

I strongly commend this book. Those who know Pannenberg will see new angles on his thought, and those who do not will be enticed into reading him.

Paul S. Fiddes
University of Oxford

INTRODUCTION

BACKGROUND, EDUCATION AND INFLUENCES, HISTORICAL, PHILOSOPHICAL AND THEOLOGICAL

CAREER

Wolfhart Pannenberg, is one of the world's leading theologians today, and also a major Lutheran figure in the ecumenical movement. He has now retired from his chair at Munich but continues to write, notably in the area of religion and science. His most famous work is *Jesus, God and Man* (Pannenberg 1977b) which has established itself as a true classic in Christology, particularly for its use of eschatology for reaching the identity of Jesus, and his discussion of the resurrection of Jesus, a *tour de force* attracting immense attention from conservative and liberal strands of theology. This ability of Pannenberg to get beyond the normal stand off of conservative and liberal theological approaches is a mark of his work, and of a very independent mind always patiently looking at the evidence. His earlier essay *Revelation as History* (Pannenberg 1969a) was a marker in German theology that the era of 'kerygmatic' theology was reaching a close following the dominance of Barth and Bultmann and their 'dialectical' epistemological approaches, for which historical research outside of faith was simply irrelevant in helping us speak about God. His three volumed *Systematic Theology* (Pannenberg 1991, 1994, 1998) takes its place as a final summa of his trinitarian theology which is constantly engaging in debate with science, philosophy and the whole field of human intellectual endeavour. His commitment to an open field of knowledge, and his development of an eschatological ontology where the future brings about the new thing, are two reasons why his work is continually stimulating, challenging and at times perplexing.

Born in 1928, he was a teenager during World War II in the Third Reich and so a different generation to that of Karl Barth, Paul Tillich and Rudolph Bultmann who were young theologians fast developing during the 1914–18 war. Just as those theologians broke with their theological teachers, the establishment figures of the day, notably Adolph Harnack the great liberal Protestant scholar, so Pannenberg and contemporaries such as Jürgen Moltmann and Eberhard Jüngel found their great predecessors needing considerable correction. Just as Barth and Bultmann were part of a theological group in their early years, so was Pannenberg the leading light in the 'Pannenberg Circle' asking radical questions of Barth and Bultmann. Pannenberg was born into a secular family and found his way to Christian faith intellectually,[1] a path that is surely reflected in his theology and again contrasting with that of the young Barth and Bultmann. Pannenberg studied under Barth in Basel in 1950, before going to Heidelberg in 1951 and Lutheran theologians Peter Brunner and Edmund Schlink. There he was also influenced by Old Testament scholar Gerhard von Rad and church historian Hans von Campenhausen. The theme of the history of the transmission of traditions was to become important in Pannenberg's theology.

At Heidelberg he lectured on nineteenth-century theology and became deeply impressed with the work of Hegel, a core influence. Here a group of graduate students gathered and gained the name of 'Pannenberg Circle' who in 1961 published *Offenbarung als Geschichte*, translated as *Revelation as History* (Pannenberg 1969a). This work set out a theological programme which was to have great influence. Pannenberg wrote his doctoral dissertation on Duns Scotus, 1954. He then lectured at the Lutheran seminary at Wuppertal as professor of systematic theology in 1958. In 1961 he moved from Wuppertal to the university of Mainz as professor of systematic theology. Pannenberg engaged in dialogue at Chicago University 1963, and Harvard and Claremont 1966/67, notably with Process theologians. In 1968 he became professor at Munich in the Protestant Faculty of Theology, where he taught till his retirement, writing prolifically.

INTELLECTUAL INFLUENCES

The foregoing brief profile of Pannenberg's career itself reveals his tremendous breadth of expertise, taking in historical and systematic theology, biblical studies and philosophy: here is a polymath whose range encompasses other areas of scholarship such as anthropology and science. Independence of mind and a principled refusal to put any intellectual question off limits marks his writing. He is determined to allow reason to play on all aspects of theology so that it can speak of God with complete integrity in the public scholarly forum.

This determination to give reason full scope in theology led Pannenberg to question what he takes to be the epistemological dualism bequeathed by Kant. For Kant reason does not have the scope to speak of God, it is limited to the realm of humanly experienced phenomena. He famously announced, 'I abolish reason to make room for faith', meaning that faith is how people should speak about God, since reason does not have the range. Kant also produced his distinction between pure reason and practical reason or moral reason, and this latter had to postulate 'God, freedom and immortality' in order to help make sense of our moral experience. Much nineteenth-century theology followed Kantian dualism; Schleiermacher based his theology on religious experience, God consciousness, to overcome rationalism and dogmatism in religion. Ritschl pursued the path of a moral interpretation of the faith, using the Kantian practical reason, dividing fact from value, critical history from meaning, in his theological system. Harnack at the end of the nineteenth century likewise pursued the dualism of faith and reason along Kantian lines, scientific reason applying to the history of religion and dogma leaving faith as simple trust in God as Father and Jesus' Sermon on the Mount as the key text for Christianity. This leaves ancient doctrines such as the Trinity and the 'two natures' of Christ 'in one person' as interesting antiques from an era when metaphysics were possible, when the church did speak of the supernatural, now deemed irrational from the Kantian angle since reason had no way of talking about the 'noumenal' which may exist but 'beyond our ken'.

Hegel was another great formative German mind of the nineteenth century, and he rejected epistemological and ontological dualism of either the Platonic or the Kantian kind. If there is phenomenal world based in the noumenal, then there must be a connection between them. Moreover it must be possible for our reason to move from the lower reaches of our world upwards to the higher levels of thinking and mind. Hegel had more confidence in the power of reason to interpret the whole of reality than did Kant. If we start with the basic simple dimensions of reality, of atoms, stones and energy, we can see that our minds classify and order these things and produce scientific laws tracking the regularities of natural relationships of things. We can then ponder the fact that our minds can reason in this way to move from objects to their patterns and scientific laws; we can reason about our capacity to reason about the phenomenon of mind and its power to understand the world. This however raises the question of how our minds do reason and raises the issue of mind behind our minds, overarching mind, the absolute mind. Hegel follows this route philosophically to argue for infinite mind or the spirit behind the whole of reality. Finite and infinite are related and not sundered. Christianity teaches this truth but in picture language, the infinite cohering with the finite in the story of the incarnation where infinite spirit realizes itself in finite conditions. Mind unfolds itself in finite history and we can ponder this process philosophically, but also have its story form in the Christian faith. Karl Marx took up Hegel's way of thinking about history, but removed the absolute spirit from it, retaining the dialectical shape of thesis, antithesis leading to new synthesis, as the way history goes forward. Hegel has profound insights as to the human subject needing to move outside itself to immerse itself into 'the other' in order truly to be itself.

His absolute spirit principle or mind, *Geist*, expounds itself self-creatively as the world, transposing its absoluteness into the relative, differentiating itself into the other, freedom becoming necessity in a dialectical self-communication. Opposites are only opposite because of their unity, there can be no distinction unless there is a prior commonality by which distinction can be made. This is the shape of logic for Hegel, it is temporal, realizing itself through time dialectically, concept amending concept, events succeeding events. We are realizing our freedom, but yet there are hidden conditionings beneath our choices making freedom and necessity not total opposites after all. The self-diversification of *Geist* into finitude accounts for our reason, and our consciousness of being ourselves in awareness of others, of losing ourselves to find ourselves. For Hegel the study of history is getting to know the nature of *Geist*, and the state of being rational is *Geist* or Mind objectified, the real and the rational are at one, in their differentiation. In his *Phenomenology* (Hegel 1977) Hegel shows that all human intellectual development is the outworking of *Geist's* coming to know itself, revealing itself to itself, a necessary process of unfolding through human consciousness, the infinite realizing itself as finite. 'Absolute idealism' is the phrase used to describe the family of philosophy following this kind of description of reality and thought, or 'objective idealism' in contrast to the 'subjective idealism' of Kant, rooted in the power of reason of the human mind and not outside it. Pannenberg takes up core ideas of Hegel in constructing his own theological system and so some basic knowledge of Hegel's thought is helpful in understanding Pannenberg. This German intellectual background is now strange to the English speaking cultures with its dominant empiricist philosophical tendency. This was not always so and Hegel had considerable theological influence on English and Scottish philosophy theology in the late nineteenth and early twentieth centuries.[2]

The fiercest critic of Hegelianism in the nineteenth century was Kierkegaard who protested at what he took to be Hegel's all encompassing system and its absorption of the free, particular individual. Kierkegaard rejected the reasonableness of faith and instead proclaimed that we need to take the leap of faith, without any aids of reason, trusting entirely in God. Here again we have a duality of faith over against reason, a rejection of the coordination or synthesis of the two. Theologically the duality of God and the world, of faith over against reason, was taken up in and after World War I by the dialectical theologies of Barth and Bultmann. Barth, like Harnack, operated a Kantian epistemological dualism of reason and faith, but unlike Harnack and Kant, Barth affirmed the inbreaking of the divine holy love in Christ, an act of revelation, enabling us to speak of God. This dialectical theology held the field of German systematic theology for decades. As Barth later said, he felt he needed to close the doors and windows of the theological house since they were banging uncontrollably as a result of the winds of outside culture. Theology needed to recover its own thought and its proper content, faith and God who discloses himself. Pannenberg represents the reverse of this movement after World War II: he rejects the shutting off of theology from the fresh air of secular cultural developments and has opened the doors and windows again. For Pannenberg there is one reality and one reason.

Looking back at the development of German thought since the Enlightenment we can see the figures of Kant and Hegel as dominating influences whose intellectual orientations have shaped and continue to shape theology. We could add Kierkegaard and Marx to that pairing as thinkers of certain contrasting casts of mind.

These two types seemingly oscillate in influence between generations. John Macquarrie speaks of the 'Hegel Marx Bloch' line of thought over against the 'Kierkegaard Nietzsche Heidegger' line as two decisive theological influences from the nineteenth century, still shaping contemporary theology (Macquarrie 1981: 393). While this is a rough distinction it points to the different sources and ways that theologians and philosophers have found most meaningful in speaking of God. The Hegelian tradition sees the Spirit at work through all history unfolding meaning and truth as we trace it rationally in our fragmentary way, while the Kierkegaardian way is to look at ourselves as individuals who must choose to have faith and to go beyond mere reason and seek God, or ultimate meaning, in our personal act of faith. This latter family of theology follows Kant in denying that reason can take us to God since God is beyond our powers of thought, whereas the Hegelian line argues that reason if followed accurately will take us to the source and sustainer of all things. The Kierkegaardian is 'fideistic', trusting to faith and relishing its paradoxes, whereas the Hegelian seeks rational continuities between the individual and the universal, the historical and the ideal. The former believes that God broke into history at the 'mathematical point' of Christ, and that our faith has this episodic character as grace breaks in upon us time and again, the needle into the cloth of history; the latter Hegelian line envisaged God as Spirit throughout the whole process of history as a gradual unfolding and development of meaning.

Pannenberg wishes to do justice to the deep significance of history and reason, taking the Old Testament history of tradition seriously, following von Rad's influence, and also wants to maintain personal faith but which has reasonable credentials and is not flying in the face of what is rational. In the history of theology Pannenberg represents a turn towards a new appreciation of Hegel, a turn now thought by many to have been much needed, albeit a turn which seeks to incorporate other insights which offset some problems entailed with Hegel for Christian thought. We will try to explain how he attempts this as we unfold his thought through the book. In Pannenberg we have a very independent mind indeed, a theologian who wants Christianity to have itself at the table of public intellectual discussion and be taken seriously for its suggestions as rational and persuasive – this goal makes him a very significant theologian for the churches. He is also a Protestant who is wholly unafraid of criticizing his traditions and being open to all others, when they can support their claims reasonably. He is a theologian who uses 'liberal' methods and yet can reach 'conservative' conclusions, notably on the resurrection of Jesus, Christology and the Trinity. There is no doubt that an engagement with Pannenberg's texts provides a rich theological education in itself, even for those not finally settling for all his conclusions about reality, truth and God, and he is almost certainly the theologian most willing to place Christian theology into the public forum as the most credible hypothesis for shaping human history, as Christiaan Mostert says, 'he exemplifies the role of the public theologian' (Mostert 2002: 238).

CHAPTER 1

HUMAN ORIENTATION IN HISTORY

FOCUSED TEXTS:
BASIC QUESTIONS IN THEOLOGY

REASONABLE FAITH

Pannenberg's concern for a theology which accepts reason as valid for faith and secular thought means that he needs to produce a convincing claim for the reality of God, a claim that commands credibility in the secular as well as sacred constituencies. At the same time, as a theologian, his notion of God has to be such that we know of God by the revelation of God, otherwise we would not be considering God in his majesty and glory: this itself is a rational claim, given the concept of God. Christian theology articulates the concept of God in such a way that this speech commands the respect of secular thinkers as well as those of faith. The concept of God has to have a power of interpreting reality within the experience of human beings or rather as they experience life, it has to have an explanatory potential rather than being an absurdity calling for a leap of faith. We might say that Pannenberg calls for a reasonable doctrine of God convincing for today's world. This means that Pannenberg regards the 'scripture principle' (Pannenberg 1970b: 1), that is, the principle that Scripture is itself a revealed and inspired text telling us revealed truths in propositional statements, as now defunct in the light of post-Enlightenment critical studies. It is, he thinks, irresponsible to call modern people to believe in the literal and inspired truth of the texts as such, but the 'essential content' of what the texts are saying, the truth of Jesus Christ and his God, should be the focus of faith and of theology. Modernity has reacted against authoritarian claims for biblical texts: 'Theology can do justice to this situation only if it succeeds in bringing modern thought again into a more conscious connection with Christian tradition' (Pannenberg 1970b: 10).

The truth of this essential content is authoritative for the church, at least until any new contrary evidence occurs, the church faces challenges of interpretation for each generation as new questions arise. The themes and concepts found in Scripture need to be understood and explicated in their contexts so as to generate powerful explanations of our human experience today. The truth of Christian doctrine is the theme of systematic theology, says Pannenberg, that is to say this truth needs constantly to be established reasonably in the public forum and in the university faculties of theology, rather than being merely asserted a priori. This is a matter 'of the universal coherence and therefore the truth of Christian doctrine' (Pannenberg 1991: 49), universal coherence being a key criterion for the truth of the Christian claim, indeed for the truth of truth itself, an important assumption for Pannenberg.

Pannenberg takes issue with those who regard the concept of God as of no public significance, and he argues to the contrary that the God being pointed to has to be shown to provide a basis for our human social and individual experience of reality, and one of the radical facets of his thought is that he upholds, on rational grounds, the plausibility of Christianity not merely as true for its adherents but as the key to understanding world history and reality. This he argues with secular thinkers who should take the Christian thesis seriously, as seriously, for example, as the secular liberal or Marxist world views. If Christianity is true, then it is true universally and it needs to be examined rationally and regularly. For Pannenberg reason is universal and globally applicable, for science, history and theology, and it must be able to test all truth claims for their coherence with accepted norms developed across the intellectual disciplines. God is the God of all reality and of the truth discovered and developed by all human reasoning.

Pannenberg in his own way takes up the task set by Schleiermacher in this theological project of commending the faith to the cultured despisers of religion, the rationalists who rejected God as unreal and inconceivable. Like Schleiermacher, Pannenberg wishes to ground faith and theology anew, away from authoritarian supernaturalism asserted by church dogma. Pannenberg tells theology that it cannot avoid reasoned debate about its claims with the secular world and it cannot hide by claiming a special authority giving it privileged access to its own sphere of truth. Unlike Schleiermacher, however, Pannenberg did not take up the path of religious feeling as the way between secular rationalism and churchly authoritarianism. Rather for Pannenberg the key category for faith and theology is not subjective feeling but history. Christianity, he argues, must be responsible and adult, must come of age in our era of rational self-consciousness and of the need for evidence on which commitment can be made. That is not to say such evidence cannot be found, indeed Panneberg argues that he has found it and wishes to argue the Christian case in the public arena of rational debate because Christianity is the best explanation we have for our modern experience of the world.

WHAT IS TRUTH?

Pannenberg turned away from the dominant kerygmatic model of the theology of the Word being spoken to us as unquestionable revelation, in order to allow secular questions to impinge on the content of faith. Modern humanity is conscious of being in history and of history, and Pannenberg argues that the Hebraic tradition, merging with Greek philosophical thought in the emergence of Christianity, was the key driver in bringing this historical self-consciousness about. Truth is not simply fixed and eternal, but has an historical character as events move on and new dimensions are experienced by human beings and new meanings come about, changing our understandings and developing them.

The question of truth itself is crucial for Christianity in Pannenberg's view as is seen in some of his early essays in *Basic Questions in Theology*. He begins his essay 'What is Truth?' with the statement: 'The question concerning the essence of truth touches a profound crisis not only of theology but also of the Christian church and Christian faith generally in the present age' (Pannenberg 1971a: 1). This question of truth, for Pannenberg, is of universal truth and the power of Christian faith to encompass all reality, including the issues raised by science and technology. Faith must embrace coherently the reality of life we experience. For Pannenberg 'the question regarding the truth of the Christian faith is not concerned with a particular truth of one kind or another but with truth itself, which in essence can only be one. It asks whether the Christian faith still contains the truth that gathers together everything that is experienced as real' (Pannenberg 1971a: 1). That is why we need to attend to the whole of reality we experience, and if this is not done then Christianity will end up as an interesting historical phenomenon. The question about the truth of the Christian faith therefore must concern itself with the whole truth, and not only with Jesus Christ as the truth, since that would cut away much important experience of the world and so the wholeness and unity of the truth. Christian theology cannot escape the kinds of questions raised for it by disciplines such as philosophy. Pannenberg's view of truth is very much a coherence view.

Pannenberg traces the history of thought about truth, and the history of human experience of truth, comparing and contrasting the Greek understanding of the essence of truth with the Israelitic view of truth as bound with history and the freedom of God as the source of all truth. Greek dualism of true being over against the world of changing sense appearances is superseded by the Hebrew view of truth not as timeless but as historical, so that 'it proves its stability through a history whose future is always open' (Pannenberg 1971a: 9). God is not to be grasped or perceived directly in history and yet is seen as we look back in retrospect in new ways at different phases of history. God distinguishes himself from present reality, acting freely anew, and this freedom Pannenberg argues, suggests a personal mode of divine presence since persons alone are free and not manipulable. This claim to truth, for Christianity, must prove itself in today's world in the critical debates it finds itself faced with, theology cannot operate with a dualistic but only a holistic view of reason and truth.

The understanding of truth in the West developed, says Pannenberg, from that of the static imprinting of truth on the passive recipient soul, the Greek tendency, towards that of the creative act of human beings. This historical move led to the turn to the subjectivizing of truth, since it became easy to merge the human creative act with truth itself: 'It seemed as if the subject, the understanding reason considered as creative, must regard itself as the source of truth.' (Pannenberg 1971a: 13) As so often, Pannenberg's incisive analysis and commentary on the history of culture and thought lights up the modern situation with great insight and accuracy: what interests the modern mind is not 'the' truth so much as 'my own' truth, is the essence of his statement. The Christian theological understanding of human thinking and truth is one of constructive creativity, as entailed in the theological phrase 'imago dei', since this puts humanity in the position of being the active ruler of the world rather than being merely the passive recipient of truth. Humanity is to engage in transforming the world with reason uncovering truth.

Pannenberg's mapping of the development of our historical consciousness of being in time claims that the rise of experimental science has its roots in the doctrine of creation, that we are given charge of the world, and freely construct hypotheses and then try to test them. Modern historical method has a similar structure, developing a picture of how things happened then seeking corroborative or negating evidence, a creative reasoning process proceeding through the flow of time. Pannenberg understands that our experience of truth requires a presupposition of the unity of truth, which is God – just as Kant postulated the concept of God to make sense of our moral experience and find a commonality for human behaviour universally:

> The agreement of human thought with extrahuman reality, and thus its truth, is possible only on the presupposition of God. Even the fact that natural science and technology find such agreement to be confirmed again and again is anything but self-explanatory in view of the creative autonomy of their thinking. Without the presupposition of God, truth is no longer conceivable in terms of agreement. (Pannenberg 1971a: 18)

The human experience of truth leads Pannenberg to track the presupposition of God and the unity of truth as basic – as an anthropological necessity to the development of our reasoning – and our ability to construct and interpret the world as a unity rather than chaos of diverse experiences.

But we live in history and many cultures have had their own particular understandings of truth in the past, and our present age will pass, raising the question of change and relativity of truth because of the passing of time. We cannot absolutize any one era or indeed our own now. The unity of truth can now only be thought of as the history of truth, meaning in effect that truth itself has a history and that its essence is the process of this history. Therefore Pannenberg asserts: 'Historical change itself must be thought of as the essence of truth if its unity is still to be maintained without narrow-mindedly substituting a particular perspective for the whole of truth' (Pannenberg 1971a: 20–1). At this stage in the essay, 'What is Truth?', which we are following, Pannenberg turns directly to Hegel. For Hegel the truth is not a finished entity, but a process in which each stage drives itself beyond itself to the next, taking up the past into the present so that the whole of history is the truth. The outcome of history, embracing all contradictions, is the Absolute for Hegel, the absolute God. The meaning of this journey is the truth itself.

This view of history, meaning and truth has connections with the biblical understanding of truth, in that it sees truth not as time-lessly unchangeable but as a history maintaining itself through change. As Newman puts it, here below to be perfect is to have changed often. Also this Hegelian view sees the whole of history as revealing the truth of the unity of all things, in all their conflicts and contradictions. The standpoint of the end of history, the eschatological point, gives this view of the whole. The future is crucial to what something really is, not just the past. Pannenberg criticizes Hegel at this point for failing to understand that the future remains open until the end and is not closed and finalized now. The biblical tradition, with its radical eschatological message, can again break in and give us a fresh understanding that the future is key to the truth as we journey on in history towards it. The early Christian disciples were led, as a result of the resurrection of Jesus, to trust in the newly arriving God, the God who comes to us in history from the future which is open in character and not final-ized, not pinned down in a concept. The resurrection of Christ pushes us beyond mere conceptualizing to trust in the God of the open future. In Jesus' resurrection the end time dawned in a pre-liminary way, and post-Easter disciples faced the future as open, history was not frozen by the Christ event, they went ahead in trust, at one with Jesus. The actual meaning of the resurrection was not known, Pannenberg says it is a metaphor of rising from sleep, an expression of human hope in the face of death. Jesus trusted in God and was vindicated by God at the resurrection, and yet the full content of this event, its full meaning, is still to be given at the end of history, is still on its way from the future as we jour-ney towards it, towards God.

The Absolute has come and yet the future is still open, we could say, because of the 'proleptic', or anticipatory, structure of our history. The Absolute is the all-including whole, running through all history, taking up the past and bringing its meaning forward in ever greater richness. Here indeed is a great difference between the Greek view of the Absolute or Logos as timeless truth, and the Hebraic historical, narrative view of truth through history with its changes and chances. Pannenberg believes that this biblical insight and tradition of experiencing reality overcomes Hegel's problem of bringing the developing meaning of history to a premature end in the concept of his philosophy of history. For Pannenberg,

> because of the proleptic character of his destiny, what happened to Jesus then is, at the same time, for us always the open future toward which we go out. The unsurpassability of the Christ event is thereby expressed in a manner much sharper than Hegel . . . was able to manage, since for him the Christ event was certainly something belonging to the closed past, which might at best still continue to operate in the present in the spirit, in concept, but could by no means be a still-open future. (Pannenberg 1971a: 25)

We should note also that the 'contingency' of events – their being not simply determined from the past but particular, individual and free rather than fixed, systematized and necessary – rests on this pattern of history and its open-textured structure moving towards God, from whom it receives its life and freedom. An English philosopher of history produced an astonishingly close description of this historical character of reality and truth to that of Pannenberg. E. H. Carr writes:

> The absolute in history is not something in the past from which we start; it is not something in the present, since all present thinking is necessarily relative. It is something still incomplete and in the process of becoming – something in the future towards which we move, which begins to take shape as we move towards it, and in the light of which, as we move forward, we gradually shape the interpretation of the past. (Carr 1961: 121)

This is exactly the shape of Pannenberg's view of reason and truth in history, probing forward and finding light from the future which we anticipate and hypothesize about, or as a sonar ray is pushed out towards the sea bed and finds orientation through its reflection back. As we move forward, so we find light which lights up what is true, and what falls away is false; similarly new ideas form and in turn are tested, probed and themselves become lit up and verified, or otherwise disappear in the flow of history. The 'absolute' becomes clearer in and through our probing dialectical questioning, a hermeneutical process moving ahead tentatively to grasp what will make sense of the past as new light occurs to us. As Carr and Pannenberg emphasize, 'it is still incomplete and in the process of becoming', the process goes on, it has not stopped and finalized itself, although for the Christian thinker, Pannenberg, the resurrection of Christ assures us of the light coming towards us which we can trust as Jesus did – yet the full meaning of this resurrection, an event but with a metaphorical character not a cut-and-dried concept, continues to develop and grow richer. It is fascinating that Carr, an atheist thinker, also realizes that the Jewish-Christian eschatological picture serves to symbolize his description of how the meaning of history unfolds. The passage quoted above continues directly by saying, 'This is the secular truth behind the religious myth that the meaning of history will be revealed in the Day of Judgement' (Carr 1961: 121).

Carr sees that the final eschatological moment of divine decision will, in Christian theology, disclose the truth of things, and that this is proleptically happening as the truth shapes itself gradually in the process of discerning the meaning of events in the past as we move ahead. The final meaning of things awaits and is not completed now. Carr, like Pannenberg, sees Hegel making the 'the cardinal error of bringing the course of history to an end in the present instead of projecting it into the future' (Carr 1961: 121). The resurrection of Jesus is the event anticipating the ultimate end of history and so disclosing its whole truth, and yet this resurrection is itself still 'open' and enriching its meaning as we move forward into the future, bringing past truth with us and forging ever new syntheses, which in turn are tried and tested and reconfigured.

Pannenberg ends this essay 'What is Truth?' by claiming that the apocalyptic tradition and its expectation of the end-time event, the context giving meaning to Jesus' resurrection, can be true for us today and our experience of the world. This is because today we are open to question beyond death, to hope beyond death, and we need to understand this questioning and hope in terms of bodily life, albeit very different to our present existence. The apocalyptic resurrection expectation, actualized in Jesus' resurrection proleptically, has an empirical fit with the nature of our probing and reaching forward for truth as we go ahead in history. If this Christian claim is true, and Pannenberg argues that it is very defensible rationally, then 'the proleptic revelation of God in Jesus is at the same time the solution to the impasses in the Hegelian concept of truth' (Pannenberg 1971a: 26). We can still own the Christian view of revelation as ours today, despite the great difference in our intellectual context from that of the early church. The Christian view of history, oriented towards the end time, which has come in advance at the resurrection of Jesus, protects the openness of the future and the contingency of events, while still upholding the ultimacy of Jesus. The end time gives us the clue to the whole of history and secures the unity of truth, and so corrects Hegel's 'cardinal error' as Carr calls it. We have a provisional picture of the whole, and this develops as we move into the future, false developments dropping away with the test of time, and new ideas, previously not imagined, occurring and setting things in new perspective.

THE HISTORICAL STRUCTURE OF HUMAN LIFE EXPERIENCE

In another essay in *Basic Questions in Theology* vol. 2 entitled 'Faith and Reason' (Pannenberg 1971a: 52ff.), Pannenberg contrasts the Greek and Hebrew assumptions about reason. For the Greek mind there is a reliable, imperturbable and unchanging reality behind sense appearances, a timelessly present reality. But for the Israelite what is reliable and true will be decided by future events, and the ultimate future, the eschaton, is the point of divine verification and vindication: 'To this extent the Israelitic understanding of truth is, at least implicitly, fundamentally eschatological' (Pannenberg 1971a: 59), and is grasped by faith since it is from the future and ultimately from God who is to be trusted as reliable. Pannenberg sees reason as probing forward and creatively active, not merely passive and receptive as in the Greek philosophical understanding of how reason relates to truth, the eternally unchanging truth. Human imagination is creative and active, bringing forth new ideas and insights in profusion, hitting upon what is utterly different.

Pannenberg here is breaking with the Kantian view of a priori reason which is outside the process of history and time. He prefers the Hegelian understanding that reason is in time as it thinks ahead and reflects back on itself, and on the difference between itself and what it thinks about. This process moves ahead in stages, forming new syntheses by this historical movement of reason, discovering the openness of reason seeking after truth. Pannenberg is also impressed by the philosophy of Dilthey and his reflection on meaning in history. The meaning of anything, individual and corporate, is gained by viewing it as a whole, and this is possible only by having it completed, by looking at the totality of its life, by looking retrospectively from the end of its life (Pannenberg 1971a: 61). A meaningful whole can only be seen in retrospect, and thus only in a provisional way because history is not finished. A foreconception of the final end needs to be made in order to gain the meaning of history, and Heidegger had this insight when he stressed that death would bring our wholeness and that we need to anticipate this wholeness. But Pannenberg criticizes Heidegger for individualism there, since the meaning of an individual can only be gained in the context of the social context of that individual, and ultimately this context is the whole human race (Pannenberg 1971a: 62).

The need for imaginative 'fore conceptions' of the final future to gain an overall perspective on human wholeness is a structure of human reason, and is not only the shape of faith. The totality of reality is constituted by the final future. Faith and reason are not to be regarded as wholly different, rather the opposite is true. Both depend on an eschatological horizon to yield meaning and truth. Both share the anticipatory structure of reaching ahead and looking for new insights from the future, which is open, which faith sees as rooted in God. Reality is laden with meaning as it moves through time, and for both faith and reason the future is the key to gaining a perspective of the totality of reality, albeit provisionally for the moment. Yes, we are on the way to fuller and fuller truth about ourselves and how things are, and this, as E. H. Carr puts it above, is akin to the way Christian theology engages with the promised eschatological day of judgement, as it calls our present life and truth in question time and again. As Carr and also Pannenberg affirm, this process of the advance of reason through history is no mere relativism, 'a night in which all cows are black', since the future arrives and brings ever new light for us to reconfigure our understanding of how things are. We can gain a provisional map of the truth, rationally arguable, rather than there being a host of maps, all equally false, which is the pure relativist position. Pannenberg's position, as Carr's, assumes that reason ultimately does make progress and takes us forward, that the bad new ideas ultimately shake out and the truth discloses itself in this gradual process.

In his essay 'Insight and Faith' (Pannenberg 1971a: 28–45), Pannenberg sets out the relationship of faith and knowledge, knowledge which is open to reason, indeed there is no other knowledge for Pannenberg. Christian faith is trustful anticipation of the future, an anticipation based on the meaning of the Christ event, the resurrection of Jesus, the meaning of the anticipated end time. This event and its meaning 'offers itself to knowledge', that is to reasonable scrutiny and acceptance. Pannenberg, as we will see, argues that this event is indeed open to historical investigation, analysis and interpretation, it is wholly reasonable to accept it as an event with a meaning gained against the background of Israel's traditions of prophecy and apocalyptic hope.

Pannenberg says that faith and reason share the same structure of anticipation reaching ahead and testing out new ideas as these occur and mesh into present theories and customs, bringing about fresh configurations and mappings of reality. Reason does not provide a different kind of knowledge base than faith, faith has no independent access to historical knowledge which is true or not true in terms of historical criteria open for anyone. The content of what reason reaches by its probing and testing, that same content is what faith understands and is persuaded by, that is the truth of the Christ event. In this Pannenberg seems to be thoroughly 'orthodox', standing with church fathers such as Irenaeus over against the many Gnostic groups claiming spiritual knowledge closed to most of humanity. Reason and faith are close partners, not in opposition to each other, rooted in their quest for truth in history and the arrival of new insights from the future. Our human experience of living in history colours both our reason and our faith in the arriving of truth from the future. Reason is in time, as is faith and imaginative insight, shaping a theory, albeit implicit, of how things hold together. Reason and faith are gifts of God, the source of all reality and truth.

Psychologically, says Pannenberg, faith is distinguishable from reason in that faith asserts its trust and assent to the truth of the Christ event and orders life on that basis. Logically however we must hold that new evidence might arise, and that the historical judgement is therefore 'provisional' and open. 'The logic of faith and its psychology must be distinguished' (Pannenberg 1971a: 32), but they combine in being based on knowledge of the Christ event. Trust expects that the meaning of the Christ event will later be fulfilled; this is a foreconception of what is later to be confirmed and verified.

This is the same shape as our thinking generally, we assume something is true and then it is confirmed definitely later on. Pannenberg happily excuses the ordinary believer, perhaps Aquinas' charcoal burner or unlettered peasant, from needing to engage in scholarly research to establish historical facts before faith can happen. Such people can rely on the strength of the work done by the church intellectually – although Pannenberg laments the scant attention paid to this task by much preaching and pastoral work.

He is utterly clear that there is not a special mode of cognition, that of commitment in faith, that can obviate normal truth testing historical research in relation to the content of the events which faith has to trust. Faith does not have its own special version of history shut off from rational discussion and critical thought:

> I would not like to distinguish the knowledge logically presupposed by *fiducia*, or which in a broader sense of the term is included in faith, from natural knowledge . . . I admit that I cannot understand any knowledge as other than 'natural'. And I cannot free myself of the suspicion that the distinguishing of a special knowledge of faith leads once again to the conclusion that the truth of such knowledge can be justified, in the last analysis, only by a decision of faith. (Pannenberg 1971a: 33)

Faith engages with the content of the Christ event, an event which is accepted as true, an objective event outside of the believer. Faith does not ground itself, and must not debase the historical content which is its true ground by manipulation of evidence, however well intentioned. Faith is not grounded in a subjective decision of faith. Pannenberg's stress on the objective content of historical events as the basis of faith entails the meaning of those events, a meaning that emerges when their context is taken into account. An event cannot have a meaning arbitrarily imposed on it by a later age, we might say in 'post modern' fashion. Rather, for Pannenberg, 'events always bring their original meaning along with them from the context to which they have been assigned by their having happened' (Pannenberg 1971a: 39). This is a controversial view in today's postmodern era commending a plurality of interpretations of events, with no decisive one either possible or desirable (Burhenn 1972).

As with Carr, Pannenberg argues that our human experience of being in history registers that events do have a meaning which will emerge and crystallize with time, and which a good interpretation will suggest and gradually confirm or reject. Pannenberg insists that reason be allowed free play on the question of the 'facts' of whether an event happened, but also on their interpretation, which cannot just be left as a matter of taste or obedience to another authority, even that of the prophets and apostles. Here we see a major break with Barth, for example, for whom the testimony of the prophets and apostles is normative for the church, independently of any historical and interpretative verification from secular disciplines, which will run the risk of distortion. For Barth faith has to precede interpretation of, for example, biblical texts and a purely secular interpreter would not find God through the texts.

The popularity of an interpretation does not, says Pannenberg undeniably, make it more or less true: 'materially and logically impeccable grounding is one thing, but the consent of man is very often quite another matter' (Pannenberg 1971a: 40). The Roman Catholic concept of the 'consensus fidelium' would not be sufficient for Pannenberg, any more than would an authoritarian papal decree 'making' something 'true' such as the 'immaculate conception of Mary' rendering her sinless and a fit mother for Jesus, an event declared infallibly true in 1854 by Pope Pius IX. Likewise the role of the Holy Spirit now is not to make an event then true, when it is not. The resurrection of the Crucified is an event that needed thorough exploration and debated interpretation, but the Spirit is linked to this Christ event, now provisionally acceptable as true, in that its eschatological content has a profound impact when understood and received for what it is. Indeed Pannenberg deplores the tradition that makes the Spirit into a merely subjective and individual agent of personal piety: 'The Holy Spirit is widely taken as a catchword for the view that the content of faith is present only for the pious subjectivity, so that its truth cannot be presented in a way that can claim binding force' (Pannenberg 1971a: 43). The content, the eschatologically rich meaning of the resurrection event of Christ, brings the dynamic power of the Holy Spirit to people, just as, presumably, the sheer force of the content of a Shakespeare play is pregnant with power to move and inform us. For Pannenberg the missionary message of the church must regain a reputation for historical truth and credibility, 'retreat to commitment', instead of being prepared to offer evidence for the Christian claims, simply damages its cause in modern society. Rational people need to be convinced of the credibility of Christ and his resurrection if the gospel message, its very content, is to be taken seriously at all.

Pannenberg here can be seen to have broken decisively with the German existentialist tradition in theology which had been so influential since 1918, with his insistence on the key importance of real historical events and their meaning for the Christian faith. Rudolph Bultmann was the theologian who had asserted that the kerygma was not about historical events in time but the liberating message of human freedom now, our real 'historicity' being existential freedom, over the merely 'historical' track of successive events. Pannenberg's essay 'Redemptive and History' (Pannenberg 1970b: 15–80) explains his position over against that of kerygmatic theology with great clarity. The reality and meaning of world history is devalued by the move which makes true historicity a matter of human self-transcendence, as we realize that history itself is relativized and emptied of ultimate meaning. He cites Heidegger's philosophy in seeking the 'historicity' of existence by going behind the 'vulgar' understanding of history into 'the anxious' (Pannenberg 1970b: 34), disdaining a final meaning to history. Pannenberg argues that the Apostle Paul's theology in Romans shows that historical continuity is vital, in Romans 9–11 with its image of the grafting in of the wild olive shoot onto the cultivated olive tree of Israel, an objective historical pathway towards a promised hope. Christian eschatology cannot simply be reduced to a moment of self-understanding, departing from the ongoing course of world history with Christ as the central meaning of that history.

Pannenberg prefers the theological wisdom of his teacher von Rad and his emphasis on the history of the transmitted traditions of Israel with their claim of divine promise being trusted and expected, whatever the current circumstances, their witness of being in a purposive history given by the creator. The New Testament needs the Old Covenant and yet sees those promises fulfilled in new and unexpected ways, 'but in such a way that the promises themselves hold good in the change of their content' (Pannenberg 1970b: 31). Pannenberg claims that this biblical tradition of historical experience and its narration has formed the western historical consciousness, our consciousness of being in temporal history which is moving on and yet is purposive. The dehistoricization of history, exemplified by Bultmann and Heidgegger, has had the effect of putting humanity in the place of God as the prime agent of history. This leads to an atrophy of historical consciousness and interest in history. The loss of Christian faith increases this process, since this faith points to the promise to be fulfilled in the future, giving meaning to all of history and giving it fundamental unity under God. 'When the historicity of man is set up in opposition to the continuity of the course of history, the last possible step is taken along the way which leads to the loss of the experience of history as well as that of historicity' (Pannenberg 1970b: 35). Pannenberg is convinced that the meaning and experience of history as a whole, and in its process, derives from the witness and experience of Israel and the Church which is crucial for human self-understanding. The eschaton has happened with the event of Christ's resurrection, but the meaning of this event will continue to develop in time while maintaining its basic content and shape. Faith is vital, but faith based on the historical events and their meaning, taken as part of the whole of human history.

This involves the totally open practice of historical critical research on the historical data found in the Bible and tradition, giving such data no special privilege over other claimed events and meanings. In holding this, however, Pannenberg does not hold to the view that historical critical procedure should a priori exclude all transcendent reality as a matter of principle. He is challenging the long-held orthodoxy of post-Enlightenment opinion which banishes any idea of the reality of the transcendent from the intellectual playing field. His view that biblical accounts of events and their meaning are not somehow privileged over against the rest of history, and so need historical critical investigation, is taken together with his view that it is not logical to exclude the transcendent necessarily from our experience of history. Historical critical work tends to be controlled by an anthropocentric presuppositional base, but this base should be rationally challenged, in Pannenberg's view.

Pannenberg here contests principles asserted by the sociologist and historian Ernst Troeltsch, for whom historical method rests on 'the application of analogy', and in this context analogy entails 'the fundamental homogeneity of all historical events'. Pannenberg is keen to accept that the history of Israel is part of a universal world history and must be set in the wider historical context of its day, in the universal correlation of all events. But this does not necessitate excluding the transcendent from the consideration of events. He rejects the practice of 'analogy' when it means that unfamiliar events are to be understood solely through our experience of familiar events.

'As a methodological principle of historical research, analogy means that something difficult to understand, comparatively opaque, is to be conceived and understood by the investigator in terms of what lies closer to him' (Pannenberg 1970b: 43). In other words we can understand the strange and difficult only in terms of what we know now. This method privileges our present sense experience, and makes that normative for understanding all events, placing our world view as a grid on all events. The future, however, is open, and the arrival of the new event cannot be ruled out a priori, says Pannenburg.

Pannenberg argues that the historian should maintain focus not merely on the homogeneity or sameness of all events but on their particularity and contingency, 'then he will see that he is dealing with non-homogeneous things, which cannot be contained without remainder in any analogy' (Pannenberg 1970b: 46). In fact the power of analogy is to reveal something different and new from comparing two things, or events or ideas, a newness arising from the comparison, not a domination of one by the other. The process of levelling all events down to the typical and analogous cuts out the different and the particular, and in fact analogy for historical research has been most fruitful when focusing on the concrete particularities being compared rather than imposing a law of historical occurrences. It is no ground for disputing a reported event that it bursts analogies with repeatedly attested events. We need also to ensure that we as knowers set ourselves in historical context, so as to avoid unwittingly viewing our own presuppositions as absolute rather than as shaped and conditioned historically.

Pannenberg is not saying that analogy should not be used and is not fruitful or necessary, but that particularity and contingency are the factors to be compared in order that a new insight can arise. And a new and opaque event may elude analogies now, but that does not mean it has no analogy at all. Analogies need to be made to help understand events, and theology has no special inspired mode of thinking to obviate the need for rigorous historical investigation and interpretation. Theology cannot escape having to proceed by normal historical methods in looking at concepts of God gradually developed by the history of Israel, using analogies and having these tested as time went by. The understanding of God is a slow process in which the character of God first disclosed itself step by step, then finally, and with ultimate validity, in the presence of the eschaton in the fate of Jesus of Nazareth. True knowledge of God is obtained from this history for the first time, and therefore cannot be presupposed a priori as something that makes it possible to grasp this knowledge. This developing knowledge gained purely from the historical events and human apprehension of them historically, corrects earlier distorted concepts of God. Pannenberg defends a subtle blend of reasoned critical historical content for gaining knowledge of God: God is not ruled out by reductionist assumptions of historical criticism but rather is a rational option for explaining our experience of life and history. Indeed only the concept of God, he teaches, can make it possible for us to conceive of the unity of history in a way that maintains the contingent and new, and again historical critical scholarship is essential for establishing the probability of God. 'How God works, and how he has created the continuity of history again and again, can only be taught by history itself' (Pannenberg 1970b: 76), and at the same time history itself can only be fully understood within the horizon of the end of history, and so ultimately of the divine judgement on history which completes and holds history together as a whole.

Pannenberg describes a dialectical pathway and pattern of the historical process, for both reality and thought. God sustains this process, brings it forward from the future, and has revealed its anticipatory structure in the the proleptic end time event of Christ's resurrection. The tapestry of history is open textured, gaining in complexity as the pattern weaves and is woven to the weaver and from him, or again, the symphony builds with harmonies and discords, with major and minor keys, with challenges and renewals, towards the great climax which still awaits – and yet has been announced in what has already been heard and played.

In another essay in *Basic Questions*, vol. 1,'Hermeneutic and Universal History', Pannenberg develops his overarching thesis of understanding being gained as we go forward in history, reflecting on the past, and new insights arise to our interpreting reason. In particular he takes up the thought of the hermeneutical scholar Gadamer and his notion of the 'fusing of horizons', that is, the horizon of the present interpreter with that of someone in the past whose texts are being interpreted. Gadamer wishes to emphasize the difference and strangeness of these horizons before any comprehension can be attained. For Gadamer,

[T]he interpreter's own horizon is not fixed, but capable of movement and expansion. In the process of understanding, the interpreter's horizon is widened in such a way that the initially strange matter along with its own horizon can be appropriated into the expanded horizon he attains as he understands. In the interpreter's encounter with his text a new horizon is formed. (Pannenberg 1970b: 117)

This process of understanding the strange event in its strange horizon entails 'the elevation to a higher universality, which overcomes not only one's own particularity, but also that of the other' (Pannenberg 1970b: 117). We deliberately acknowledge the distance of our horizon from that we are seeking to understand, and in order to develop our understanding we project another horizon to try to encompass ancient and modern in the widest horizon possible, relating to all known reality. Pannenberg disagrees with Gadamer's view of such interpretation as a conversation, since the text cannot speak as a 'thou' without the questioner first asking questions of it and enabling it to speak.

Language is indeed crucial to the hermeneutical process, but not as an event transcending careful interpretation of content and in historical context. This involves a conception of the actual course of history which unites the past and present and their different horizons. Pannenberg argues that history and hermeneutics are vitally bonded together: the historical contexts of events and ideas, contexts including the thought world of the day, are critical in reaching interpretations. New horizons of meaning are constructed from dialogue with the inherited tradition from the past. The new understanding of how things are and hold together, this understanding has to prove itself in the contemporary realities of life: the new concept has to show itself as a powerful way of explaining things in the concrete reality of current life. This relation of concept to historical reality will be seen to be an important theme in Pannenberg's way of interpreting history and meaning: both the 'ideal' and the 'real' are historical and in the process of history as understanding develops. The progress towards horizons that can unite disparate insights, as their contexts and contents are unfolded and understood, anticipates an ultimate horizon giving a final meaning for the whole of history. History and hermeneutics cohere as the real and the rational, as being and meaning.

As E. H. Carr's formulation puts it, as we project new understandings they are confirmed or not as new events occur to 'judge' them positively or negatively and take things forward accordingly. This very process is the criterion of truth, as we move forward so the truth emerges and discloses itself, rejecting the false from the past and developing the seeds now seen to be of truth. For Pannenberg, our experience of life involves that of encountering new events which are not predictable, and which point to a freedom rather than a fixed determinism of history. The future, events that as yet have not arisen although they may have been hinted at already in human guesswork, prediction and hypothesizing, cannot be mastered but will always have new events to surprise us in ways which are sometimes epoch making. History for Pannenberg, therefore, is not convincingly explained by atheistic materialists, for example Marxists, who see everything determined and necessitated from the past. Rather there is indeed a stability to reality, but there is also an unpredictable novelty about events that raises the question of God as a concept that could better account for the freedom experienced in history, certainly better than the rigid grid of materialist determinism. Pannenberg's hermeneutical drive is towards the universal meaning of the totality of all things, yet from particular contingent events: the dialectic between the two will be found running through his understanding of reality, and the freedom of the individual events and persons comes from the future orientation of history, creating self-creative contingent agents.

RAISING THE QUESTION OF GOD

Pannenberg takes history to be the key category for understanding our human experience in the modern world. We experience new insights as we move on in time, seeking to orientate ourselves by projecting ever new horizons of meaning in order to reach convincing new syntheses accounting for the evidence we have. We are woven into a hermeneutical historical process of developing interpretation as we are open to new events, both concepts and happenings, all in their own contexts of meaning: interpretations are confirmed or weakened by the arrival of new events. We are open to what is new and cannot freeze the present moment as the eternal key to truth, things change and stimulate new understandings. Each new phase of understanding claims to give the best overview of things, the best interpretation of the whole of reality and its meaning, and yet this will be superseded until an end point is reached. This, as Pannenberg repeats, was Hegel's way of understanding truth and reality, but

Hegel absolutized his own theory as the final revelation. The Christian claim is that the final moment of meaning is to come at the end time, but that Jesus and his resurrection enacted that moment in advance, and yet the full interpretation of this event still develops in time. History is inherently meaningful, is a hermeneutical process.

'The Question of God' is an essay probing the question in the secular modern world. The term 'God' is felt by modernity to be irrelevant to modern concerns, and to be a private matter with no place in public rational debate. Pannenberg, as we have already seen, seeks to unfold the implication of our modern human experience of living in the world as an experience of living in history, and to unfold it rationally, explicating how we gain our understanding of how things hold together in the light of new discoveries, theories and events coming to us as we move into the future. Thus far we have seen Pannenberg's commitment to the Christian portrayal of reality and truth as a legitimate claimant on the public and academic world stage to express the truth of how things are – the best thesis – to account for all the factors known to human experience in the face of all the tests put by secular scholarship. This Christian thesis, however, is itself continually open to face and engage with new evidence as it may arise.

Our self-understanding as historical beings raises the question of God, even in the form of human atheism and rejection of God; 'God' remains a concept to be rejected, and so curiously remains on the agenda of modern consciousness. Human experience makes itself a question to itself in the hope and despair that mingle in the human breast, 'the hopeless gap between the question of man and the silence of the universe', according to Sartre quoted by Pannenberg (Pannenberg 1971a: 216). Man is 'open to the world', *Weltoffenheit*, but as George Kehm in his 'Translator's Preface' brings out, this word includes man's ability to question every given content and condition in the world, and to imagine something beyond any given state of affairs, hence the meaning of Pannenberg's use of the term must include the factor of the future (Pannenberg 1970b: xiv). As human beings we are able to go beyond every situation, and we can change our environment to a considerable extent; we are 'eccentric' in being able to transcend our own situation and not be locked into the present experience. We can adopt a standpoint towards ourselves that gets above our situation and reflects on ourselves. Ernst Bloch's view is taken up by Pannenberg, describing the human race as reaching 'beyond everything that has happened by means of his anticipations, wishes and hopes' (Pannenberg 1971a: 216). Humanity entails a question of itself which it cannot avoid without lapsing into a sub-human state, and this question is part of our basic structure, not merely a metaphor. Our inquiring and probing of the world and our situation entails an implied answer, which we have not yet reached but reach towards with our projections and anticipations. As the answers arise we move beyond the present situation.

This phenomenon of human questioning raises the question of God as the possible content for which we search, as that which we feel as yet we lack, without which our souls are restless; it is a possible option with perfectly good rational credentials. The characteristic human questioning might be merely an expression of human creativity, but it also might be suggesting that a supporting ground is a reality and that God is a concept evoking our inquiry, albeit this is not directly the concept of a personal God. The projections of answers, entailed in the questions asked by humans, are certainly on the one hand creations of the questioners, but shallow questions are shattered by events and good questions are not. The questions are therefore not simply about individual taste and creativity. Events correct and shape the nature of the questionableness felt by humanity. Religions express conviction of the reality behind all things and philosophical reflection takes up the religious suggestions in the form of human questioning or shaping this questioning. 'To this extent', says Pannenberg, 'we must agree with Barth's thesis that the human question is first disclosed from the side of the answer' (Pannenberg 1971a: 226). But Panneberg broadens this out to all religions, although from the Christian angle non-Christian religions are based on an unclear form of the answer, the answer given in greatest clarity is the history of Jesus: the dialectic of the particular and universal again shows itself.

Our very experience as humans therefore raises the question of God as a possible answer to our predicament, an answer springing from our very capacity to ask questions and to learn to shape better questions with the arrival of new insight and truth as we advance in time. The concept of a personal God is raised by our reflection on 'the all determining reality', that which rules over all things in the cosmos, a description which any definition of God must include. Such an all-determining reality cannot be manipulated and has, by conceptual definition, to be free over the world reality of which it is the deity. This deity cannot be reducible to being a mere object at hand to the created reality, it has to be free and sovereign if this is fulfilling the best concept of God. Religious experience tends to speak of this kind of power making a claim on the religious person. For Pannenberg the experience of Israel is special in knowing of the freedom of God in history, of faithfulness and of the promise of the future of God's public reign over all reality. 'The future of God will bring the answer to the questionableness of every phenomenon in the world of nature and of mankind that still remains open in the flow of history' (Pannenberg 1971a: 232). The Christian framing of this questionableness means that there is an ongoing openness in the answer given to us, the question is not ended, the answer given in the death and resurrection of Jesus continues to generate new questions. The factor of novelty in history which is ongoing has a strong place in the Christian answer, which Pannenberg finds implicit in the human questioning of itself as human.

CONCLUSION

From his essays in *Basic Questions* we have seen the shape of Pannenberg's historicist ontology and epistemology, one of meaning arising from events being interpreted rationally by human beings in the light ultimately of the widest possible horizon of the end time, but initially in the particular contexts of the individual events. The particular widens out to the universal perspective, a crucial part of Pannenberg's view of meaning. Reason is historical and God given, and seeks to find out the best theory to make sense of the coherence of things in our historical experience, and for Pannenberg the Christian thesis of the proleptic end time come in Christ is the best option, albeit provisionally. We have seen Pannenberg articulate a system, and yet one which includes freedom and not determinism, one which fosters free critical thinking and allows the new event to be conceptually possible. We now turn to examine the same reality of history, and human reasoning about the real, from the conceptual angle of revelation.

CHAPTER 2

REVELATION AS HISTORY

FOCUSED TEXT:
REVELATION AS HISTORY

INDIRECT SELF-REVELATION

Pannenberg announced his theological agenda with colleagues in 1961 by the publication of *Revelation as History* (Pannenberg 1969a). This was a collection of essays edited by Pannenberg in which he contributed the introductory essay with the same title, and an essay entitled 'Dogmatic Theses on the Concept of Revelation', and a postscript to the second edition of the symposium. The 'Preface to the American Edition' (Pannenberg 1969a: ix) sums up the aim of the essays, and we see the themes of *Basic Questions*, discussed in Chapter 1, configured anew in this symposium but from the angle of the concept of revelation. The essays bridge the gulf between exegesis and systematic theology, and this means a consideration of the concept of revelation in the light of historical critical exegesis of the texts of the Scripture. The introduction provides a discussion of 'the modern concept of revelation' and a reinterpretation in terms of 'the comprehensive whole of reality'. This is an ongoing temporal process of a history not yet completed, but 'open to a future, which is anticipated in the teaching and personal history of Jesus' (Pannenberg 1969a: ix). Revelation is open to critical questioning and is not a matter of authoritative tradition, nor is it understood as a supernatural disclosure nor deep subjective experience. This theological programme is a deliberate break with the 'neo-orthodox' positions exemplified in Barth which are deemed to be authoritarian claims for the divine Word, irresistibly breaking in upon us now. Likewise Bultmann's claim for the existential experiential moment of revelation, not related to reason at all, is rejected by Pannenberg. The open rationality of the Enlightenment is preferred to these modes of theology. But Pannenberg retains 'a concern for the substance of the Christian tradition', presumably because that tradition is still credible as a way of understanding the human situation.

The first half of his programmatic introductory essay examines the way the term 'revelation' is used in theology, and indeed this examination is of the highest importance for theology because, as Panneberg says, Protestant theology for most of the twentieth century has articulated itself through this rich theological concept. Barth in particular sought to ground all theology in revelation as a term entailing not merely epistemology but also ontology. This move continued that made by Ritschl in its exclusive focus on Jesus, albeit in a different mode, rejecting philosophical metaphysics as a way of speaking about God. Kantian influence can surely be found behind both Ritschl, in his focus on morality as the ground for theology, and Barth in his epistemological dualism rejecting natural reason as any pathway to Christian theology. Pannenberg is correct in holding that the concept of revelation was made to carry a huge pivotal burden. Revelation is deployed in several ways in modern theology, but underlying them is the 'consensus that revelation is in essence the self-revelation of God' (Pannenberg 1969a: 4). Revelation is not the making known of a set of arcane truths but the self-disclosure of God, the axiom developed by Barth. For theology before the Enlightenment revelation meant truths that were given authoritatively by God in the form of texts and traditions. This view came under the criticism of the Enlightenment attack on superstition and claims to knowledge that avoided scientific scrutiny.

Early twentieth century theology restricted the term to divine self-revelation and the implication that this entailed a single, full and unique self-manifestation of God. The revelation of God to the created order of being is always going to be through a creaturely medium of some kind, but in the case of the self-revelation of God claimed to be in the man Jesus Christ, this creaturely medium is united to the divine so that this medium is not separable from God. Pannenberg puts this point succinctly and suggestively: 'The creaturely medium of revelation, the man Jesus Christ, is caught up to God in his distinctiveness and received in unity with God himself' (Pannenberg 1969a: 5). Here is a uniting of the finite with the infinite, the relative with the absolute, the particular with the whole, as God reveals himself through himself to mankind. The Holy Spirit alone allows us to apprehend the self-disclosure of God: by God alone can God be known. This strictly defined concept of revelation, the key to Barth's trinitarian theology, has deep roots in the thought of Hegel, and this is not necessarily a bad thing, for Pannenberg – if not for Barth, a critic of theology shaped by such German idealism.

And this tightly defined understanding of revelation, developed by Barth, entails the uniqueness of revelation, as opposed to a multiplicity of revelations for which no one instance could qualify as 'the' revelation and so none would give the true self-revelation of God. Pannenberg accepts this logical move of Barth's doctrine of revelation, that divine self-revelation is unique and unrepeatable if it is true, no single act among many acts would be the authentic self-revelation. This strict view of revelation entails that the 'special means by which God becomes manifest, or the particular act by which he proves himself, is not seen as distinct from his own essence' (Pannenberg 1969a: 7), a key point developed by Barth who stressed the unity of Jesus with God as a unity in revelation and so a unity of essence. But Pannenberg thinks that Barth endangers his insight by insisting that the form of divine revelation, or unveiling of God, is simultaneously the veiling of God, since 'the conception of a God who by nature has a veiled form of manifestation (the veiling is not just against those who misunderstand) runs contrary to the unity of revelation as the self-revelation' (Pannenberg 1969a: 7). This, for Pannenberg, conflicts with the insight of the strict definition that the essence of revelation is self-disclosure and that the form of revelation reveals God in fullness, and does not veil him.

Having endorsed the meaning of revelation as self-disclosure for modern theology as the most convincing interpretation of this concept, and what it needs to encompass, Pannenberg goes on to explore the biblical evidence for this concept, and quickly concludes that the actual terminology of the Bible has no expression for this notion of the self-revelation of God. The divine announcement of the name of God might be an equivalent, since a name was not separable from the being holding the name as it is now, but full self-disclosure does not seem to be included in this biblical usage. Likewise the 'Word of God', argues Pannenberg, does not have the personalistic resonance that the full self-disclosure model has. In Luke-Acts 'when the author speaks of the Word of God he has in mind the apostolic kerygma. Here, too, is an entity whose content is clearly distinct from God himself' (Pannenberg 1969a: 11). Perhaps teasing his kerygmatic theological opponents, he comments likewise on the Johannine Prologue and its doctrine of the Word: 'one could argue that the Gnostic concept of revelation has been broken by its connection with the tradition of Jesus, because its connection with that tradition gave it an element of indirectness totally foreign to Gnosticism' (Pannenberg 1969a: 11). By this Pannenberg refers to the dualistic Gnostic view of revelation which is of a totally direct intervention into a world wholly antipathetic to the revealer and understandable only to the very few elect capable of spiritual knowledge, gnosis.

Rather, the biblical usage of revelation concerns the history of Israel and the content of its traditions in articulating the Word of the Lord. The modern personalistic idea of the Word as a 'Thou' directly engaging the hearer is more like the Gnostic than Israelite understanding of revelation in history. Nor can it be said that the giving of the Law on Sinai correlates to the direct self-revelation of God in modern theology, rather God is known prior to this event of Law giving. Pannenberg finds no biblical justification for the modern view of revelation as direct self-disclosure. He concludes programmatically:

Instead of a direct self-revelation of God, the facts at this point indicate a conception of indirect self-revelation as a reflex of his activity in history. The totality of his speech and activity, the history brought about by God, shows who he is in an indirect way. (Pannenberg 1969a: 13)

That statement crystallizes the new direction in which Pannenberg takes the doctrine of divine self-revelation, maintaining the concept developed by Barth but radically revising it in what he claims is a more biblical understanding, as well as a properly reasonable and responsible understanding which offers a world view. This new programme entails mining the category of history and the content of history, gained by a view of eschatology from the apocalyptic tradition. Universal history, a category developed by the tradition of Israel as it reflected on the God of all creation, is inseparable from

God and the revelation of this God. The tiny particular people of Israel proposes the notion of a purposive meaningful totality of history, the universal and the particular come together.

The third part of Pannenberg's rich and seminal introductory essay, looking back as it does to German idealism and also forward with the horizon of biblical apocalyptic, takes the reader into the apparently difficult notion of full self-revelation which is yet indirect and a reflex of divine activity in history. This, moreover, accepts Barth's definition of the unity of revealer and revelation, a unity not simply of act but of essence, so that the form of self-revelation equates with the divine essence and does not conflict with it. Direct communication goes to the recipient without a break, the content being directly knowable. Indirect communication involves a break so that the content – always an important term in Pannenberg's theology – first 'reveals' its actual meaning 'by being considered' from another perspective. Moreover Pannenberg says that indirect communication is on a higher level, 'it always has direct communication as its basis, but takes this into a new perspective' (Pannenberg 1969a: 14). What Pannenberg is saying here is that the revealed content, which is the content of divine self-disclosure of a totally unique kind, needs to be processed by our minds; we need to think about this content so that its meaning emerges to us from the divine, hence with a 'break' to any directness. Here we encounter an Hegelian move, from direct experience to that which the mind ponders and considers so as to reach the height of truth about how things are. The cognitive content comes through the processes of human historical inter-pretation (to coin a new spelling in order to emphasize a point!).

The directness is not necessarily a matter of immediacy: a messenger can deliver a message directly from the sender, but the content of the message arriving directly for the mind to grasp immediately is the point here. Indirect communication can likewise arrive straight from its sender, but its content is such that it requires consideration before the meaning is gained, the indirectness – a higher level of understanding in the eyes of Pannenberg – requires the mind to work out the content. This reverses, very deliberately, the dominant Protestant view of revelation since 1918 stressing the immediacy of divine revelatory action, apprehended not by rational cognition so much as surrender of the self in faith and worship, putting aside detached rational critical judgement.

Another way of putting this is with reference to Kant's legacy of dividing pure reason from practical reason, that is, critical reason from moral reason. Bultmann and Barth accept this division and freight their theological task epistemologically away from the realm of critical reasoning and into that of meaning, value and faith. For both Bultmann and Barth, critical evidence from and about historical events is irrelevant to the content of faith: faith is a separate realm with its own mode of apprehending, and being apprehended by, its object, the majestic and free Lord. Worship is the immediate mode of response to the self-disclosing God, for Barth. But for Pannenberg 'indirect communication is distinguished by not having God as the content in any direct manner. Every activity and act of God can indirectly express something about God. This is the change of perspective, that the content of the divine revelation is not felt as a direct impact, it is 'perceived for its own value' by a reflection on the event first perceived, on the religious experience felt in the event which stimulates our thinking about this.

Here we may indeed feel 'perplexed', since Pannenberg has told us that he is working with the 'strict' view of revelation developed by Barth, that is the self-disclosive model of fullness of revelation of divine being, but 'indirectly' and not an immediate experience of being overwhelmed and brought to worship by the sheer direct majesty and holiness of God. Pannenberg is calling for an indirect self-revelation by way of historical events which are reflected upon and then yield up their meaning. But, as he says, there are many events that cast light on God indirectly:

> As acts of God, these acts cast light back on God himself, communicating something indirectly about God himself. That does not of course mean that they reveal God or that God reveals himself in them as their originator, for every individual event which is taken to be God's activity illuminates the being of God only in a partial way . . . Thus no one act could be a full revelation of God. (Pannenberg 1969a: 16)

This fact of the multiple events and meanings taken as divine acts 'destroys the strict sense of revelation as self-revelation of God' (Pannenberg 1969a: 16), which is needed if we are to understand the totality of God's action as his revelation. The totality of all these many events as divine acts must equate to divine self-disclosure communicated to us 'indirectly', through our mental processes and interpretations, as we journey forward to the eschatological end of the continuum of history when all will be revealed. We are in this hermeneutical web of history, dynamically moving to, and receiving its being from, the future freedom of God.

Pannenberg has broadened, or universalized, the cognitive or hermeneutical 'content' of revelation to include the meaning of history as a whole, whereas Barth envisages Christ as the full self-disclosure of God, directly to world history and to us now, not as world history or its quintessential meaning. In Barth's mature theology Christ is the way of the Son into the far country, the history of the trinitarian God into the history of human misery, sin and disobedience (Barth 1956a). There could be no 'considering the content' of this revelation of the Son of God and making up one's mind intellectually about it for Barth, rather divine self-revelation in Christ is an embrace of forgiving love not to be interpreted but joyfully accepted.

Pannenberg has, as it were, spread out the hermeneutical content whereas Barth personalizes it, and Bultmann makes it an intense event of the individual subjectivity. Pannenberg is clear that his move aligns him with German idealist thought, interpreting history with divine self-revelation: 'Hegel gave systematic formulation to the conception of universal history as an indirect revelation of God in connection with his explication of the concept of self-revelation' (Pannenberg 1969a: 16–17). As Pannenberg says, the German idealists, notably Hegel and Schelling, were seeking to blend their idea of revelation with biblical narrative as well as provide a sound philosophical vision of reality. But for biblical theological work, there is a problem with Hegel's view in that the Christian vision entails one great event in history giving its final meaning, the Christ event, so how can the ongoing process of events equate with that claim, how can one specific event claim to be absolute truth? Also, if the totality of history is to be taken as the self-revelation of God then the full course of history needs to run its course, past the Christ event, for the full divine self-manifestation to happen. Hegel argued that the development meant the developing understanding of the significance of the Christ event, but Pannenberg wants to insist that there must be 'a development in the facts themselves' also, the future remains open and new facts may emerge, in theory at least. This is where Pannenberg ends his introduction to the symposium.

DOGMATIC THESES ON THE DOCTRINE OF REVELATION

Pannenberg ends his introductory essay and rather teasingly hands over to his colleagues in biblical studies and church history to give their essays on the subject, before returning with his second essay, 'Dogmatic Theses on the Doctrine of Revelation' (Pannenberg 1969a: 125ff.), which in effect gives his answer to the problem he left at the end of his introductory essay, taking up points he made there and taking some further in the light of the biblical and historical material given by his colleagues in the intervening essays. The major point being made in his seven dogmatic theses is that the resurrection of Jesus, taken in the context of the apocalyptic thought world of its day, suggests an eschatological meaning for this event, subject to a historical critical scrutiny of the evidence and an attitude of provisionality lest new evidence arise. The Christ event, taken in its cultural context, is arguably the 'end time event' come in advance, and therefore is the prefiguring of the moment giving meaning to the totality of history. It will be worth going through the seven theses, as they constitute the spine of Pannenberg's theology, whether seen from the sacred or secular aspects, a dualism of these perspectives being ultimately wrong.

The first thesis is that 'The self revelation of God in the biblical witnesses is not of a direct type in the sense of a theophany, but is indirect and brought about by means of the historical acts of God.' He looks at the Old Testament traditions and finds them to express Jahweh's deity and power shown in events such as the exodus from Egypt, in the clusters of events interpreted by the Deuteronomist as showing Jahweh's identification with Israel, and in the prophetic declarations of salvation and self-vindication of Jahweh as the nation falls. The apocalyptic tradition envisages the final manifestation of God in his glory, and Jesus shares this horizon. Only within this horizon is it credible to regard Jesus' resurrection as a reflection of the eschatological self-vindication of God. Pauline texts are close to the apocalyptic conception in their teaching about the glory of God: the glory of God is visible to Paul in the fate of Jesus, whom he emphatically proclaimed as the crucified one (1 Cor. 4:6). God is indirectly revealed in the fate of Jesus. The apocalyptic revelation of his glory in the end judgement has come to pass ahead of time in this fate. The content of the gospel of the early church entails the inbreaking of the divine life and glory, which the Christian congregations know and experience as the eschatological gift of the Spirit. This first generation experience and belief is taken forward by the next generation in a way that links the claim of the Spirit's presence to the past event of Christ its content. Pannenberg looks at the process of the history of developing tradition. The content of this theology of divine acting in history, culminating with the Christ event as the end event ahead of time, needs to be understood cognitively and indirectly as divine self-revelation.

The second thesis is, 'Revelation is not comprehended completely in the beginning but at the end of the revealing history.' The content of revelation is continually revising itself as traditions develop and show, for example, the deity and power of God through events and their meaning. These are taken up and forward, and seen not as final but as steps along the way to the disclosure of the universality and purposiveness of God the creator and saviour. The manifestation of God at the end of history means that the course of history is taken up into the self-revelation of God and therefore of his essence. This has some echoes with Barth's doctrine of election in which God elects to be for the world in Christ, so making the cause of the created order his own cause, although of course critics of Barth argue that this achieves precisely the reverse of what Pannenberg aims to achieve by his move away from the start of history to its end as its matrix of meaning and purpose.

But this end point draws to itself the very course of history which preceded the end, and without which the end would not be the end, and so God reveals his very being as always in unity with the total course of history. Pannenberg can say that 'although the essence of God is from everlasting to everlasting the same, it does have a history in time' (Pannenberg 1969a: 134). Divine self-revelation takes the form of world history, and we recall earlier Pannenberg insisting that the form of mediating this self-revelation has to be in unity with God, not separated from God's being: here now we see this working out in Pannenberg's doctrine of revelatory history, which is however known and finally established only at the culminatory meaning of the totality. Divine essence does have a history in time therefore, and this is indeed self-revelation and indirectly so. God is revealed as the universal God of all people at the end of history and the Christ event anticipating this led to the inclusion of the Gentiles as well as the Jews in the scope of the gospel message. At this stage we might conclude that for Pannenberg the whole of historical meaning is indirectly God's very being spread out in time, that the Son is the significance of all history, all finitude – a distinctively Hegelian idea. There is certainly a deep identification, if not identity, of God in Christ with history in its totality – but this identification, as we will see later, includes a differentiation. And this is certainly not a necessary process, but freely enacted by God and revealed in Christ.

Thesis three says: 'In distinction from special manifestations of the deity, the historical revelation is open to anyone who has eyes to see. It has a universal character.' Here Pannenberg is reinforcing his point that revelation is apprehended through the normal rational processes and is not open in a special way to some and not others, a way he thinks is Gnostic. The historical events, notably the end-time event come in advance, are open to all for consideration and assessment. Taken in context, 'God has proved his deity in the language of facts' (Pannenberg 1969a: 137). By apprehending these facts and their meaning rationally, faith and trust in God are generated – Christlike trust exercised towards the future.

Thesis four is that 'The universal revelation of the deity of God is not yet realized in the history of Israel, but first in the fate of Jesus of Nazareth, insofar as the end of all events is anticipated in his fate.' Pannenberg claims that the biblical view of the one universal God revealed through history is richer and wider than the Greek philosophical view of God as the structuring principle of the cosmos, since the biblical historical view includes the contingent event rather than only the same structures of the world. The eschatological event establishes the Lordship of God over all things and the resurrection of Jesus, this event in advance, does that also, proving the deity of this God over even death. Pannenberg tells us that in the fate of Jesus God is revealed as the hidden God, notwithstanding his criticism of Barth for his language of veiling and unveiling. But what he means is that the revelatory event is so densely packed with meaning that no one can fully see all its implications and exhaust its meaning.

From the human angle we need to realize that the event of revelation is inexhaustible in its depth of meaning and to understand this is to ensure against the misunderstanding that revelation as history might be taken to entail the encyclopaedic knowledge by a human of absolutely everything. Clearly Pannenberg envisages the knowledge of revelation as history to be a qualitative rather than compendial form of knowledge, a grasping of the depth of meaning of all things, proleptically disclosed in Christ. This revelation discloses that the being of the God of Israel belongs to the Son and Spirit as well as to the Father (Pannenberg 1969a: 143), rendering the revelation present at all times in history. The revelation of God is both particular in an event or complex of events in history, and universal in expressing the deity of God over all history totally.

Thesis five states that 'The Christ event does not reveal the deity of the God of Israel as an isolated event, but rather insofar as it is a part of the history of God with Israel.' Jesus' authority was defined against the background of prophetic and apocalyptic expectation of the end, and his resurrection even more so gained its meaning from the Jewish eschatological expectation. Again the indirectness of divine self-revelation is clearly seen here in Pannenberg's view of things. This is not a direct revelatory impact on a person so much as the interpreting of events against their background to discover their true meaning, in this case the deity of God.

Thesis six is that 'In the formulation of the non-Jewish conceptions of revelation in the Gentile Christian church, the universality of the eschatological self-vindication of God in the fate of Jesus comes to actual expression.' Here we have another expression of Pannenberg's view of the development of truth as history goes on, or rather as it is drawn into its future towards its climactic revelation. The initial Jewish thought world gave birth to the revelation of the deity and universality of God, and quintessentially in the life and fate of Jesus, that fate culminating in resurrection from death. This truth, giving the key to the shape of reality as a whole, was taken forward by the Jews of the Greek diaspora and then by Gentiles of Hellenistic culture. The fact that the church widened out to take in Gentiles marks the universal significance of the content given by the resurrection of Jesus, and the engagement of this content by the Hellenistic philosophical culture helps to clarify this significance.

Pannenberg argues subtly that the early church's encounter with Gnostic thought, with its teaching of direct revelation for the select few and of God revealing himself in human form, did influence Christianity notwithstanding the biblical-historical view of indirect divine revelation through historical acts and events. The notion of incarnation, says Pannenberg, had roots in Gnostic understanding of revelation, but the Christian faith integrated this Gnostic idea into its own historical and apocalyptic structure. The incarnation of Christ is a kind of summary interpretation of the revelation of divine self-vindication of God in the earthly life and fate of Jesus:

> The concept of incarnation expresses the *development* of the process of God's revelation and its coming to fruition in the one man Jesus of Nazareth. This is the development from the distant majesty of God to his imminence that is revealed for all time in the Christ event. The statement of the incarnation is a final résumé of the God of Israel's history of revelation. (Pannenberg 1969a: 151)

The doctrine of the incarnation must be understood as a secondary reading of the biblical-historical revelation, a summary of indirect self-revelation, not as the primary non-historical event from which revelation is interpreted and dehistoricized in dualistic fashion.

The final thesis, seven, states that 'The Word relates itself to revelation as foretelling, forthtelling and report.' The concept of the direct coming of the Word of God might be influenced by the Gnostic tradition, but is also clearly found in the Old Testament, raising the question of its relation to revelation. The direct divine self-manifestation, a clear Gnostic emphasis, is not to be confused with 'God's multi-pronged involvement in the concrete execution of the history of revelation by means of his authorised word' (Pannenberg 1969a: 152). Pannenberg points out that history entails meaning, rather than just raw facts, and that history involves understanding hope and remembrance, a developing understanding in the processes of culture and time. E. H. Carr's previously cited formulation of the gradual process of validation of some ideas over others as time goes on expresses Pannenberg's point again. History is a process of transmission of meaning and its development in the light of new discoveries and challenges. 'The events of history speak their own language, the language of facts; however this language is understandable only in the context of the traditions and expectations in which the given events occur' (Pannenberg 1969a: 153). The resurrection of Jesus as an event of some kind, with a meaning to be derived from its context, fits into this hermeneutical pattern.

To what extent, asks Pannenberg, are the words authorized by the God of Israel and Jesus to be related to the history that he activates? The Word of God is promise, and this is a vital aspect to the understanding of revelation. The interlinking of the foretelling of the prophetic word with historical events prophesied establishes the promises of God in the tradition of Israel. God vindicates his deity, his Lordship over all reality, in this way and this again is a part of the totality of revelation, of the way Israel was taught of the rule of God. This prophetic word of promise and fulfilment is included in the apocalyptic teaching of the end time and the nearness of the kingdom of God. The culmination of all prophetic promise and warning is seen in Christ, the anticipation of the end of all history.

The Word of God is also 'forthtelling', the declaration of the Law of Israel entails the universal deity and holiness of God which is to be vindicated and not mocked, the end of days will see the vindication of the ways of God and the judgement of the wicked. The forthtelling of the Word as law therefore cannot be said to be direct self-revelation but to contribute to the understanding of God alongside his acts by indirect consideration. Likewise the forthtelling of God's law presupposes Jesus being the bearer of divine authority and the divine self-disclosure, fulfilling the law of holiness and grace. This forthtelling of holy love is, again, not direct self-revelation but indirectly participates in that content derived from indirect self-revelation as history.

The Word of God as kerygma is most aptly described as 'reporting' that the Christ event is the Word 'of the cross', or 'of redemption', or some key aspect of the meaning and significance of the life and fate of Jesus, which is also the self-vindication of God. This 'reporting' however is not simply detached chronicling, but embodies the note of proclamation and faith in the content reported by the apostolic message about Christ and his significance for us now. The kerygma does involve 'notification' of events, of facts and their meaning: 'The events by which God demonstrates his deity are self-evident as they stand within the framework of their own history. It does not require any kind of inspired interpretation to make these events recognizable as revelation' (Pannenberg 1969a: 155).

Thus Pannenberg declares the sheer facticity of the Christian message, that it speaks for itself once the facts, with their contextually driven meaning, are allowed to speak for themselves. This message then elicits a decision to trust in the Christian hypothesis about the meaning of all history as given by God as revealed in Christ.

Pannenberg is deliberately rejecting the tradition of kerygmatic or dialectical theology, obviously against Bultmann's complete abandonment of the field of history as relevant to the message of salvation, epistemologically and ontologically. And he is rejecting

Barth's epistemological view of the need for faith as a prerequisite for seeing divine self-revelation in and through the history of Jesus narrated by the apostles and prophets. Without this a priori attitude of faith and worship, in Barth's theology, that history notified by the traditions of scripture is merely Ancient Near Eastern history, open to the critical studies of the historian, but is not revelation (Barth 1975).

Pannenberg says that the content of this history, open to the careful and reasonable reader, itself declares the deity and love of God: these events are sufficient, with proper interpretation, to mediate the divinely given meaning to the reasonable person. Sermons, moreover, are reports of the revealing history 'and an explication of the language of fact which is implicit in this history' (Pannenberg 1969a: 155). Preachers should be getting the historical probability of the Christian message across to congregations, not whipping them into making emotive leaps of faith. Since the 'content' of this history is so rich and meaningful it will indeed impact on the lives and decisions of the hearers of this Word of God as kerygma, will call for response to the meaning of the facts and bring consolation.

In his final 'Postscript to the second edition' of *Revelation as History*, Pannenberg explains further what he means by this very objective view of the proclamation of the Word as reporting the historical facts with their meaning, in response to critics who accused him of a rationalism and a detached objectivity over against the very object of faith, God, who surely must be approached only in worship and not critical questioning. Pannenberg explains against Günter Klein that 'what matters is precisely the way in which we are affected by the event' (Pannenberg 1969a: 188) which befalls us, that is the event of hearing the reports of the life and fate of Jesus – presumably exemplified by the preaching of Peter in Acts, leading to many repenting and having faith in Jesus. The object of the reporting is such that a proper cognitive apprehension could not be of mere interest since the content of knowledge about this object lays claim to a person's whole life. Moreover this knowledge, as all knowledge of all content, is subject to the testing of time and new factors coming up to challenge or confirm the content gained in the knowledge:

The process in which human beings are affected by an event befalling them becomes fully intelligible only when we see that human life is realized always in contexts of traditions that are either confirmed or modified by our experiences, that perhaps can also be broken through, and in certain circumstances broken off. (Pannenberg 1969a: 189)

The reported events gain their meaning from their contexts of tradition, and these can bring the deepest possible impact on people. We also need to note the relation of knowledge to faith: we need knowledge to rely on for faith, but the priority of knowledge to faith is logical and not a temporal one. Some theological adjudicators, however, have read Pannenberg as heavily rationalist, for example, John Macquarrie (1981).

For Barth, the glory of the Word speaks for itself in the world, the glory of the Son of God in his priestly self-giving which is at the same time the glory of the 'royal man' exalted to partnership with the Father: for Pannenberg the content of the meaning of the history of Jesus, his life, death and rising from death, also speaks for itself by the language of facts. The intriguing contrast is over the 'content', for Barth the '*Sache*', of faith and theology: as a young rising theologian Barth had been engaged by the great Adolph Harnack, a most eminent liberal Protestant, over this very question – what is the object of the theological task, to what is it responsible? (Rumscheidt 1972). Harnack was insistent on rigorous historical critical scholarship as vital for theology, with faith a matter of private moral discipline. Barth insisted that God was the content of theology and so needed a response of faith and worship, appropriate also to theological reasoning, transcending history and moral reasoning. Harnack was no Hegelian, however, and rather was loyal to Kant's view that God was 'beyond our ken', outside our field of knowing altogether. Unlike Pannenberg, Harnack regarded Jewish apocalyptic as primitivist myth to be stripped away and not taken seriously as the context for Jesus' life and fate. Pannenberg sees his work as going beyond Harnack and liberal Protestantism while upholding his commitment to critical histori-cal research, and also as taking forward Barth – notably his definition of the 'strict' view of revelation as the hinge for faith, the way from the history of Israel and Jesus to the self-disclosure of God. Harnack's historicism lies under the kind of 'analogy of history' challenged by Pannenberg in his rejection of Troeltsch's handling of history considered above, that is to say Harnack would not allow for the possibility of a new happening or that the course of history could reveal anything about God. For Harnack the secular and sacred are divided clearly, and history falls under the auspices of the former and critical scholarship: the Kantian dualism that Pannenberg attacks.

For Pannenberg, as we have seen, 'secular' historical scholarship can analyse data and identify events which, taken in their context of thought, will yield meaning and there is nothing to rule out a meaning that points to the divine. As he says in his 'Postscript': '"Unprejudiced" perception of events revealing God is directed precisely to their position in historical context, to their original meaning, mediated through the context of traditions into which they entered' (Pannenberg 1969a: 190). The totality of history and its meaning is, as we have seen above, the overarching context for all traditions and questions, which are preserved and developed and ultimately superseded in the whole. The resurrection of Jesus is the anticipation of that overall meaning – an anticipatory meaning which, however, will itself develop in meaning and face new challenges as they arise. The Christ event is no *deus ex machina* arriving as an alien event in the mist of time, but rather is the climax of the whole proleptic structure of history, which is always reaching forward and either confirming or undermining current orthodoxies with the arrival of what is new, as new insights cast light back onto present and past understandings.

This very structure, as E. H. Carr puts it, is what Christian eschatology says, that the end of history has the last judgement on events, behaviour, theories and world views, and somehow this future judgement comes to meet us ahead of time. Or we might illustrate this shape of 'revelation as history' in the light of the Christian liturgical calendar where Advent is listed four weeks before Christmas. Advent, strictly speaking, is about the 'second coming' of Christ in judgement and final rule over all things: Christmas celebrates the birth of Jesus as a baby, the Christ child, the Messiah long expected. The churches using this calendar celebrate the coming in 'great humility' of the one who is to come in 'glorious majesty' as supreme judge, and at the same time regard the former as ultimately having the divine identity of the latter – and of course as the former is taken up by the latter a radically new understanding, or revelation, of the glorious, majestic divine judge is given. The form of the proleptic revelation is taken up into the divine essence, leading to the trinitarian understanding of God's very being. The 'last judgement' is a process working in history now, testing, criticizing and remaking events and ideas, refining them, taking them forward into clarity and truth, for Carr; for Pannenberg there will in fact be an actual end-time event of judgement on history.

Pannenberg's doctrine of revelation entails the divine self-definition as being that of the God whose very being is unified with that of the crucified and risen Jesus – intriguingly akin to Barth's way in to Christology and Trinity, with the necessary adjustments of epistemological method. We certainly see a dialectic in Pannenberg's view of revelation between the proleptic and the ultimate end point, each enriching the full meaning of the other. In sharp distinction to Barth, of course, Pannenberg is claiming that this argumentation for divine self-disclosure in the Christ event can be conducted on the basis of critical scholarly reasoning on the same basis as is all such historical interpretative work – although as will become clear later he has his own way of allowing the Spirit's activity to be part of this human project of discovery. 'The proleptic structure, which determines the form of all acts of knowledge is proper to the knowledge of the Christ event also precisely in view of its content' (Pannenberg 1969a: 199). And this, like all knowledge, is provisional in the sense of being open to the judgement of new evidence and insights that will emerge from the future, and ultimately of course, 'Only God's future will bring the final disclosure of what took place in the Christ event' (Pannenberg 1969a: 199). That great day of final reckoning and judgement holds the ultimate verification and vindication, the deepest meaning of what happened in and to Christ, in relation to the God he called Father.

OVERVIEW OF PANNENBERG'S DOCTRINE
OF REVELATION

In Pannenberg's seminal text, *Revelation as History*, he sets out a doctrine of revelation that is dynamic, and historical in the sense of a moving history, not merely an antiquarian looking back to the past for a fixed criterion of meaning, but a movement linking the past, present and future as they move ahead drawing the past forward and distilling its best insights to engage with new questions, in order to gain a world view consistent with all the information known to us now. Only the end of the process, the eschaton in Christian language, will give the moment of total truth and the whole picture or rather its meaning, qualitatively rather than quantitatively. We use a provisional map which we have to adjust as new terrain or weather conditions or other factors are encountered, and this is both revelational and reasonable. Perhaps one might say that a new form of 'logos' is emerging at the centre of Pannenberg's doctrine, albeit in historicist mode, linking reason and revelation, rooting both in the giving of the God of Israel, Jesus and the totality of all things. This new mode of logos might be 'prolepsis', the structure of looking forward and back simultaneously in order to gain a purchase on how things are, to anticipate the future and reconfigure the meanings of the past. Reason, for Pannenberg, is not an a priori capacity but an historical structure of 'sketching and reflecting' and with 'an essential openness to a truth always presupposed but never grasped in the act of thinking out the sketch' (Pannenberg 1969a: 198). Individual events, or clusters of events in their cultural contexts of tradition, can be revelatory of aspects of the divine in an anticipatory way. But only the totality of meaning as it supersedes, takes up and climaxes all prior nexuses of meaning, can equate with revelation 'strictly' defined, that is, self-revelation of the very being of God and the ultimate meaning of all history and reality. And yet, dialectically, we have a foreshadowing of that final meaning in Christ, the sketch plan proving itself now and into the future, and yet again – dialectically – provisionally. This dialectic is a moving one, Hegelian and not Kierkegaardian, clearly structured as temporal prolepsis, an historical form of logical development, seeking to yield provisional but accurate sketch plans of reality. The proleptic structure of the Christ event means that this is no mere bare assurance planted into history extrinsically, but it reveals and enacts the human and the divine interweaving as we are drawn to trust in the God of the future eschaton, made present here and now.

This describes our lived experience and gives its logical shape in our own personal lives. But also the widest possible canvass of truth and meaning is given eschatologically and so also proleptically in Christ to us, who otherwise would be in the dark trying to make sense of things religiously and rationally. This Christ event gives us the plan of how reality is and so how our lives fit, or should fit, into this great web of divine meaning, and indeed how God relates to it and us. History is akin to a great drama, the great story of divine disclosure, revealed in fullness only in the final moment of the play when we know 'the play', when the various plots and sub-plots forge together to give us the whole message and meaning:

> [R]evelation, which is substantiated through the course of history, can be an event only at its ending: that is, after the totality of events has run out, which for their part acquire their definitive light only in virtue of the end. (Pannenberg 1969a: 206)

The whole is vital, and while in a play, for example, a Greek drama, we can see 'the end' as inevitable, a tragic fate of the gods that cannot be prevented or changed, in the tradition of Israel this is not the case, since God is free and will bring about the new and unpredictable thing. And the traditions of Israel are, for Pannenberg, decisively important, not a priori but because of their content and power to map reality convincingly. He goes on to say that,

> The peculiarity of the end event in relation to the total course of history is indeed decisively connected with the fact that in the Israelitic sense the course of history is not to be understood as development. Its individual constituents do not yet carry within themselves what they are in truth. Instead, it is in the light of the end that the meaning is decided of the whole way and of its individual factors . . ... The end event not only reveals but also alone decides the meaning of all that is provisional; and, by thus constituting history as a whole and the true meaning of individual figures and factors, it finally reveals God as its creator (thus absolutely for the first time in its full meaning.). (Pannenberg 1969a: 206)

The whole of history, rather like the whole of a play, has its message 'given' entirely by its ending which reads back over the events of the play to declare the meaning of all the 'factors', all the clusters of events in different contexts bundling up together until that final 'secret' discloses itself and every thing else with it. We know now, in advance, that the Christ event holds the key, in its contextual world of the Israelite traditions: and so we know that this event does hold the clue to all things, and yet cannot be 'grasped' or domesticated, to use Kierkegaard's term. 'It' is in fact the self-revelation of God, and so engages our lives and decisions accordingly.

Pannenberg's doctrine of revelation claims to be both rational and biblical, a perfectly reasonable theory of how things are for all to consider without any special pleading by way of a leap of faith or subjective warmings of the heart prior to engagement with the 'facts' mediated through the historical records and the 'history of transmission of traditions'. He has made a clear break with the dominant twentieth-century German Protestant model of the Word speaking to us now, through Scripture and the church witness as the Spirit acts to bring the message to life in us and for us. This approach uses a duality of knowing in relation to revelation, a faith mode as against the secular critical mode, this mode has to be one of worship and faith since revelation reveals God, not simply another object in the universe, and that revelation is 'direct'. Pannenberg as we have seen insists on our normal cognitive processes in relation to 'revelation as history' which is 'indirectly' mediated to us as we consider the facts and evidence until the content emerging from our consideration shows it to be about divine disclosure in the Christ event, and this content moves us to engagement with God in trust.

The structure of all life also prompts us to ponder on our past as the future becomes the present, bringing fresh insight and change of perspective with it. Israel's experiences and the teaching of the prophets raised the question of divine universal rule and holiness of God, to be confirmed at the end of days and trusted till then. 'Strictly defined' revelation, divine essence being disclosed, is an eschatological event but prefigured by such world historical insights as Israel kept and were taken forward in the early church with a Hellenistic bent. All manner of manifestations and teachings did disclose facts about God, leading up to the Christ event.

Pannenberg therefore teaches that reason is thoroughly compatible with revelation, that the two mesh and complement each other, that the *conceptual* gain of 'self-revelation' disclosing divine essence combining with the *happening*s of the Christ event in the context of Israel's traditions do yield the ultimate meaning of all things, proleptically. We should note that Scripture becomes, in Pannenberg's theology, a set of texts associated with the history of Israel and its claims to insights given it from the God who creates and sustains all things, also with Israel's bringing forth of the man Jesus as the product and the climax of its spiritual journey, the messianic figure whose life, death and resurrection unfolded the meaning of the vocation of Israel for the world. It is the sheer content of the texts, not a matter of special textual inspiration but the record of the prophets, chronicles, wisdom, apocalyptic hope from beyond the political corruptions of this world, that content is the important matter about Scripture. We could compare it to the Shakespearean canon, a canon important for the quality of its dramatic literature itself, the actual content we find there told by the words of the texts. The authority of the Scripture is a matter of its substance, and the texts are fully open to scrutiny and interpretation. This substance, looked at in the light of the Christ event, tells us of the world as created reality, as free and formed, and as upheld by the divine life disclosed as trinitarian. And again, all this theologically imbued history, with all its particularity and strangeness, rolls up, or rather is taken up, towards the Christ event to open up its depth of truth, truth as given in and through history by God, according to Christian Scripture.

We can find a parallel line of theological support from the leading Greek Orthodox theologian, John Zizioulas, who contrasts the New Testament view of truth with the Hebraic historicism on the one hand and Greek philosophical thought on the other. The Old Testament idea of truth is eschatological, the truth is to come but is not already here, as it is in Christ for the New Testament. Likewise in contrast to the Greek metaphysical view, Christ is an historical being and is the truth, which challenges the Greek view of timeless truth, 'since it is in the flow of history and through it, through its changes and ambiguities, that man is called to discover the meaning of existence' (Zizioulas 1985: 71). It is not clear, however, whether Zizioulas would give the degree of provisionality, formally at least, to the self-revelation of God in the Christ event to give space for new discoveries to arise and possibly challenge it.

We should note here that for Pannenberg, historical events, which are clusters of events in their cultural contexts, do have a correct interpretation which will emerge at the end of the day – again as E. H. Carr's dictum also indicates, since the future will evaluate competing ideas and interpretations and the dross will drop away with the test of time. So the resurrection of Christ has to be theoretically 'provisional' while being the most probable understanding taking account of all the evidence available now. This view entails a version of the eschatological verification principle, that is the truth will be revealed in the future, Christ will judge all history, being a myth in Carr's words, but for now we walk in faith, which is very credible, reasonable and probable for Pannenberg. In this assumption that there is ultimately one convincing and true interpretation Pannenberg flies in the face of 'postmodernity' and its stress on the diversity of reason, truth and meaning, indeed the deconstruction of such foundational matters. It would be very interesting to see how Pannenberg would respond to the postmodern attack on Enlightenment 'rationalism' and foundationalism. There is little doubt that he would point out the hazards of the postmodern attack undermining its own claims – after all they do claim to offer 'the' overview of how things really and permanently are, an overview, or 'metanarrative', itself liable to deconstruction. Pannenberg perhaps represents the Enlightenment's ability to take care of itself intellectually. He certainly does uphold the 'metanarrative' of reality as reasonable, but also as free and provisional and open to what is new, all criteria vital to the postmoderns.

His *Revelation as History* can be seen as the seminal text for the rest of his theology, the structural frame, or principles which he develops and expands theologically and philosophically, and indeed anthropologically, into his very large subsequent corpus of theological writing. The strict concept of divine self-revelation, indirectly gained through human consideration and reflection, and at the same time given to human understanding in events and ideas flowing from God, enables Christianity to see the true meaning of Jesus' resurrection as the divine self-disclosure, opening up whole new vistas of meaning and being. This definition of revelation, rooting back through Barth to Hegel according to Pannenberg, is the matrix for faith and theology and indeed ontology. Revelation as history is one side of the same coin of reality, the other is the statement of an historicist philosophy of reality, coherent with Christian eschatology, as Carr realized, moving forwards historically so we can look back and correct our ideas retrospectively as the new amends the old, as concepts are verified by events, as the particulars are taken up in the expanding horizon leading to the universal.

TRUTH AND CONCEPTS OF GOD

Having launched his theology on the basis of his doctrine of revelation, Pannenberg returns to it again at the end of his career, his *Systematic Theology* (Pannenberg 1991). There Pannenberg places his interpretation of revelation after initial chapters dealing with the question of God in terms of philosophy and religion. This reminds us sharply of Hegel's approach to religion and its treatment first of the *concept* of religion then the concrete religions themselves (Hegel 1998). Pannenberg, in fact, acknowledges his admiration of Hegel in this project, and defends him from the charge of holding a purely intellectualistic and abstract concept of religion: 'Awareness of God', for Hegel, 'the concept of deity, is indeed the basis, but the concept of religion reaches its culmination in the cultus' (Pannenberg 1991: 173). Cultus, for Hegel, means all forms of bridging the gulf between humanity and God. The final form of religion will be that which God brings about, in convergence with the human attempt to reach after the divine. The path from concept to concrete reality could be said to characterize Pannenberg's theological technique: a concept develops and refines itself, then is put to the test of concrete history.

Revelation is going to manifest itself finally in all the debates and controversies of life. 'The manifestation of divine reality even within the unresolved conflicts of religious and ideological truth claims is called revelation' (Pannenberg 1991: 171). This restates the thesis of revelation as history, linked to all the phenomena of the historical flow, isolated from no part of it. Christian theology must exist in this continual struggle to uphold its truth claims against all manner of criticisms and rivals, and divine self-disclosure comes in and through this complex and contested context. The *Systematic Theology*, consistently with *Revelation as History*, insists that Christian theology cannot simply base itself on assertions which are not subject to critical questioning by unfettered reason. But 'the knowledge of God that is made possible by God, and therefore by revelation, is one of the basic conditions of the concept of theology as such', says Pannenberg; 'Otherwise the possibility of the knowledge of God is logically inconceivable; it would contradict the very idea of God' (Pannenberg 1991: 2). This logical deduction from the concept of God, that God, if he is God, must disclose himself rather than be an object of human discovery akin to some sort of supra-object, does not close the question of how this revelation is made and how human kind apprehends it.

Pannenberg rejects the distinction between natural theology and revealed theology, as if the former were the product of some 'God-free zone' of human enterprise. Revelation comes in and through the processes of history, subjective and objective. He affirms this as a matter of epistemology, rejecting a fideist starting point. Yet as a matter of logic, at the start of the *Systematic Theology* vol. 1, he is able to say that,

> [R]ecourse to the incarnation is indispensable [explaining that] Only from the standpoint of God's saving action that seeks to bring creatures into fellowship with himself can we maintain their participation in the deity of God (without prejudicing their distinctiveness), and therefore in theology as the science of God. (Pannenberg 1991: 6)

Theology can only speak of God if we can know of God in the world's reality, and therefore incarnation seems indispensable to this enterprise. But has it happened, and can we uncover it in the vast flow of history? For the Christian faith it has, and the incarnation is a way of stating the case, although it is not the epistemological starting point, as we have seen.

We move from chapter 1 of his *Systematic Theology* vol. 1 entitled 'The Truth of Christian Doctrine as the Theme of Systematic Theology', to chapter 2, 'The Concept of God and the Question of its Truth.' Chapter 3 takes us to 'The Reality of God and the Gods in the Experience of the Religions', prior to chapter 4, 'The Revelation of God', and chapter 5 'The Trinitarian God'. The pattern is clear. We move from the insistence that Christian doctrine prove itself, rather as a maths teacher might ask a child to demonstrate why the answer given is true. Doctrine cannot simply be asserted by authoritative *diktat*, not that of the Emperor Justinian (Pannenberg 1991: 10), nor that of the consensus of the church, nor the idea of a Koranically kind of inspired Scripture. But Pannenberg does regard the content of Scripture as basic, and all creeds, 'confessions and dogmas are in fact summaries of the central themes of scripture' (Pannenberg 1991: 16). The subject matter of the Scripture, not because of an authoritarian ecclesiastical claim but because of its traditions of prophecy and apocalyptic which cohere with our experience of being in history, through all the processes of interpretation, is what produces church consensus, according to Pannenberg. His view that theology must continually renew itself in the light of the developing exposition of Scripture, and so regard itself as provisional, similarly echoes an evangelical note, *semper reformanda.* In other words, his *Systematic Theology* is a Christian theology, positing the doctrine of Christ and finding Scripture fundamental content: but these doctrinal claims must always be tested, must prove themselves as true in the process of human experience and history, in the light of the whole realm of human intellectual enterprise – and might be wholly discredited intellectually by some future discovery or criticism.

The shape of Pannenberg's thought emerges again as positing a question or idea, and then a confirming of it: a kind of di-polar elliptical process which does not end – until God confirms finally the truth of Christian doctrine at the eschaton. In this way Christian truth claims are ultimately provisional until 'that day' (Pannenberg 1991: 16). Theology articulates the Christian understanding, but also tests its truth and confirms it, rather than presupposing this truth as given beforehand. A kind of bracketing of initial certainty is entailed in terms of the objective intellectual quest, and this will ultimately 'confirm' personal subjective faith (Pannenberg 1991: 50). Pannenberg is keen to argue that truth cannot depend upon my individual act of faith, rather truth is connected to the concept of God, as he commends Augustine for teaching. This in fact is another way of putting his contention about revelation as history: divine being cannot be separated from divine self-disclosure in historical event and interpretation. He develops this point by suggesting that the concept of truth entails the criterion of truth, 'can that be a criterion of truth which is not part of the concept?' he asks (Pannenberg 1991: 53), and thinks that the concept itself becomes ontological. Truth relates to being, and to God: 'God alone can be the ontological locus of the unity of truth in the sense of coherence as the unity of all that is true' (Pannenberg 1991: 53).

But again, this truth will be definitively confirmed only at the eschaton, and the biblical understanding of truth 'does not seek to grasp it as that which is present behind the flux of time. It seeks to grasp it as that which shows and confirms itself to be lasting as time progresses' (Pannenberg 1991: 54). Christian dogmatics then takes the form of postulated hypothesis making sense of reality and conceptuality. Dogmatic statements are assertions, but modestly made. They are propositions laying claim to the truth of what they assert, but are open to question by other disciplines and dialogue partners. Mindless acceptance honours these propositions less than their invitation to testing and confirmation. Dogmatics is really a systematic doctrine of God, and since the world exists, it also concerns the connection of God with this world, including the debateability of

God in the light of human experience: this debateability is not only a matter of the order of knowing, but also of the order of being for God, since God has given himself into the process of history in a real way so that the outcome of history affects God ontologically. This radical doctrine also shows how meaning, for Pannenberg, unites knowing and being as his ultimate ontological category.

Pannenberg's system does not permit the idea that faith builds onto reason as if the two were initially separate and needed to be reintroduced. The two are intrinsically related. For Pannenberg, as we saw in the previous chapter, reason has the same hypothetical structure as faith, and faith is suffused with reason: again, two sides of the same coin. Christian faith understands life in the world on the basis of the self-revelation of God in the resurrection event of Christ, and believers move forward through life believing this to be true and trusting in the revealed God of Jesus, the God of the open future. Psychologically believers are sure, but logically they are open to new evidence – which might contradict their working hypothesis and bring it down, as we saw in his *Revelation as History*.

Philosophically, the historic 'proofs' of the existence of God are no longer convincing. They can be treated as merely projections of human longing for a primal reality sustaining all things, along with the atheistic criticism developed by Feuerbach. But Pannenberg understands the function of the proofs as pointing to the concept of God as essential to a proper human self-understanding. This can be in relation to human reason, or other human faculties, our moral sense, for example. Pannenberg cites Hans Küng's theory that all humans exist presupposing a deep trust that things hold together and are sustained, that the same conditions will continue hour by hour, making life possible. This deep trust in the coherence of things, alongside Pannenberg's own stress on the accompanying newness of events in history, is an anthropological axiom of humanity. It is constitutive of the human condition. The believer refers to this deep basis of things as God. Pannenberg also argues that human freedom is a phenomenon deeply problematic for the atheist to account for, and that it points to an origin in God.

This is not a claim to proof in any strict sense, but rather 'what is maintained is that we are referred to an unfathomable reality that transcends us and the world, so that the God of religious tradition is given a secure place in the reality of human experience' (Pannenberg 1991: 93). As interpreted anthropologically by Kant and Hegel, says

Pannenberg, the proofs of God usefully bear witness to the need of humanity and human reason to rise above the mundane finitude of human existence to the thought of the infinite. The cosmological arguments are important because they refer all reality to the one origin. Pannenberg views the arguments as helping to clarify the concept of God in relation to the world, and so helping to develop a critical, purifying function for theology. The divine is constantly at work in all manner of ways, mediating itself in and through such conceptual philosophical theology, refining the concept of God – which will of course be decisively confirmed and verified at the eschaton. The Spirit of God is at work in the human conceptual development of arguments for his own existence.

RELIGIONS AND REVELATION

Religions in general, not only Christianity, likewise must be relevant to our theological considerations, and here Pannenberg takes an unusual – but surely important and contemporary – course in his *Systematic Theology* by devoting an early methodological chapter to 'the reality of God and the Gods in the experience of the religions', this after his treatment of natural theology. This radical move ought not really to have surprised us, since the religions are part of human history just as much as philosophies and of course make claims about the divine to be tested and evaluated as hypotheses without fear or favour. The history of Christianity and biblical history is not to be picked out a priori as a special, inspired, strand of history, rather we are one open field of knowledge and experience, religiously and cognitively; Pannenberg's commitment to rational testing and debate is never lost in all his theology.

Pannenberg after all has consistently taught that human existence is at its deepest level of being, *Weltoffenheit*, open to the world and what sustains it, and that this points to an inherently religious openness to the future, the future anticipating the final promised end summing up the totality of meaning (Pannenberg 1970a). He has consistently argued that God is indirectly 'co-given' in world history, not directly given or accessible, not, as Heidegger would have put it, 'at hand', like a commodity in the supermarket of the universe (Pannenberg 1976: 301). In ordinary experience of meaning, he teaches, the totality of meaning is only implicitly anticipated, that is to say as the implied grand context for any particular meanings, whereas in religious experience there is already present 'a form of explicit awareness of the total meaning of reality, even though it is only an indirect assumption within the awareness of the divine basis of all reality' (Pannenberg 1976: 333). Logical implication coincides here with religious sense in his understanding of a less than fully worked out content of religion. The combining of logical unfolding of concepts, with historical development, is vital to Pannenberg's thought, again a clear link to Hegel's style of thinking, both logical and encyclopaedic, in its attempt to grasp the grand unfolding meaning of the universe (Pannenberg 1994: xiii).

Pannenberg is very alert to the issue of the plurality of religions in the world, and the problem that this poses for Christianity. Contradictory truth claims compete with one another, and Christianity cannot escape being classified as one of them. Pannenberg insists on being honest about the clash of religious assertions, and he believes that glossing over this plain fact increases public secular scepticism about religion in the West.

> Only a so-called theology of religions in the industrial societies of the West closes its eyes to this truth, depicting the many religions as in principle unconflicting ways to the same God. In the event this type of theology plays into the hands of the prejudice that the advanced secularism of the modern public has against all religious truth claims, treating the differences in religious confession merely as private matters of no public interest. (Pannenberg 1994: xii)

Christianity must cling to the truth it perceives as coming from the revelation of God given by the resurrection of Jesus, but constantly take responsibility for defending this truth in the light of the many challenges of other disciplines and criticisms.

Pannenberg has an unusual interpretation of the rise of the secular mindset in the West. He does not attribute this to the rise of science or to intellectual criticisms, rather the savage European wars of religion, especially the Thirty Years' War, set back the cause of religion as a public good as societies turned to secular structures to avoid religious feuding. Religion became a matter of private devotion, not a resource for public values and policy making. In the era following September 11, 2001, the extremist Islamic terror attack on the United States, this point has become of great interest and importance as Western secularists and indeed Christians had the political aspect of one branch of a world religion made painfully clear. It is less and less obvious now that all religions do actually make the same truth claims about God. Likewise the assumption that religion is a private matter, detached from wider public relevance and criticism, becomes decreasingly plausible. The moral imperative to respect people of different faiths, and none, can less easily blur into a homogenization of the truth claims of these faiths, *as if* they were the same. Pannenberg, in other words, wants to distinguish tolerant politeness from the question of truth as debated between the positive religions.

He regards a religious dimension as being constitutive for being human, not consciously known or conceptualized until the stage of positive religion – when the concrete religious systems must of course compete, as just indicated, to show which best makes sense of human experience in the world. Human development of cognition, of awareness of objects other than ourselves, presupposes a religious dimension, he argues, 'that which can become the explicit object of religious consciousness is implicitly present in every turning to a particular object of our experience' (Pannenberg 1985: 72). Development of human experience of life entails rising levels of consciousness of other things and of the self as a being in relationships, and of being finite or bounded. Pannenberg draws on a doctrine of the *imago Dei* originating in the work of Herder, who interpreted this divinely given image not as an original state of perfection but rather as a destiny given to us and fulfilled by divine agency. From our earliest days 'we are set before a transcendent mystery in the sense that the silent infinity of reality that is beyond our control constantly presents itself to us as a mystery' (Pannenberg 1991: 114). Later in life this is recognized as having been 'nonthematic' knowledge of God, which is not however properly real knowledge of God.

Pannenberg teaches that we all have a 'sense and taste for the infinite', or a 'dissatisfaction with the finite', very often not brought to the level of intellectual formulation, but that this can be connected to the definite question of God which will be gained from an actual religion. Pannenberg cites Paul's teaching in *Romans* to back up this thesis that in the history of humanity there has always been in some form an explicit awareness of God which is linked to experience of the works of creation, and hence our creaturely perception of creation. Pannenberg, again perhaps like Schleiermacher and his audience of 'cultured despisers of religion', is keenly aware of the need to take seriously the challenges and concerns of contemporary society. This is a generation, in the West at least, in which all talk about God is reduced to subjectivity. Accordingly Pannenberg wants to attend to the fashionable vogue for the religions and the anthropological elements of truth that he might be able to take from this approach, so as to take them up into a theology focusing on the primacy of God and divine revelation. The history of religions and the conceptual development of monotheism, connected to the understanding of the unity of the human race, are significant in Pannenberg's analysis of religion. God is 'the all determining reality' (Pannenberg 1991: 159). As ever, he applies his principle of the need for truth claims to be tested and confirmed in human historical experience.

> In other words, the gods of the religions must show in our experience of the world that they are the powers which they claim to be. They must confirm themselves by the implications of meaning in this experience so that its content can be understood as an expression of the power of God and not his weakness. (Pannenberg 1991: 167)

This seems difficult for the 'theology of the cross', but Pannenberg takes this into account and applies a kind of 'test of time' criterion. Conceptual testing is included, a point that can be forgotten in Pannenberg's analysis, and the concept of revelation as divine self-mediation has become decisive in the history of religious self-testing. God reveals himself in the world, human effort does not reach deity by unaided effort: this notion, he claims, has attracted such widespread agreement so as to become a definitive concept (Pannenberg 1991: 171).

Placing revelation after a treatment of religion in his definitive *Systematic Theology* clarifies Pannenberg's approach, making him very unusual among Christian theologians, but within that tradition of theology so keen to make links with contemporary culture and to begin with the questions it is asking – that of the religions being one of growing importance. Pannenberg is acutely aware of the pluralist approach to religions now prevalent in the West, and the effect of this to relativize all religious claims into the realm of private taste. It is therefore vital to take up this issue with all seriousness in doing Christian theology. Pannenberg accepts that religions can pervert and mythicize the relationship of God to the world, as Barth stressed. But Pannenberg thinks that the revelation of God transcends the dangers of human construction of idolatrous religion, and that in the course of the history of religion the God of Israel emerges as the God of the universe. The claim of Christianity, one of the religious claimants, is that it will prove itself as true. This is better put that the God of the Bible will prove himself to be the one God of all people, the one God disclosed in Jesus Christ. Historical revelation confirms the concept of the one God, the all-determining reality. Christian theology takes the form of explicating and confirming the truth claim about this God, starting with the historical revelation. Theology is at the same time a theory or hypothesis of the meaning of history, rooted in the person of Jesus and the God he trusted.

Revelation recapitulated in the context of religions

The thesis of 'revelation as history' is reaffirmed in the *Systematic Theology*, with some attention to his critics' concern about the displacement of the 'word of God' model of revelation. Pannenberg maintains his use of the apocalyptic idea that the final truth, now lying hidden in historical events, will appear at the eschaton, together with the idea of provisionality before that day. He emphasizes the varied nature of the experiences of Israel in relation to God, and claims that his view of 'indirect self-revelation' has the 'systematic function of integrating the various experiences of revelation to which the biblical writings bear witness' (Pannenberg 1991: 243). Again Pannenberg stresses that the decisive concept of revelation is crucial, the concept of the self-revelation of the very being of God, the concept claimed to be realizing itself as real, as historical. This truth becomes clear in retrospect as the processes of interpretation engage with the historical events set in context.

We are placed in a sort of historical dialectic: on the one hand the future will manifest the truth of God, 'on the other hand, there are preliminary revelations of this final event that is still hidden in the future' (Pannenberg 1991: 247), in prophetic and apocalyptic insights. Jesus' proclamation of the kingdom of God is similar to these preliminary disclosures of end-time events, but the coming of God's kingdom actually occurs here, the power that shapes the future.

> The future of God is not merely disclosed in advance with the coming of Jesus; it is already an event, although without ceasing to be future . . .. In this special sense we can speak of an anticipatory

revelation, in Christ's person and work, of the deity of God that in the future of his kingdom will be manifest to every eye. (Pannenberg 1991: 247)

Pannenberg also retains his original view that special subjective 'supplemental' inspiration to understand revelation is not necessary: the content of that revelation is sufficiently convincing and self-interpreting, the apostolic message is Spirit filled in virtue of its content, and so can impart the Spirit. The most proper understanding of the 'Word of God' is Jesus Christ, the quintessence of the divine plan for creation and history, and their final destiny, yet already come in advance. The Christian revelation and its intellectual outworking will constitute itself to be the consummate religion, of all religions: 'just as the thought of revelation becomes a comprehensive one for God's action and thus takes the place that myth has in other religions' (Pannenberg 1991: 257). All religions, however, all have their aspects of truth, which are part of the overall process of the self-manifestation of the deity, and indeed the state of religions, their diversity and unity, reflects the unity and diversity of God and this process moves towards the end time (Pannenberg 1991: 171). Revelation, however, holds the key to this ultimate disclosure, and 'Christian speech about God can be verified only in such a way that it is the revelation of God itself which discloses that about man and his world in relation to which its truth is proved' (Pannenberg 1971a: 206–7).

Israel discovered that history is the plane on which divine self-manifestation happens, and Christianity inherits this true insight, taking it to the culmination of Christ, the proleptic universal end for of creation. World religions constitute a vital part of world history, the totality of which constitutes revelation in the strict sense, so they are bound to be taken up into the whole meaning of God and the history woven from the divine future, a future culminating in the Christ event. The historicity of the resurrection of Jesus is crucial factor in the uniqueness of Christianity (D'Costa 1990: 96–106).

TRINITARIAN CONCLUSION

Revelation as history has been followed through to include the history of religions and concepts, all subject to reasoned scrutiny and all material for the sketching projections trying to make sense of our overall experience of life in history. The provisional anticipatory projections are themselves part of the web of history and time, and they are proven or disproven with the arrival of new events. The faith of Israel is that God is at work in history, and will finally vindicate his rule of all things at the end of days, the moment of ultimate revelation of the very being of God. This concept is validated and realized in the Christ event, if that event did happen in some way, and it is quite credible that it did. Here we note a key procedure found throughout Pannenberg's work, the dialectical process of moving from experience or historical event to a conceptualizing of that, then to the test of that concept in historical events and an adjustment or confirmation accordingly. This is a procedure very akin to that deployed by Hegel – the taking up, superseding and inclusively transcending, of the past as history moves ahead in the Spirit. The great and vital difference, as Pannenberg points out clearly, is that the process of history is not driven by a necessity of inner logic so much as drawn onwards by the free God of the open future. That is the whole point of his programme.

History is accessible through reason which can probe its true meaning to reach the notion of revelation and divine purpose and reign, a kind of 'natural theology', which at the same time is a revelational way of looking at history. Reason and faith cohere perfectly, and the ongoing provisionality of the content of revelation requires reasoning for the sake of faith. The concept of revelation as divine self-revelation means that only God can prove it to be true, and the Christ event, with its surrounding debates, is precisely given by God and yet remains provisional as such. The dialectic of openness, confirmation and openness to new confirmation or negation, continues as history moves on to its final promised end. The stimulus to gaining meaning from events 'derives from the event itself' (Pannenberg 1969a: 15), in an objectivist, rather than subjectivist, mode of interpretation. Pannenberg has exploited what C. K. Barrett refers to as 'the natural affinity between apocalyptic eschatology and philosophical idealism' (Barrett 1973: 53), and the interweaving strands of apocalyptic provisionality in the light of the final vindication (Pannenberg 1991: 210).

This doctrine of revelation is clearly an economic trinitarianism:

In the fate of Jesus, the God of Israel is revealed as the triune God. The event of revelation should not be separated from the being of God himself. The being of God does not belong just to the Father, but also to the Son. The Holy Spirit also shares in the being of God by virtue of his participation in the glory of God that comes to life in the eschatological congregation. Hegel and Barth are correct in the principle of grounding the doctrine of the Trinity in revelation. In all periods of history, one can experience with special force the incomprehensibility of God in that the dualism of the one and the many, which always guided Greek conceptualization of God, is here overcome. All of this is connected with the fact that the doctrine of the Trinity formulates the concept of God as a historically experienced revelation (Pannenburg 1969a: 143).

Pannenberg's thesis of Revelation as History is deeply trinitarian, the Father as the free God of the open future and 'all determining reality', the Son the proleptic self-revelation of the very being of God, the Spirit integrating the meaning of all history together and enabling the new to synthesize with the past into the present. Pannenberg offers a dialectical movement of the God of the open future into the finite form of time as the sovereign free God reaching into the bonds of time and space as temporal human being.

This economic trinitarian ontology integrates God into history and history, in its fullness, into God, an immanentist doctrine of God protecting divine freedom and sovereignty from being imprisoned in history, by the future tense: God is free as the God of the future. At the end of days, the final eschaton, God will become the God of the 'future perfect tense', God will always have been this God, it was always going to have been this way since God freely invested his being into this history and not another history, so its openness was real and yet was always going to be realized in the way it actually worked out – from God's free love. The dialectic dynamic moves from end to beginning and vice versa, the time line has, as it were, joined both its ends together into an elipse. Epistemologically we participate in this from the temporal finite perspective and so, as we discover *through the concept of revelation* this historical ontology, what is the real shape of reality, we discover the reality of the divine life in and through history, as history even, leading to the worship of the glory of the Lord.

CHAPTER 3

JESUS' ESCHATOLOGICAL IDENTITY

FOCUSED TEXT:
JESUS GOD AND MAN

PANNENBERG'S ESCHATOLOGICAL
HISTORICIST CHRISTOLOGY

Jesus God and Man (Pannenberg 1977b) is the title given to the English translation of Pannenberg's magisterial treatise on Christology, *Grundzüge der Christologie*, first published in 1964. Pannenberg in this rich study sets out to explore the problems of Christology in the light of his theology of history,

> characterised by the concept of the prehappening of the end of history in the activity and destiny of Jesus. This idea must be subjected to the question of its verification in terms of the entire range of Christological problems. Moreover, the thesis that God's revelation can be known from its historical manifestation in the history of Jesus can find the necessary clarification only by carrying out the interpretation of the Christological traditions as the development of the significance inherent in the activity and destiny of Jesus. (Pannenberg 1977b: 12)

We remember that events ultimately bear their own inherent meaning, taken in their contemporary cultural contexts, and that the true interpretations will emerge with testing and proving of time in the traditions flowing from the original event. The work, he tells us, engages with issues of ontology and epistemology related to the issues of the meaning of Jesus, ultimately of course relating to the widest possible horizon, that of the end time. His work is to continue his reasoned theology of an eschatologically oriented ontology which will help clarify, and be clarified by, Christological explication.

He has a particular early warning for 'whoever finds enjoyment in it' to 'continue to measure my talk about knowledge and reality with the standard of a positivistic understanding of being and knowledge in order in this way to discover to his general surprise its inappropriateness' (Pannenberg 1977b: 12). Pannenberg is not a positivist philosophically, not a reductivist, but rather a thinker who is interested in events and meanings arising from them, in concepts relating to events and the movement of thought progressing through history. For Pannenberg, the Kantian division between critically appraised 'fact' and moral 'meaning' does not reflect reality or how we think. We need therefore to attend to the doctrinal traditions of Christology and also to the critical historical study of Jesus. The history of doctrine itself needs to be charted in relation to contexts and to the philosophical questions of truth, and the lasting truth in this Christological tradition only discloses itself to a critical appropriation that grasps and tests the Christological models. We see again the interweaving of conceptual history set against contextual historical reality, interpretative tradition meshing with today's questions and with the Jesus of history in his context: the history of the development of Christological doctrine ultimately needs to show that it gives us the best interpretation of Jesus' history and significance. This entails that Jesus has a clear meaning which can accurately be transmitted through human thought and witness down the years, so that its content is open for us to examine, accept or reject according to its interpretative power.

As seen in the previous chapter, Pannenberg argues that the meaning of Jesus, gained from setting his life and fate in Jewish apocalypticism, is universal and so claims the totality of history – historical 'fact' and the 'meaning' of everything become one. The development of Christological traditions, with all the transformations and reconfigurations attempted, follows from the logic inherent in the activity and destiny of Jesus, which we can see as historians of doctrine in retrospect as we try to discriminate between successful and misleading theological suggestions. Pannenberg signals his intention to conduct his Christological work through a historical review of Christological transmission of traditions, and readers will be very aware of being given a wonderful education in the history of theology as they proceed through the text. But this shape is also theologically important because the succession of interpretations belongs to the historic essence of the subject matter to be interpreted, as its claimed universal significance relates to new and wider understandings and events, producing new interpretations. The real is the rational, and reason is in time. Pannenberg does not claim to produce an encyclopaedic history of Christological tradition but to confine himself to key aspects of the topic and typical tendencies. The notion of unchanging dogmatic statements, frozen in time, must be abandoned in favour this more historicist mode of approach with its keen recognition of the truth and its expression being debated and refined as new discoveries and hypotheses arise. But the meaning of the Christ event is not an arbitrary matter of interpretation being imposed on the subject matter, rather the history of Jesus carries its meaning in itself, and will ultimately resist interpretations that fail to accord with the original dynamic of Jesus in his context – although this can in theory be changed by new evidence.

It might be worth noting here that Pannenberg's structure of thought suggests comparison with some Roman Catholic thinking about the development of doctrine, notably that influenced by Newman's work written in self-justification of his acceptance of the Roman Catholic dogmas and authority. Newman jettisoned his Anglican position, resting on the patristic doctrinal formulae as normative Christian interpretations of the Bible in the church, for a position of developing tradition enriching itself as it went on in history. Like an idea, expanding and increasing in depth and width as it engages with philosophies and cultures, Christianity changes while staying the same, indeed in order to stay the same: 'here below . . . to be perfect is to have changed often' (Newman 1845: 40). Pannenberg has a much greater concern for the historical Jesus as a criterion to test novel doctrinal suggestions than has Newman, for whom church authority expressed by the papacy becomes the infallible test of suggested developments. Pannenberg's theological procedure is very ecumenical indeed, but he would not accept an infallible human oracle to determine truth from falsehood, rather he trusts to high-quality critical and hermeneutical reasoning to sort the 'wheat from the chaff' in terms assessing developments, and trusts the future to judge.

Pannenberg is far more philosophically self-aware than Newman, who is writing an apologia for his change of mind to accepting

Roman Catholic doctrines and practices that cannot be grounded in the New Testament nor the early patristic Fathers, and so appeals to change and expansion: the river is broader and deeper the *further* from the initial stream of the Apostolic Church. Pannenberg wishes to correlate doctrinal development with the history of Jesus scholarship, and put this into a universal context not just a church context. But he is indeed very concerned to take full account of the community of faith and its experience of Jesus in its spiritual life through the centuries. He says in his first chapter that, 'Christology deals with Jesus as the basis of the confession and the faith that he is the Christ of God' (Pannenberg 1977b: 21), and begins his treatise by taking very seriously Christian experience in the church. He accepts the importance of this experience of faith, reviewing Schleiermacher, Kähler and Hermann in this regard, but registers the caution made by Hermann that we need to beware of basing faith on 'something that is perhaps not an historical fact at all, but is itself a product of faith' (Pannenberg 1977b: 23); although Hermann also rejects grounding faith solely on the basis of secular historical research. In particular Pannenberg rejects Bultmann's Christology which dismisses Jesus' temporal history as significant, opting for an appeal to faith experience alone. For Pannenberg we must go back historically, that is using proper historical methods that will command respect among historians generally, behind the New Testament text to Jesus himself. And only this will reveal the reason for the unity binding the different New Testament texts together, that is, the person of Jesus on whom they all focus: they must be read as an historical source, not just a preached text.

The basis of our faith in Jesus of Nazareth is surely Jesus of Nazareth, says Pannenberg, and while this basis must continue to prove itself in the face of new challenges, and be confirmed anew by its power to interpret our modern experience of the world today, yet this basis of Jesus itself lies in the past events which we must explore as best we can – using modern methods and questions, sliding back and forth along the Pannenbergian dialectic of past-to-future-to-past, the continuum of fact and meaning. Present spiritual experience of the church depends on what happened in the past, and only on that basis do we know that Jesus is the exalted Lord:

[O]nly in trust in the reliability of the report of Jesus' resurrection and exaltation are we able to turn in prayer to the one who is exalted and now lives, and thus to associate with him in the present. Christology has the task of unfolding the church's confession of Christ as Lord but above all with grounding it in the activity and fate of Jesus in the past. (Pannenberg 1977b: 28)

The matrix for proposing that this Jewish man Jesus is the Christ, is revelation: 'How else is the history of Jesus supposed to substantiate faith in him except by showing itself to be the revelation of God?' (Pannenberg 1977b: 29). The task of Christology is to bring out this revelatory character inherent in the history of Jesus. We note here that Pannenberg is a critical historical scholar in all fields of study, notably biblical interpretation as his reading of the titles given to Jesus in the New Testament immediately shows: he goes behind the text to see how the various titles developed and were written into texts, their cultural contexts and purposes. But, as he insisted, he is no positivist or reductivist in his outlook on reality as a whole: the new event is philosophically possible.

'CHRISTOLOGY FROM BELOW'

Pannenberg tells us that there are two approaches to Christology, 'from above and from below', and that he is clearly using the latter approach. The former belongs to the era of the patristic theology with its Logos theology of the divine person assuming human nature. Contemporary theologians also use this approach, notably Karl Barth in his theology of the 'history' of the Son of God taking the way of self-giving into 'the far country' of the sinful human world in order to save it and reconcile man to God. Pannenberg gives three reasons why such an approach from the eternal triune Son into the world can no longer stand. First, this presupposes the divinity of Jesus, which is precisely what needs to be shown from history. Second, this top-down approach produces difficulties in integrating the divine with the human, and it detaches Jesus from his Jewish background so as to make it incidental; the particularity of Jesus the Jew as a real man fades into unimportance. Third, we do not have a God's eye view of reality, as moderns we can only begin from the continuum of history where we find ourselves. All this is not to say that two millennia of Christian teaching and faith about Jesus as the Logos enfleshed has been a colossal mistake, but that tradition needs to be reappropriated in the light of new consideration of the evidence. Pannenberg indicates that the way of conducting this work will be to investigate Jesus and his relationship of unity with God: there is no question of following the steps of reductivist theologians who posit the man Jesus independently of his link to God and attitude to God. Indeed Jesus brings about a new take on the word 'God', so that Christology and theology cannot be separated.

Pannenberg proceeds through soteriological motifs in the history of Christology as he asks how Jesus has been understood as divine, that is to say how Jesus the man has been interpreted as saving us. Patristic tradition saw Jesus' humanity as assumed into the deity thus saving us and recapitulating human life experience in a holy way, removing our sins by his act of penitential suffering and obedience. For Anselm, the vicarious self-giving of Jesus the man on the cross satisfied what is owed to God. For Luther, the man Jesus is the one who humbly stands before God to represent us in respect of divine wrath against evil. Post-Enlightenment theologians turned inwards to the human subjectivity, and Schleiermacher produced this theology of Jesus the prototypal religious man, the perfectly God conscious man, and the power of this God consciousness is the divinity of Jesus. Ritschl saw Jesus as the perfectly moral person who founded the community of moral people, the kingdom of God in the world. These neo-Protestant theologies, for Pannenberg, have very modest concerns for the problem of salvation in that they care little about overcoming death or the hope of resurrection, and they look at the issue of forgiveness of sins from the angle that we can all in theory live the good life from the impetus of Jesus. The cross of Jesus becomes something of an embarrassment, and salvation becomes a matter of what we make of life on earth.

Pannenberg again concludes that we must focus on the person of Jesus himself, the historical figure, rather than his effects on us: 'Soteriology must follow from Christology, otherwise faith in salvation loses any real foundation' (Pannenberg 1977b: 48). Looking back to the past is no mere matter of digging up brute facts in the positivistic sense, since meaning is inherent in the activity and fate of Jesus, who understood life as a gift from the Father. Objective fact with meaning must precede our subjective experiences of this content of faith for theology. He turns to Jesus through historical scholarship, but with a wide philosophical lens which takes in the relationship of Jesus with God; this must be discussed first, before any claim to his fulfilling human existence in general can be considered.

The universal significance of Jesus could only be given from God, the Lord of the universe. Part 1 of the book is therefore 'The Knowledge of Jesus' Divinity', and it begins with Jesus' resurrection as the ground of his unity with God.

JESUS' REVELATORY RESURRECTION

Concept of resurrection as credible

Jesus, ministry was ended humanly by his unjust execution, but the Christian claim is that God, whom he trusted as Father, raised him from the dead in an objective yet 'metaphorical' way ungraspable by human words and concepts. Pannenberg begins his discussion of this in *Jesus God and Man* by considering Jesus' oblique 'claim' to authority, made in Hebraic Old Testament terms, for example, in the signs of the kingdom being 'at hand', enacting prophecy and messianic allusions in deed and word. But Pannenberg, while accepting on historical critical grounds that the oldest stratum of sayings about the Son of Man are from Jesus himself rather than editors, does not think that such claims are sufficient to ground a Christology: 'Rather, everything depends upon the connection between Jesus' claim and its confirmation by God' (Pannenberg 1977b: 66). Once more we see this dialectical to and fro between a contested concept and its validation from the future in terms of an event – an event that will gain its meaning, or divulge its meaning, in light of the previous context and concepts pointing towards it. Jesus, claim to be the truth is to be put to the test of history. Pannenberg finds a strongly proleptic element in Jesus' claim to authority, notably in the Son of Man sayings with their resonances of the Danielic apocalyptic texts.

Interestingly the hypothetical significance of the resurrection is then examined, before the historical data is examined: the possible meaning before the possible fact, or rather of the possible fact taken in its contemporary Jewish context of thought. This is a common mode of exploration in Pannenberg's writings: an event validating a concept and yielding decisive meaning – and yet with the provisionality that more data may arise to change things in a fresh synthesis. Pannenberg makes six points (Pannenberg 1977b: 66–73) about the significance of Jesus' resurrection, if it did occur, and they are all determined by the apocalyptic theological expectation of Jesus' cultural context. First, if Jesus has been raised, then this is the inauguration of the end time, since the resurrection of the dead is an event of the end time, along with the giving of the Spirit as part of this eschatological radical revolution. The Spirit is closely associated with Jesus being raised, according to Paul's teaching in Rom. 1. Second, this must be the act of God for a Jew, and it confirms the pre-Easter ministry of Jesus. Third, Jesus' resurrection places Jesus in role of the eschatological Son of Man, the Danielic figure, this is his identity. Fourth, if Jesus, being raised, is taken to God, thereby beginning the end of the world, then God is finally and ultimately revealed in Jesus. Jesus' resurrection spells the summation of all things, the meaning of all things, and this can be only the act of God: 'Only because the end of the world is already present in Jesus' resurrection is God himself revealed in him' (Pannenberg 1977b: 69). The glory of God is revealed in the man Jesus, and as the early church became Gentile and used Hellenistic concepts, this began to move towards the notion of incarnation of the Logos of the Cosmos in human history. This is the key point to pick out: the resurrection event constitutes Jesus the eschatological revelation of God. Fifth, Jesus' resurrection motivates the mission and inclusion of the Gentiles and all peoples in history. Sixth, the words attributed to the risen Christ are to be seen as the content of the earliest tradition of the disciples, explicating the inherent meaning of this event, word and event belonging together.

Pannenberg probes the concept of resurrection, and stresses the metaphorical structure of language used, since this language refers to a mode of life beyond and transcending this life and our experience. Resurrection is not mere revivification of a corpse back to the same sort of finite life it had before death, but a transformation in the biblical hope of resurrection, a transfiguration to a new way of being. The question as to the validity of the apocalyptic framework of hope for us today is raised, the question of hope beyond death and whether this is still a question for us today. Pannenberg here claims thinkers such as Ernst Bloch and his work on the principle of hope for anthropological insight, chiming in with the Hebraic wisdom about living in history:

The phenomenology of hope indicates that it belongs to the essence of conscious human existence to hope beyond death . . . Human *Weltoffenheit*, openness in relation to the world and *Umweltfreiheit*, human freedom in relation to his environment.

More precisely this concept involves an openness that goes beyond every finite situation . . .. Thus, because of the structure of human existence, it is necessary for man in one way or another to conceive of the fulfillment of his destiny and indeed the totality of his existence beyond death. (Pannenberg 1977b: 85–6)

Pannenberg puts in place a modern anthropological factor in his consideration of the concept of death and resurrection, suggesting that the same point and questions raised by the Israelite hope beyond death, places the concept of resurrection at the heart of human meaning and destiny as a concept to be seriously considered. Suppression of such reaching out in metaphors and concepts to ask this question of our very being and meaning is unhealthy, says Pannenberg: this kind of probing is part of being fully human. The kinds of imagery developed in this speculation can be tested conceptually, notably the suggestion of the survival of the immortal soul and resurrection of the dead.

Pannenberg thinks that the concept of the immortal soul is not plausible now in the light of what we know of the holistic nature of humanity, making Platonic dualism impossible to consider: any idea of soul must now be understood as the transfigured whole life of a person – the notion put forward by those holding to the resurrection of the dead. The notion of the immortal soul focuses, moreover, on the sameness of our present existent self rather than a future transformed self, and so this concept again looks weak and unhistorical. The resurrection of the dead is a strong concept in that it entails the universal resurrection, a common destiny for all, so it has the power of portraying an eschatology for the whole of reality. Pannenberg has added a layer of conceptual clarification meshed with some contemporary anthropological suggestions about hope and the structure of human life as it yearns for completeness in the face of death. At the very least, the notion of resurrection, the metaphor of rising from sleep, is not absurd to modern people, at the conceptual level the claim should be taken seriously. Here we have a modern version of the Hebrew apocalyptic view of life, that it is provisional and lives in hope of what is to come to vindicate life here in the present; thus Pannenberg is not simply asking us to believe the apocalyptic worldview as it stood then, since its basic thrust is still credible now and is expressed in modern culture. It could of course be argued in opposition to this that there are modern thinkers and analysts for whom life is absurd, Sartre being the most obvious, rejecting any orientation to be open to the world and beyond. But Pannenberg appeals to anthropology for the phenomenon of hope in humanity.

Historical analysis of the resurrection evidence

We now move to the issue of Jesus' resurrection as a historical problem. We have heard that language about the resurrection must be metaphorical, since it deals with a mode of life transcending anything known to us in space and time here and now, and the resurrection cannot be pinned down precisely as to its content. But the metaphorical structure of our language about the resurrection of Jesus does not mean that the data cannot be considered by historians. Pannenberg is committed, we recall, to treating biblical data on the same basis as any other data and with normal historical critical methods, and he thinks that probability is the only mode of 'proof' that history can render, answering the question as to what is the most likely judgement to account for the evidence available now. He identifies two different strands in the Easter traditions of primitive Christianity, the traditions of the appearances of the risen Jesus and the traditions of the finding of the tomb of Jesus empty, and he wants to treat them separately rather than unifying them, as he feels has been the tendency in biblical studies. One of his points concerning the credibility of the traditions is that contradictions exist in and between the traditions, showing that evidence has not been tampered with by editors trying to harmonize them.

Primary attention is given to the appearance tradition, in particular to the contribution of Paul of Tarsus and his understanding of it. Paul, it should be emphasized for Pannenberg, claims to have encountered the risen Christ, as he says at the end of his list of those who were so encountered he places himself, 'last of all' in 1 Cor.15:8. Paul wrote this letter to the Corinthian Christians approximately in 56 AD, making his list probably the earliest there is in the New Testament. His account of his experience is given in the book of Acts, an experience of encounter with Christ some time after the 'forty days' of the Gospel stories of the post-Easter appearances of the risen Jesus. Paul did identify the figure who met with him as Jesus risen from the dead. Paul links his experience to those in the early traditions circulating before being written down in the Gospels.

It is arguable that the appearance tradition was a pure invention and deception, but Pannenberg regards that as unlikely in terms of motive and incentive. Also the tradition could be the record of deluded people who were psychologically confused and so produced experiences of a purely subjective and hallucinated kind. But Pannenberg finds this explanation of the data unconvincing for two reasons. First, there were several appearances distributed over a period of several years. Perhaps the tension of early Christians, their frustrations and hopes, could have induced a series of visions, but this theory does not account for the complexity of the appearance tradition (Pannenberg 177b: 96–7). Second, the theory of subjective visions does not seem able to account for the transformation of the disciples from being broken and disappointed after Jesus' death into being enthusiastic, confident preachers of the new message of the Gospel. The texts of the New Testament indicate that the disciples did not expect Jesus to rise from the dead. Pannenberg says that such Jewish people would expect the general resurrection of the dead at the end time, not the resurrection of Jesus before then. In the light of these factors of a lack of expectation and disappointment at the humiliating death of Jesus, Pannenberg argues that an actual event did happen, the resurrection, and that this event and the appearance of the risen Jesus is the most plausible theory to account for the fact of the transformation in the disciples.

The empty tomb tradition, while less significant in Panneberg's view, adds substance to the view that an objective event did occur. The claim that the tomb was empty was made in Jerusalem and could have been refuted by showing the dead body of Jesus, which would have quashed the growth of the fragile Christian movement in the Synagogue; there is no refutation of any such claim opposing the emptiness of the tomb in the New Testament texts, or other data. The emptiness of the tomb is likely to have been true, in Pannenberg's historical judgement, given the state of the evidence. Again, this is formally speaking a provisional judgement, falsifiable if convincing counter evidence should emerge. Pannenberg thinks that the two traditions were, from the historical critical angle, initially separate, and that 'the tomb tradition and the appearance tradition came into existence independently, then by their mutually complementing each other they let the assertion of the reality of Jesus' resurrection, in the sense explained above, appear as historically very probable' (Pannenberg 1977b: 96–7). Pannenberg takes this position to be in place until more evidence comes to light to affect the judgement on the probability one way or the other.

Pannenberg argues that we should not be imprisoned by the assumption that the unique event cannot happen, as we have seen in regard to his discussion of the historical law of analogy of all events debated with Troeltsch. Pannenberg therefore argues historically as above for the probability of the resurrection as the best provisional judgement on the data, and also philosophically that this judgement should not be suppressed on the basis of a naturalistic view of history and reality. Philosophically Pannenberg criticizes the modern secular understanding of natural laws as ruling out a decisive event, in the future or the past. It is not possible to predict the future for two reasons, one being that a scientific 'law' must always be open to falsification or moderation rather than being absolutely certain in the sense that future experience is now of no concern, since new factors can emerge. For Pannenberg natural laws are contingent, depending on discoveries by scientists who are developing their understanding of reality. It is also the case that events comprise more than the accounts natural laws are able to analyse completely, there is a novelty to each new event. Because we cannot prescribe what can and cannot happen beforehand, therefore the resurrection cannot be in theory discounted as a possibility, and the resurrection would not be incompatible with science. There is no reason why a new event should not occur and why God should not have acted in this way. Historians have contested this claim on the grounds that their commonsense body of knowledge cannot have space for acts of God who lies beyond their critical grasp. The resurrection may have occurred, but a pure historian cannot prove it or go beyond ruling out other explanations and leaving a question mark over the data (Burhenn 1972).

JESUS' REVELATIONAL UNITY OF ESSENCE WITH GOD

How does the resurrection affect our estimate of Jesus' identity? Some characters in the Old Testament after all were claimed to have been taken directly into heaven, notably Elijah. Indeed in the Roman Catholic dogmatic tradition Mary is said to have been assumed bodily into heaven, and this doctrine must be accepted as an infallible teaching of the church since 1950 – another interesting dialectic between the 'now' and the 'then', with meaning developed centuries later allegedly creating an historical 'fact', although Pannenberg would be insisting on historical evidence for this event. Pinchas Lapide, a Jewish scholar, is not averse to accepting the resurrection of Jesus from the dead as an historical event, but does not think that this fact necessitates accepting divine status for Jesus any more than for Elijah (Lapide 1984). Lapide, an Orthodox Jewish scholar of the New Testament, mounts a surprising argument that the resurrection of Jesus was a historical event. He points out that the birth of a baby ultimately is a bringing of new life out of dead matter, and he sees the Easter story as bringing the message of God to the whole world, in consonance with Judaism, and so being providential. Here is a sympathetic reading of the evidence, but not leading to the divine status of Jesus.

Why then does Pannenberg think that the resurrection, now deemed probable as an event, albeit an event of the most elusive kind by its very nature of linking space and time with what transcends it, leads to the recognition of Jesus as divine? If we read the preaching of Peter recorded in Acts, the first proclamation of the Christian message, we see that the earliest church regarded the death and resurrection of Jesus as fulfilling Old Testament prophecy directly, this was the Messiah predicted of old, the suffering servant of God, whose body 'did not see decay' since he did not sin, hence the resurrection was a vindication of Jesus as the one for whom Israel had waited so long, their saviour. Pannenberg's argument from revelation seems to have room to take up and take in this very early line of Christian theology, resting on the holiness of Jesus, his Messianic identity and his oneness with God. Pannenberg's stress falls on the universal meaning of history and Jesus' place as that point where divine and human interpenetrate, a finite expression of the transcendent verdict on history. This apocalyptic framework, in its widest sense, is utterly crucial for Pannenberg:

[I]f the apocalyptic expectation should be totally excluded from the realm of possibility for us, then the early Christian faith in Christ is also excluded . . .. One must be clear about the fact that when one discusses the truth of the apocalyptic expectation of a future judgement and a resurrection of the dead, one is dealing directly with the basis of the Christian faith. Why the man Jesus can be the ultimate revelation of God, why in him and only him God is supposed to have appeared, remains incomprehensible apart from the horizon of the apocalyptic expectation. (Pannenberg 1977b: 82–3)

The event of Jesus' resurrection, suffused with the meaning of that final eschaton of God as revelation, means that Jesus is the self-vindication, the self-revelation, of God, and so inseparable from the very being of God. This is because, as we saw in the discussion of *Revelation as History*, the strict concept of revelation now inescapable for modern thought means that true revelation entails disclosure of true being: there can be no gap between revealer and revelation if it is a transparently true revelation. Pannenberg therefore speaks of the revelational unity of essence of Jesus with God.

God is present in Jesus in this mode of revelational presence, God has disclosed himself in this life and fate and so Jesus shares the very essence of God. This human history, culminating in its conquest of death, is that of God, the God whom Jesus called Father. This historicist mode of divine presence, rather than the Platonic mode of eternal Logos, wholly other to human changing history, or than the mode of adoption of a good man inspired by the Spirit, is how Pannenberg can unite the full humanity of Jesus, with the God of universal history, who is the God of Israel. Revelational presence, using the strict Barthian definition of revelation, entails essence, 'the Christ event belongs to the essence of God himself' (Pannenberg 1977b: 129). The concept of revelation proves to be the core of Pannenberg's Christology, linking history and eschatology to the being of God in Christ. This revelatory presence is the only appropriate way of understanding the presence of God in Jesus. Moreover the identity of the essence of Jesus with God means that God is not to be defined apart from the Christ event, God reveals himself as the God who raised Jesus, and the form or medium of this revelation is not alien to God but discloses the depths of God uniquely and decisively.

Pannenberg has developed an eschatological identity for Jesus the man, his truest identity is that of the self-revelation of God, enacted and disclosed at his resurrection from the dead, which was divine self-vindication, as Barth puts it 'the verdict of the Father' (Barth 1956). This is thoroughly biblical: Jesus is clearly the bringer in of the kingdom of the universal God, the one who is to come has come, the hope of Israel has arrived. The identity of Jesus is a divine identity because his life and fate are at one with God, they are the self-disclosure of God himself, that is the content of who he really is. He is human, and yet this human being shares the very essence of God as revealed and enacted from the eschatological future arriving at the resurrection. He is human, bearing the future of humanity and revealing what that is.

RETROACTIVE FORCE OF EASTER FOR JESUS' PRE-EASTER IDENTITY

For Pannenberg the end-time significance inherent in the resurrection of the man Jesus constitutes his divine identity and being. Meaning, for Pannenberg, seems to constitute being and identity, and Christology is the theological theme showing this most clearly. Who is Jesus? He is one with God in his very being, which is taken into God and was always given by and from God. His life was marked by his 'filial dependence' on God whom he called Father, whom he trusted and obeyed despite the darkness this involved when he went to Jerusalem for the last time, hoping and trusting in the vindication of his Father. The resurrection confirmed the manifestation of Jesus' 'divine Sonship' which had been lived out by Jesus in his life and death, this identity was vindicated by the resurrection and its revelational meaning.

Pannenberg here asserts that this divine identity of Jesus was not only retrospective but retroactive, not merely a matter of the order of knowing, but of the order of being, that Jesus' revelational unity of essence with God was constituted by the resurrection 'retroactively'. This is one of Pannenberg's most difficult, perplexing and interesting theological doctrines. The retroactive significance confirmed who Jesus was but also made him who he was, in that had the resurrection not occurred he would not have had this essential identity, he would not have been who he was without the Easter event. Again we see here the structure of to and fro, advancing into the future from the future, from the past to the future and back again, Jesus' life contained claims to divine authority, made in the idiom of his own religious culture, and these claims were validated by his resurrection – without which they would not have been true. Therefore there is an ontological reading backwards from the resurrection to Jesus ministry and anticipated Lordship, shown in the signs and preaching of the kingdom, for example. His life anticipates his vindication in the future, that future confirms his identity all along. This again is a Christology of the future perfect: this was always the case, we know it could not in fact have been different – since the resurrection did occur.

Pannenberg says that this structure of meaning applies generally. The future decides what we are to be and who we are to be, and yet we ourselves work at being what we are and hope to be: 'the essence of a man, of a situation, or even of the world in general is not yet to be perceived from what is now visible. Only the future will decide' (Pannenberg 1977b: 136). Pannenberg is saying here that the true identity of a person is given at the end of their life when 'all will be revealed', and there are examples of surprising verdicts of history. For example, Wolfgang Amadeus Mozart died as a pauper and was buried in a pauper's grave with very little regard or esteem. Now he is judged to be perhaps the world's greatest composer and musical genius, in the light of his corpus music and its impact on the world since his death. The totality of evidence, as interpretation has engaged with it, discloses this meaning and his true identity. His meaning constitutes his being. This constitutes Mozart's identity 'backwards' and yet confirmatory of the genius shown in his music and not fully recognized during his life. This concept of retroactive validation is difficult and perplexing, but such examples can help us to understand something of what Pannenberg is suggesting.

I think that if we go along with my interpretation of Pannenberg's ontology that meaning constitutes being, then the idea of retro-activity makes sense, again in a dialectical way: the future when all is revealed decides on the truth and meaning of an event or person. In the case of Jesus, he died condemned by the religious and political authorities as a blasphemer, says Pannenberg, but his future given by the event of his being raised from the dead reversed this verdict and confirmed his sense of closeness and Sonship to God, his Father. Jesus' identity was an eschatological one, fully open to God and trusting wholly in the end-time vindication of God alone; the mean-ing of the resurrection event, in all its metaphorical character, gives the final decision as to who Jesus really is, a decision bound up with the ultimate self-revelation of God, the very being of God.

We can say that Panneberg's idea of 'Christology from below' seems better expressed as Christology from 'before', from the future of history, since God's self-revelation is not from a transcendent dimension outside history so much as from the future of history itself, the final occurrence of its culmination. Pannenberg's ontology rejects the Platonic view of a timeless transcendent dimension over against the created world of time and space, a dualistic ontology, in favour of an historicist and more immanentist understanding of

God in relation to the world. Some commentators interpret his ontology as that of Process theology (McKenzie 1980) although Pannenberg rejects the Process view on the grounds that his God of the open future is free over history and not its victim. He rejected Logos theology as the basis of Christology because the timeless Logos could not be properly integrated into the processes of history as a kind of *deus ex machina* inserted into the fabric of history from eternity. The Christology rooted in Jesus' revelatory unity of essence with God overcomes this dualistic problem. Pannenberg had rejected the Christology of the pre-existent Logos but he later rehabilitates the term as a description of important aspects of Christology arising from the revelatory unity of essence, a secondary deduction from the primary source of revelational unity of essence enacted by the resurrection.

Pannenberg is surely correct to point to the end of Jesus' life, and the glory of the resurrection, as the matrix of the Apostolic message, in the light of which the New Testament was written, and in the light of which the earliest church lived. The doctrine of the incarnation was developed on the basis of the belief in Christ crucified and risen, and Logos theology, in the context of Hellenistic thought, and came to eclipse its origin. This brought with it Platonist assumptions about God and the world causing problems with the doctrine of God and the potential of God to relate in a real way with the created order (Young 1991). Pannenberg recognizes that the divine identity of Jesus, enacted at Easter, carries back into the very heart of God:

> Viewed from the confirmation of Jesus' claim by his resurrection, the inner logic of the matter dictates that Jesus was always one with God, not just after a certain date in his life. And in view of God's eternity, the revelatory character of Jesus' resurrection means that God was always one with Jesus, even before his earthly birth. Jesus is from all eternity the representation of God in the creation. Were it otherwise, Jesus would not be in person the one revelation of the eternal God. We can no longer think of God in his eternal deity without Jesus. This is, indeed, the meaning of Jesus' resurrection. (Pannenberg 1977b: 153)

And yet of course, in human historical terms, this claim is provisional, since new evidence may still arise undermining the whole thesis, only the actual – rather than the proleptic – end-time event can finally verify and establish this. From the divine angle similarly, history is free and its outcome genuinely affects the divine being, as we will see later.

We again find ourselves in Pannenberg's dialectic, not of above and below, nor finite and infinite, but of both 'before and after' linked with 'concept and event', synthesized, in my reading, by 'meaning' emerging necessarily from the combination of event taken in conceptual context. The concept of universal history and its unificatory end is actualized proleptically in the resurrection of Jesus revealing the very being of God as inseparable from Jesus' life and fate. This actualization reads back over Jesus' life and confirms his divine status and reveals that the very life of God is Christlike: the 'humanity' defining the divinity and the divinity 'taking up' the humanity. The dialectical 'history' of Jesus Christ in Karl Barth's *Church Dogmatics* unites into one life the divine self-humbling with the exaltation of the man Jesus. For Pannenberg a very similar dialectical history plays out on a timeline: the human Jesus' resurrection defines the divine being as self-giving and Christlike, and God the Father exalts this man Jesus to divine status – 'taking up'[1] therefore this complex status into God and so into what always has been the case. The conceptual claim to divine status implied in the ministry of Jesus is validated by the resurrection which then reads back this divinity to the man Jesus, whose very meaning always was going to be found to be that of the divine Son in revelational unity of essence with his Father.

The fact that the resurrection did occur means that the anticipatory concept is realized, the rational is the real. But yet there is more provisionality about the concept and its full interpretation until the real end, when again the event verifies the claimed Christian hypothesis for the world and reads back into all universal history this truth, which always was the case in retrospect and would not have been the case without the actual ending given by God, the Father, the God of the open – but now closed and completed – future. The conceptual hypothesis is projected forward, or projects itself since it arises from the inherent meanings of events, to explain the essence of things, creaturely and divine, that essence being realised by the end time as it unifies all things in one divine perspective of meaning – revelation as history.

The concept of the unitive totality of universal history and its inherent meaning arises from human thought about the shape of history, and that concept is realized by the summation of all events.

The dialectic of events under analysis, giving rise to their conceptual meaning and provoking wider and deeper conceptual hypotheses, which are then tested by events, giving rise to new syntheses, this rolling dialectic finds its truth and completion, its incarnation, in Christ and the eschaton. We move forward while looking back and so gain the truth of the past as history moves ahead, till the final denouement when an ultimate looking back is granted, and this gives a Christocentric perspective of meaning and interpretation, showing that true being is in Christ. This is the way to try to understand Pannenberg's difficult yet intriguingly attractive doctrine of retroactivity from the future back through the present and into the past: it presumes an ontology of meaning, of events and their ongoing conceptualizing through human thought. The past is pregnant with the future and the arriving future decides on the meaning of the past. The arrival of the future knits up our fragmented understanding by bringing ever new unifying hypotheses, horizons of meaning, to unify their diversity. But then the present new hypotheses break open again as the future reconfigures the past – until the anticipated and promised final end.

THE UNITY AND DISTINCTION OF JESUS WITH HIS FATHER – RECIPROCAL SELF-DEDICATION

Pannenberg considers that the doctrine of the Trinity arises from the interpretation of the ministry and history of the historical man Jesus. He certainly was in a deep relation to the God he called his 'Father' in a radical closeness and sense of immediacy to God (Pannenberg 1977b: 229). Jesus is totally open to the Father, and also, in the experience of the Spirit of the end time, makes the rule of God present now. The resurrection confirms Jesus as the divine Son, one in being with God the Father, and because of the 'revelational unity of essence' with God it is no longer possible after Easter for those who accept the Easter message to think of God the Father without Jesus. But since God is eternal, his relatedness to Jesus as 'Son' must be eternal too: again we note this ontology, and epistemology, of the future perfect tense, ranging forwards to the perfected end, then backwards through the prior process with the perfected truth of the end. Therefore, two different aspects in the historical reality of Jesus come to be distinguished: the human aspect that took its beginning in time and the divine aspect (his Sonship) that belongs to perfected eternity.

This is not only a question of cognition, as we have seen, but also of reality, but a reality that is claimed on the basis of the historical Jesus and is not independent of that particular history. If Jesus had not been raised, he argues, he would not be the Son of God. Nor would we know of any Son of God. This is not only the question of knowing, or simply retrospection, since if such knowledge occurs, it also involves being – being is not independent of time. This even applies to the very being of the God whose kingdom or rule Jesus proclaimed to be coming: if the kingdom were not to come about, then this God whom Jesus announced would not be real. But it has, so he is – and there is no real question about this real state of affairs: the future has been perfected, proleptically. After the kingdom will have come, future having been perfected, we shall know that Jesus' God existed from eternity. But yet that eternal existence depends on the future of the kingdom. Had no world come into being, God conceivably could have enjoyed his existence without a world. But since there is a world, the existence of God cannot be affirmed without his sovereign divine rule being established in this world, God being by definition the all-determining reality. This is the reason why the very existence of God will continue to be debated until the end, when his kingdom will have been decisively established. The orders of knowing and of being converge in meaning, which constitutes being, even for God.

The content of what is revealed is that God is the God of Jesus Christ who is the Son; and also that the structure of all reality is itself proleptic, at the heart of all being and knowing. We might even say that here is Pannenberg's reworking of the Nicene 'homoousion', the doctrine of the unity of being between the Father and the Son, but in Pannenberg's case the unity of being is given through his matrix category of revelation as being, and the Jesus of history is the real content of 'the Son' rather than a heavenly entity called the Logos which is almost impossible to integrate into the historical narrative of Jesus and his eschatological identity. The identity of Jesus is disclosed as that of the Son, because his unity with the Father is revealed as being included into the divine being, God is the Father in union with the Son, and in differentiation from him.

The resurrection confers the identity of Jesus as the divine Son, and since this is true for God's essence it was also so – and yet would not have been so had the event not occurred – again the future perfect perichoresis of being and knowing. Pannenberg stresses that the true Christological matrix is the Father–Jesus relation, not the Word–Jesus relation, although the latter may be a valid way of expressing what is true on other grounds. The historical relationship of the man Jesus and his God, the God of the open future, whose coming kingdom Jesus proclaimed, this is the central relationship for trinitarian doctrine, which is of the essence of Pannenberg's whole ontology. He establishes the doctrine of the Trinity in eschatology, to reintegrate it into organic connection with finite reality. Thus the revelation of God in the event of Jesus means that the relationship of Jesus' openness to God is included in the essence of God. In the fate of Jesus, the God of Israel is revealed as the triune God. This surely is a very healthy theological development in showing the doctrine of the Trinity to be no matter of speculative metaphysics but deeply rooted in the saving act of God, who proves himself threefold in giving himself to the created order out of pure free love. However one assesses Pannenberg's historicism, his intellectual achievement in moving the centre of theological gravity to the man Jesus as the eschatological saving and revealing essence of God lived out in human conditions is quite remarkable and a landmark in the history of theology that will remain intriguing, suggestive and vital.

Pannenberg argues that 'If God has revealed himself in Jesus, then Jesus' community with God, his Sonship, belongs to eternity' (Pannenberg 1977b: 154). Galloway sums up Pannenberg's theology aptly: 'The eternal communion within the Godhead between the Father and the Son is not some ghostly metaphysical transaction. It is precisely what took place between them in the birth, life, death, and resurrection of Jesus of Nazareth' (Galloway 1973: 102). Pannenberg has been consistent in taking, retroactively, the life and ministry of Jesus prior to the resurrection into his divinely revealed and constituted identity as the Son. He works this out in terms of the Sonship of Jesus and the Father–Son relation established by the resurrection. This relation contains a distinction rooting back to Jesus' historical life and ministry: his attitude of humble refusal to claim equality with God, or as Pannenberg puts it, his self-differenti-ation, or self-distinction, from God. Jesus' history and his person now belong to the very being of God, and therefore the distinction that Jesus maintained between himself and the Father also belongs to the divine being. The unity includes differentiation, the self-humbling of Jesus before his Father: this is true in history and in God's very life.

The essence of God has the dialectic of the freedom of the God of the open future, the Father, and the Son, the man Jesus. God's revelational activity, his self-disclosure, embodies the temporal appearance as essence of the Father–Son relation, which is divine. A reciprocal self-differentiation of Father, Son and Spirit is revealed in the Christ event: 'God himself has come out of his otherness into our world, into human form, and in such a way that the Father–Son relation that – as we know in retrospect – always belonged to God's essence now acquired corporeal form' (Pannenberg 1977b: 156). God is the God who releases finitude from himself into temporality, and yet is always distinguishing himself from these events in his freedom and ungraspability. Jesus, in the structure of his life, was wholly open to the future and was thus in harmony with it. Jesus' life, therefore, shows the proleptic structure, the union and differentiation with God coming from God. Indeed, Christianity is the crown of all the religions because Jesus was the epitome of openness, which reveals God as the ever-new and free God of the future: the God who can be trusted even beyond death, the God who decides the truth of all being eschatologically. The history played out between Jesus and his Father, in the Spirit, therefore becomes the trinitarian history, and by the principle of the future perfect, always was going to be so, and so eternally always was so.

Pannenberg's trinitarian doctrine, it is again worth noting, is in fact a claim or suggestion, made to the secular as well as to the faithful, about reality. God really is this relational being, bringing all things into being, and the clue to this lies in the resurrection of the man Jesus and his identity revealed as ultimate and divine. The pattern of humble self-distinction on the part of Jesus takes us to the heart of reality, to the very being of God. Pannenberg means the actual concrete history of Jesus, and his temporally lived life of prayer and witness, and ultimately death, when he speaks of this self-distinction. This is no Platonic image reflected in history; the actual historical revelation is what is meant as being true for God, affecting God, and coming from God. The Logos is this structure of relationship.

Pannenberg stresses sovereign Lordship of the Father, the God who comes to us in freedom from the open future, and at the same time Jesus' pointing to that and laying down his life in obedience to God. Jesus refuses divine Lordship in all humility; his Lordship is to proclaim the rule and kingdom of the Father. The Father however hands over Lordship to the Son, to receive it back: the Father therefore makes his Lordship dependent on that of the Son's glorification of the Father. This reciprocal self-distinction reveals that the Father not only 'begets' the Son eternally, but hands over all things to him, 'so that his kingdom and his own deity are dependent upon the Son' (Pannenberg 1991: 313). We recall that Pannenberg teaches that if a world does exist, then God must be its sovereign to meet the conceptual conditions of deity. This Lordship, it is revealed, is Christlike and not mere worldly power play.

'The deity of Jesus Christ cannot, therefore, have the sense of undifferentiated identity with the divine nature, as if in Jesus, God the Father himself had appeared in human form and had suffered on the cross' (Pannenberg 1977b: 159–60). This trinitarian insight is developed increasingly by Pannenberg. The self-distinction of Jesus from the Father is part of his union with the divine being. God is revealed as being the Father of the Son, with this particular relationship. Jesus trusted his Father, for example, as he sought to fulfil his vocation and went towards unjust death. He trusted the God of the open future, and by his resurrection he was vindicated against the unjust judgement of the world, and he distinguished himself from God throughout his ministry. This openness to God as Father, in all humbleness and obedient love, is key to Pannenberg's view of the Trinity: Jesus' self-effacing, humble self-differentiation from deity is itself taken up into the life of God as having been the case in eternity. 'If Father, Son and Spirit are distinct but coordinate moments in the accomplishment of God's revelation, then they are so in God's eternal essence as well' (Pannenberg 1977b: 180). All hinges on the strict conceptual definition of 'revelation' entailing the being of the revealer, disclosed now as a relational being revealed proleptically in the resurrection as confirming the life and fate of the man Jesus. 'In the vital movement of such reciprocal dedication of Father, Son and Spirit, the divine unity consummates itself in the revelatory history' (Pannenberg 1977b: 183).

God is the Father of this Son and not otherwise. Here we have a doctrine of the Trinity which connects, through revelation, the life of human history with the very being of God. The economic Trinity, the work of the triune God outside of himself, is inseparable from the immanent Trinity, God in himself. There has to be a distinction between immanent Trinity and economic Trinity, according to Pannenberg, because if God's revelation in Jesus Christ involves the trinitarian structure, then there must be a trinitarian structure in the eternal reality of God himself – prior to the existence of creation. On the other hand, the economic Trinity is not merely an image (in the Platonic sense) of the eternal trinitarian structure in the being of God. The immanent Trinity is dependent on the process of history, hence on the economic Trinity.

JESUS THE MAN BEFORE GOD

The first third of *Jesus God and Man* concerned 'the knowledge of Jesus' divinity' through the revelation of the resurrection of Jesus' Sonship in his revelational unity of essence. The second third of the book, to which we now turn, is entitled 'Jesus the man before God' and this gives the thrust of how Pannenberg unfolds the relevance of Jesus to us now, how we have community with God through Jesus' life, work and eschatological resurrection. Jesus is the 'true man' revealing true humanity and human destiny. This destiny is revealed in Jesus' life acts and his resurrection. He had announced his significance for human destiny in his life and called for response from his hearers, and Pannenberg has argued that his message and associated actions imply an identity with God, confirmed at the resurrection. He had been commissioned to issue and implement the divine decision about humanity, and this commission, or office, was sealed by God at Easter. A person's relationship to Jesus decides what a human being is in the sight of God. For Pannenberg the crucifixion of Jesus proved to be a sign of judgement on all those who rejected the Father in the Son.

Salvation, for Pannenberg, consists in the fulfilment of openness to God, which is proclaimed by Jesus. It has in fact already become present, come to those hearers of the message of Jesus who accept this message of the nearness of the kingdom of God. Repentance means turning to God's future, being open and trusting towards God for all things. Jesus is not only a teacher of righteousness and wisdom, he lives out the life of righteousness, he accepts his place under the Jewish law and seeks to live out that law as a man before God, and he is seen in the New Testament as someone with a dominating consciousness of God very close to him. We can see a likeness here to the picture gained from the evidence by the Jewish scholar Geza Vermes (Vermes 1993), who sees Jesus as conscious of God as his Father, utterly close to all aspects of his life. Pannenberg of course goes beyond Vermes in interpreting the Fatherhood of God in relation to the Sonship of Jesus, an eschatological identity mapped onto the man Jesus and so an identity inseparable from the divine judge of all reality. But Pannenberg also goes beyond Vermes in seeing that the humanity of Jesus has soteriological power for us now, not a power stemming from the potential of humanity itself, as if Jesus triggered an awakening of this neglected spiritual possibility which we then actualize. This saving power stems from Jesus' particular and unique relationship to God, revealed at the resurrection.

The universal significance of Jesus' particular life and fate has been stressed throughout by Pannenberg, and this theme again is claimed as key to the doctrine of salvation, which involves human community with Jesus: without this universal significance there would be no possibility of our having such community with Jesus and of finding ourselves in the figure of Jesus (Pannenberg 1977b: 205). The theology of Paul shows that a fundamental element of this universal significance is found in Jesus' death on the cross. The resurrection event claims the universal meaning that in Jesus' rising from death the hopes and deep longings of all humanity are fulfilled. In sharing Jesus' life we share in the life of the man who was totally dedicated to God and 'God conscious' to the superlative degree and so, as Schleiermacher taught, was the fulfilment of the creation of human nature (Schleiermacher 1928: § 89). Schleiermacher is correct in reclaiming this theological insight about Jesus' soteriological significance for us now, but failed to see that this was an anticipatory completion of human eschatological destiny and that the church's community with Jesus gives us a preliminary taste of our final eschatology humanity, according to Pannenberg. Schleiermacher did grasp the key significance of Jesus as the new Adam, the true human being who has the power from God to renew our openness to God and liberate us from sin, from turning away from God as the ultimate reality. But Schleiermacher drastically narrows the scope in how the true man Jesus, the new Adam, represents us before God, both in terms of how Jesus has a divine identity and how he lived and suffered in the blood and tears of actual history, leading him to suffer an agonizing death on a Roman cross of execution.

Schleiermacher's stress on the vital importance of human openness to God is shared by Pannenberg, notwithstanding their very different explications of how Jesus' openness to God relates to ours:

The close association of God's revelation through the anticipation of the eschaton and the revelation of man is finally established in the fact that the essence of man, like his salvation, the fulfillment of his destiny, consists in openness for God. Openness for God is the real meaning of the fundamental structure of being human, which is designated as openness to the world in contemporary anthropology . . . . Only when man lives in the openness of this question, when he is completely open toward God, does he find himself on the way leading toward his destiny. (Pannenberg 1977b: 193)

Salvation means fulfilling our destiny in the whole of our life, and this cannot only be a matter of our own effort and decision in our earthly existence. Our essence, our deepest being, comes to us from the future, meshing in with our openness towards God and with what is already realized in us or is not so: our destiny lies beyond what we already are. The history of Jesus, as he went to Jerusalem for the final time, in obedience, fear and trust, reveals the taking up of our past life into the future of God, and the bestowing of our identity and essence by God. Human destiny to openness for God constitutes not only the object of Jesus' office and calling, but it is at the same time fulfilled by Jesus' own conduct in life. Jesus enacts the divine will, not merely teaching it.

Jesus lived as the man completely dedicated to God, as God's authorized representative to humanity: he simultaneously represented the human situation to God. We could call the office his messiahship, which Jesus clearly follows as his vocation rooted in the Hebraic traditions. Jesus' calling is to stand before God as the new Adam, and it is because he does stand in this position that his death, in the light of the resurrection, can have vicarious meaning for humankind. The destiny of universal humanity is revealed in the fate of Jesus, that is to say what happened to him at the resurrection thus confirmed his pre-Easter life acts and teaching, and revealed the particular life of Jesus of Nazareth as universally significant rather than confined to the particular context of his cultural time and place. Pannenberg unites the particularity of the works of Jesus pre-Easter, contrasted with the universal meaning and being of Jesus given at the resurrection, his fate or what happened to him independently of his human efforts. The 'office' of Jesus is aligned by Pannenberg with Jesus' active human works before Easter, his 'fate' with what happened to him at the cross and resurrection.

The traditional three 'offices' of Christ, prophet, priest and king, for Pannenberg in *Jesus God and Man* can only apply to Jesus' work before Easter and to the post-Easter Son only as mythical in form but expressing important meaning, and he prefers to use them in terms of the immediate historical Jewish context of Jesus. Pannenberg can derive theological value from the threefold 'offices' by taking them indirectly and typologically. Thus he agrees, for example, that Jesus, fate shows that he took the place of the priesthood and sacrificial rituals found in Israel and other religions as a human confession of ideal holiness before the face of God. He reserves the threefold offices for Jesus the man. But in *Systematic Theology* vol. 2 he modifies this position, since the Sonship of Jesus entails the work of Jesus the man in actual history (Pannenberg 1994: 446). Pannenberg does not wish to conduct his Christology by presenting Jesus as the God-man in his works, a worker of thaumaturgy of a docetic kind:

> Whenever the tradition about Jesus is interpreted as the action of a divine human person without considering the indirectness of the language about God and thus Jesus' divinity, one over-looks the incisive significance that the crucifixion and then the resurrection have for the whole of Jesus' life. (Pannenberg 1977b: 224)

Jesus is a man whose life history is all important in gaining his identity as one in being with the Father, his death at Calvary was a catastrophe and not merely an episode in the earthly career of a God-man, a catastrophe overcome by the divine act of raising him from death to open up the way to new hope for all those who wish to have community with him.

Pannenberg returns to the New Testament for the human activity of Jesus which he finds a more real way of treating what theology has categorized as the threefold offices of Christ. Jesus calls his disciples to the kingdom of God by his expectation of its imminence: it is 'at hand', is present in the presence of Jesus and his acts of restoring creation on the Sabbath, the day when creation is complete and at rest. The Fatherhood of God and his fatherly goodness is taught, prayed and lived out in the life and work of Jesus, producing a life of love and forgiveness, which opens up new possibilities for working with the God of the open future. The love taught by Jesus comes from hearing the word and trusting the promise of salvation, creating a community. Here is the essence of true humanity, being open to God and to one's neighbour. In this Jesus fulfils his kingly role, as he helps those in trouble and disability, those ignored by society in general. Here is the messianic calling of Jesus and his willingness to embrace it to the full. This calling to love is not only on the individual level but fans out into the social order towards a caring society, not one that is crystallized into a particular political order but one which will leaven the dough of societies of different structures: the kingdom of God lies ahead and is not finalized in human history. We certainly cannot transfer structures from the earliest church to the present day without taking account of the historical contextual differences, we cannot universalize that particular situation as if a template for all time without achieving what Jesus did not intend (Pannenberg 1977b: 240).

JESUS' VICARIOUS DEATH ON THE CROSS

Jesus' death is taken by Pannenberg to be something that happened to Jesus, not something linked to what Jesus actually did, unlike Jesus' actions announcing the nearness of the kingdom of God, although Pannenberg does concede that Jesus may have had a good idea of what fate was in store for him, and we might surely add that he was free to quit his pathway to conflict with the political and religious authorities of the day who were increasingly worried and threatened by his ministry. There seems little need for Pannenberg to press the distinction between human works and the activity of the God of the open future at this point. The images used by the New Testament writers for the death of Jesus are many and varied, and Pannenberg picks out that of the just person suffering for his people as the most meaningful for today. Jesus may well have had such thoughts in mind during his passion. It is vital that his passion has a vicarious element if it is to be relevant for us now, 'the common situation of selfish entanglement in personal concerns designated by the term "sin" is thereby transformed' (Pannenberg 1977b: 250).

Pannenberg controversially stresses Jesus' conflict with Jewish teachers of the law and the Jewish law itself: Jesus' claim to an authority on a par with God meant that he was a blasphemer in the eyes of the law, and his crucifixion was as a blasphemer. His resurrection gave the divine verdict to Jesus and against the teachers of the law, confirming Jesus' teaching about the law and indeed deciding that those who condemned Jesus were the real blasphemers. The resurrection, says Pannenberg, means that the law itself became invalid, and Jesus' message of love, revealed in his activity and fate, takes up and supersedes the tradition of the law. The resurrection was the verdict of the God of Israel for the emancipation from the Jewish law.

The substitutionary interpretation of Jesus' death arises, thinks Pannenberg, from the Lord's Supper tradition and also from Jesus' saying about serving others given in Lk. 22:27b and Mk 10:45, and in fact Jesus' whole life was a life of service to others. Therefore, if his death were a supreme act of service that would be deeply fitting, but how his death could be related to an act of service to humanity is a difficult question. Pannenberg points out that every act of service is vicarious in meeting a need of another unable to meet it himself. The early church clearly looked to the Old Testament figure of the Suffering Servant of God to interpret Jesus' death as vicarious, but the appropriateness of this presupposition needs to be examined, and Pannenberg proceeds to look at the issue of substitution by Jesus for Israel and for humanity. As regards a substitutionary role for Israel by his death, Pannenberg again looks to the resurrection as disclosing that Jesus was vindicated by God as not being the blasphemer and as such condemned to die, but that his judges were found by God to be the blasphemers, and thus Jesus bore their punishment: he was a substitute for them. Pannenberg argues that the Jewish judges were only doing what the law expected them to do, and therefore all Jews of that age were similarly blasphemers, and Jesus bore their punishment deserved by the law. Jesus died as a substitute for Israel.

At this point we need to note one of Pannenberg's very few changes of mind in his theological position over his long career, and it relates to this area of the meaning of Jesus' death and the Jewish people. In his *Systematic Theology* vol. 2 Pannenberg stresses that in Jesus' resurrection the God of Israel,

> not only cancels the condemnation of Jesus as a deceiver but also expresses God's faithfulness to the election of his people. For Paul, then, the cross of Jesus was certainly the end of the law (Rom. 10:4; cf Gal. 3:13), but not the end of the election of Israel.

In his footnote to this sentence, he emphasizes this distinction as 'normative for correction of my own 1964 discussion of Paul's doctrine of Christ as the end of the law and the judgement that for

Christians the cross of Jesus means the end of Judaism as a religion.'
He adjusts his position having seen that he then held,

> far too an undifferentiated a view of the Jewish religion as a
> religion of law, which according to Paul had come to an end in the
> cross of Jesus, instead of seeing the essence of Jewish faith in
> the same way as the proclamation of Jesus i.e in terms of faith
> in the God of Israel, in antithesis if necessary to the legal tradi-
> tion. (Pannenberg 1994: 342)

Pannenberg continues his logic and widens the significance of
Jesus' death as vicarious for all humanity, arguing Paul's claim that
Jesus represents all humanity in his death, since all are blasphemers
against God in their universal sinfulness. Pannenberg sees this as a
universal substitution, or 'inclusive substitution': everyone must
indeed still die, but their death can now be in hope for the life of the
resurrection of the dead in community with Jesus. Pannenberg
explains this notion of inclusive substitution most clearly in his
Systematic Theology vol. 2, where he contrasts inclusive with exclusive representation. Exclusive representation is the notion, used by
Anselm for example, that Christ pays our debt exclusively for us, we
have nothing to do with the moral 'payment' offered to God on our
behalf. This, he argues, is not biblical: after all we do all die. 'Christ
is not the representative of humanity insofar as he is outside it
but insofar as he *is* it, representing in himself what is the same in
all individuals' (Pannenberg 1994: 429). This corresponds with
Pauline second Adam Christology and its inclusion of all humanity
in the work of Christ, the representative of all, hence an 'inclusive
representation' – a better phrase than inclusive substitution in
explaining what he seeks to say, since 'substitution' can imply an act
by Jesus, outside or excluded from humanity.

Pannenberg interprets human guilt socially rather than individually, we are all bound together in a web of relationships in society,
and substitution is part of being in society generally. There are always
people in society who are suffering, in various senses; Jesus suffered
unjust execution at the hand of religious and political authorities of
unjust society and its sinful ways deserving of divine judgement – and
so their death was suffered by him. 'God himself, who raised Jesus,
had laid on him the punishment for blasphemy through the actions
of his legitimate office holders' (Pannenberg 1977b: 269), those who

condemned him. But the resurrection transforms our hopelessness and Godforsakenness, in community with Jesus. The uniqueness of Pannenberg's treatment is its focus on Jesus' condemnation for blasphemy and his logic of this injustice being reversed by the divine justice in a way opening up forgiveness and hope to all humanity. Pannenberg agrees with Barth that Jesus took up and overcame our death with its dimension of divine judgement and destruction, but for Pannenberg this is a historical action by Jesus the man before God and what happens to him, his life of service culminating in the catastrophe of his supremely unjust death. In terms of the classic models of Christological atonement this takes in that captured by Aulen in his phrase 'Christus Victor' (Aulen 1931): the view of Jesus as the one who obeyed his Father throughout his life even unto death and overcame the power of evil in so doing, thus defeating the power of sin as it controls us and leads us to sin against God (Pannenberg 1994: 412).

But Pannenberg also includes a strong emphasis of vicarious penal suffering in his understanding of Jesus' death. The innocent Jesus bore unjust execution as a consequence of human sin,

> thereby effecting representation in the concrete form of a change of place between the innocent and the guilty. The innocent suffered the penalty of death, which, as the harmful result of sin, is the fate of those in whose place he died. This vicarious penal suffering, which is rightly described as the vicarious suffering of the wrath of God at sin, rests on the fellowship that Jesus Christ accepted with all of us sinners and with our fate as such. This link is the basis on which the death of Jesus can count as expiation for us. (Pannenberg 1994: 427).

Pannenberg is unfashionably content to uphold the notion of penal sufferings from God borne by Jesus as our representative. The human historical Jesus, concealing the meaning, and thus being, of the eternal Son, suffers unjust execution at Calvary but 'the fate of execution that overtakes Jesus is also seen to be an act of self offering on the part of the incarnate Son of God, who is at work in this history' (Pannenberg 1994: 448). Jesus the man accepts his impending fate as not only imposed by his enemies, but from God, as the Gethsemane story shows was the mind of the earliest church. The Son of God present but concealed in Jesus life and work, makes himself an offering in obedience to the Father (Pannenberg 1994: 440). Pannenberg is surely correct to stress the self-offering of the eternal Son to the Father, as P. T. Forsyth puts it, the atoning work of Christ is fundamentally a trinitarian dynamic, God offering himself to God (Forsyth 1938). Pannenberg's Christology carefully distinguishes the human historical from the eternal eschatological dimensions of Jesus the man and the eternal Son for this purpose, so as to avoid the idea of an innocent young Jew being given brutal suffering and death to appease an angry deity.

There is a 'great exchange' but of judgement: God inverts sinful human judgement on idolatrous politics and religion. Jesus is vindicated for his total trust in the God of the open future, and his suffering gains a divine valuation as the new way of being, the way of hope and trust in the coming kingdom. Divine reconciliation through the death of Christ is, for Pannenberg, following Hegel (Pannenberg 1971a: 149), God absorbing the pain of the negative in the totality of history, negating the negativity arising from the freedom of creation, and this can well be portrayed in human historical form as Christus Victor, the finite Jesus overcoming human negativity and sin, transforming it towards the rule of God. The Hegelian note is also present in Pannenberg's view that the death of Jesus effected a transition from his particular individual existence as man to the eternal Son, from the finite to the eternal; Jesus gives himself into the hands of his Father in total obedience to his fate for the sake of the kingdom, and by giving up his individual particular human life he made room for the death and life of others (Pannenberg 1994: 433): the particular dies to become universal.

Jesus is the true man before God, including us in his work of bearing judgement but not excluding our own repentance and acceptance of his resurrection life, which bonds us into community with him. 'No longer must anyone die alone and without hope' (Pannenberg 1977b: 269), because our community with Jesus gives community with God. It is worth noting that the Holy Spirit receives little mention in Pannenberg's account of Jesus the man before God, but this is in line with virtually all western theological interpretations of the ministry of Jesus, including his death. Pannenberg does however buck this western trend when it comes to his profound consideration of the resurrection, where he finds the role of the Spirit to be vitally important.

THE DIVINITY OF CHRIST AND THE MAN JESUS

We close this exposition of Pannenberg's *Jesus God and Man* by sketching its final third, in which he seeks to go into more detail about the relationship of the divinity of Jesus arising from the resurrection event and its revelatory declaration of the unity of being between this man and his Father, and the human activity of Jesus, the man before God.

Incarnational Christology: the two natures in conflict ?

The first subsection of this final part of the book gives the reader a critical review of classical Chalcedonian Christology and its difficulties raised by theologians down the centuries, from the side of biblical theologians and post-Enlightenment critics. Christology must keep itself rooted in human history and eschew speculative metaphysics. Karl Barth's Christology comes under the same criticism, despite his use of the category of 'history' in elaborating the 'Way of the Son into the Far Country' (Barth 1956: 157): 'here history means nothing else than the incarnation event, not the earthly *historia* of Jesus.' Barth's early use of the term 'event' seems to equate to the Kierkegaardian 'moment' of the inbreaking of the divine into the finite web of human history, and his later deployment of 'event' is identical with 'the life of Jesus Christ' including a temporal duration (Pannenberg 1977b: 302–3). Pannenberg insists that history is history, open to critical scrutiny and interpretation, ongoing and provisional, one open field of being and knowing – and meaning. The history of the Chalcedonian mode of Christology, however remodelled by such theological doctors as Karl Barth, fails to overcome the dilemma of divine-human contradiction in Christ. There can be no true integration of the divine in the human under the Chalcedonian model.

Pannenberg then restates his thesis that the resurrection of Jesus is the one point of departure for recognizing the unity of Jesus with God. The retroactive meaning of the resurrection confirms the claims of Jesus' pre-Easter ministry, implicit and explicit, and 'makes it possible to conceive what is true from the perspective of the resurrection as true for the totality of Jesus' person from the beginning onward' (Pannenberg 1977b: 307). This retroactivity of meaning overcomes the dilemma between Jesus' unity with God being either initiated already from birth as with Chalcedon, or only realized through a subsequent event in Jesus' life. Pannenberg here takes up the Christological idea of 'kenosis', the self emptying of God as the way of postulating a divine human Jesus ab initio and offering a resolution to the two natures problem (Pannenberg 1977b: 307–23). The kenotic theories themselves fail to deliver the resolution of uniting the man Jesus with God, in Pannenberg's critical survey, but kenotic Christology has had the beneficial effect of stimulating thought about God in the Christological debate. God is the living God who in his eternal identity can become something and in so doing remain true to himself, the same God. God becomes and is the same in becoming who he is, and Pannenberg is clear that to hold this means that there can be no inner and outer layers of God, the latter being able to change with the former unaffected. Any change in God does not affect the divine identity, who God is. This means that eternity and finite history are not mutually exclusive, so that God's eternity can and has been affected by events in history, that God is the God who freely allows this to happen.

Developing work by Rahner, Pannenberg takes up the implication from the incarnation that God is the God of self-differentiation whereby 'God can be himself in creating what is differentiated from himself in devoting himself and emptying himself to it' (Pannenberg 1977b: 321). This Hegelian trinitarian doctrine is the presupposition for God's possible unity with what is differentiated from God, that is to say with the man Jesus. The resurrection of Jesus decides the totality of his life and meaning retroactively, and also decides that this is the case for God's eternity. Here again we run into the most perplexing aspect of Pannenberg's thought, the relation of time to eternity, and the very nature of eternity. He is claiming that eternity itself is such as to be affected by a temporal event, the Christ event. The resurrection of Jesus constitutes Jesus' revelational unity of essence with God as always the case. 'That is true from all eternity *because* of Jesus' resurrection' (Pannenberg 1977b: 321). It was hidden before that event, and probably hidden from Jesus who was so concerned not to identify himself as divine but to distinguish himself from God. 'It was hidden because the ultimate decision about it had not been given' (Pannenberg 1977b: 321). And moreover this decision and its significance remains contested until the final end, when the proleptic end given at the resurrection will be conclusive and all debate about the status of Jesus will be ended. This proleptic – confirmatory structure of Christology, an eschatological structure, achieves what the kenotic Christologies attempted, a genuinely human Jesus who is divine by identity. Pannenberg sums up his Christological suggestion to define the incarnation:

> [O]ut of his eternity God has through the resurrection of Jesus, which was always present to his eternity, entered into a unity with this one man which was at first hidden. This unity illuminated Jesus' life in advance, but its basis and reality were revealed only by his resurrection. (Pannenberg 1977b: 322)

The particular historical man Jesus is revealed to be in unity of essence with God, and the basis of this unity is from God, although we can perceive this unity only from history, not from a heavenly standpoint as with Chalcedonian Christology. Once more we have to accept Pannenberg's own unique ontology of the elliptical future perfect tense as true for God and for creation: the free sovereign Lord mediates eternity into history and gives himself to it, uniting himself to it in the man Jesus, whose rising from death is true for God's eternity and always was – although if it had not happened it would not have been. We now find that eternity has been defined by God's own self as self-differentiating and purposive, able to relate and unite with the man Jesus so that this man is revealed as the divine Son.

Jesus and the Father: personal unity with God

Pannenberg's penultimate chapter is entitled 'Jesus' personal unity with God', with the thesis sentence being 'only his personal community with the Father demonstrates that Jesus is the Son of God'. He is now concerned to focus on the nature of the revelational unity of essence and its character, which must be one of a unity of person, and on how the eternal Sonship of Jesus relates to his particular historical humanity. Jesus' self-consciousness is discussed, and his own awareness of not knowing the things of God and of the need to wait for the eschaton, a matter reserved for God. Jesus' true human freedom and openness is shown in his ignorance and his desire to trust only in God, and his lack of knowledge is a condition of Jesus' unity with God. According to critical scholarship of the New Testament, Jesus probably did not claim to be the awaited Messiah nor accept as true confessions of messiahship by others. He may well not have been aware of being the Messiah, or unique Son of God, his unity with God expresses itself only indirectly through his activity reflecting prophetic expectation and his sense of deep communion with God as his Father, his 'filial dependence'. Karl Rahner suggests that Jesus had a deep awareness of God as Father and that this consciousness of God was overwhelmingly how Jesus lived his life, focused intensely on God and his kingdom and not on his own 'identity', thus, according to Pannenberg, being 'indirectly' the Son and not aware of the fact 'directly', being so taken up in the concerns of the kingdom of his Father. Rahner's theology of Jesus' self-differentiation of himself from God meshes into Pannenberg's analysis of Jesus' self-awareness and total dedication to his Father's will, rendering his own status and identity unimportant to himself. This of course is of the essence of 'kenosis', self-humbling before God.

Pannenberg's 'dialectic of Jesus' Sonship' is on the plane of history, the divine dimension coming from the future and God's sovereign freedom rather than from 'above' as a metaphysical realm wholly disconnected from the created order of time and space. Therefore, Jesus' consciousness was of the Father and not of directly being the divine Logos. His Sonship is mediated indirectly. Jesus gives his whole person, his very self, to his Father. This axis, not the Logos-Jesus axis, is that of Christology, the unity of Jesus with his Father, a unity which entails a self-differentiation and self-humbling. This is the 'detour' by which the unity of the man Jesus with the eternal Son arises: 'Only the personal community of Jesus with the Father shows that he is himself identical with the Son of this Father' (Pannenberg 1977b: 335). His personal communion with the Father is revealed in the conduct of his life and ministry, and in what happened to him at Easter. Jesus' trust in the Father through the darkness of his unjust condemnation and crucifixion shows the absolute depth of his personal dedication, a personal dedication confirmed by God at the resurrection. As we have seen, Pannenberg's interpretation of revelation entails the being of the revealer, and Jesus therefore is of the divine essence, this includes Jesus' dedication to the Father and self-differentiation from him, it is a 'personal' unity of being.

Personal community is the essential community of being, since personal being exists in self-dedication to another. For the second time in the book Pannenberg quotes Hegel on personhood in relation to the Trinity, that it is 'the character of the person . . . to supersede its isolation, its separateness' through dedication. 'In friendship and love I give up my abstract personality and win thereby concrete personality. The truth of personality is just this, to win it through this submerging, being submerged in the other'[2] (Pannenberg 1977b: 336). Immersion in the 'Thou' of the other is also participation in the being of the Thou, and in this way Jesus can be seen to share in the divine being and to be the divine Son. The mutual dedication of the Father and Son constitutes the trinitarian unity of God, and also the deity of Jesus as the Son: Jesus' relation to the Father as the Son is true for the eternity of God and for the 'historical Jesus', integrating eternity and time and replacing the metaphysics of Logos trinitarianism. The trinitarian mutual self-dedication of Father and Son is the historical mutual self-dedication, an economic trinitarian reality. This is not detached from space and time and imprinted onto history 'from above' in a structure of divine self-correspondence, as found, for example, in Barth's *Church Dogmatics*. Rather the history of Jesus is from the Father and to the Father from the Son, whose identity is that of Jesus – as the resurrection event decides. Pannenberg teaches a dialectic of Jesus and the divine Son, each illuminating and confirming the other, meeting at the point of the resurrection when each maps the other, revealing the true God to and for us, while actually being the very life of God:

> His humanity is not synthesised with a divine essence, but it involves two complementary total aspects of his existence. These aspects are as different from one another as God and man are different. Nevertheless, with the special relation to the Father in the human historical aspect of Jesus' existence, his identity in the other aspect – that of the eternal Son of the eternal Father – is given. (Pannenberg 1977b: 337)

The dialectic of Jesus and eternal Son connects to the dialectic of knowing and being: epistemologically, we know of Jesus' identity by considering history drawing together his life of total immersion in his Father's will and what happened to him at Good Friday and Easter, ontologically this identity is found to be rooted in the very being and life God.

Pannenberg therefore rejects the doctrine of '*enhypostasia*', the doctrine that the divine person is the person of the human Jesus, the divine Logos including the human nature. Jesus lived in dependence on the Father, not on the Son as in the *enhypostatic* idea. The *enhypostatic* doctrine fails to distinguish between the personal community of Jesus with the Father and the identity of person with the Son, and this has to do with a failure to understand persons as relational. A person's history is worked out in community with others, in give and take, acting and receiving. In this kind of way Jesus is integrated into the person of the divine Son through Jesus' continual intercourse with the Father, trusting and receiving – right up to Calvary and Easter Day's divine gift of the divine life itself. Pannenberg speaks of the identity of the divine Son hidden in the man Jesus, and this has to be his 'essence' arising from his ultimate meaning, read back retroactively. Instead of the dialectic of the changeless divine Logos incarnated as the man Jesus, we now have the dialectic of the future perfect: the divine eschatological meaning takes up the man Jesus into full divine essence, in unity and distinction. The person of Jesus, his identity, is divine meaning, and relational meaning, including the meaning of all history: he does not break into it in judgement and grace from 'outside' history.

We could well conclude that Pannenberg teaches the revelation of the Trinity, rather than the Logos made flesh: the resurrection discloses and decides how God is God, in this threefold economy of self-dedication, the resurrection proving the great historical event of God, and so an event of eternity – an eternity that redefines itself as historically unfolding itself, while always being what it was going to end up being. The triune God is the reconciler of the world, since the Father's act of raising Jesus from death constitutes Jesus' identity as the eternal Son. Thus the trinitarian God is revealed and enacted between the Father and Jesus, and the Spirit who raised the Son of David and declared him Son of God in power (Rom. 1).

Jesus' Sonship, moreover, fulfils human personality by virtue of his total openness and trust. We receive life from God our Father and respond to this by trust and self-dedication, finally becoming our true selves at the completion of our life which is a matrix of our act and divine gift interweaving together, preserving humanity and divinity. Jesus has pioneered this way, and God has sent us the Spirit of this Sonship, so we too call God 'Father' (Gal. 4.6). Jesus was a normal man, his sinlessness was a matter of his whole life and its vindication by his Father, and he overcame sinful human behaviour, Christus Victor, the obedient New Adam representing humanity before God. The historical life of Jesus vis a vis the Father in the Spirit is one of openness, obedience and loving trust, and this is the role of the Son vis a vis the Father in the trinitarian life.

The Lordship of Christ

The final chapter of Pannenberg's Chistological magnum opus concerns the Lordship of Christ, the kingship of Jesus. The early church asserted this Lordship – despite the fact that Jesus pointed to the Father as the sovereign Lord of the universe – as a post-resurrection fact established by the Father, who delegated the kingship announced by Jesus to Jesus, the Son. The difference between his proclamation of the kingdom and the eschatological reality of its arrival in the resurrection was superseded in Jesus' own person (Pannenberg 1977b: 67). The Son's Lordship is to bring all creation to worship and obey the Father; Jesus is himself the kingdom of God established for us already. The future remains the future in our historical continuum, and the kingdom of the Father remains in the future, however it has arrived proleptically in Christ. Pannenberg's theology hinges on the differential of past, present and future, even to the extent of the trinitarian persons' relationship effecting and being affected by these tenses: 'the difference between Father and Son is also lost with the loss of the difference between future and present, between the Lordship of God and Jesus' own historical activity' (Pannenberg 1977b: 370). The kingdom of God is present as the future of God's final reign proleptically arrived in Christ, and yet the future holds the fullness of this reign and our participation in it. The Father has the role of the end time towards which the Son and Spirit open themselves and open creation, and from which they have been sent, as the resurrection discloses.

Here, as elsewhere in this Christology, for example, the treatment of Jesus' sinlessness, there is a remarkable absence of a treatment of the Spirit in the work of Jesus as he faces the Father representing the human race, and readers should go to *Systematic Theology* vol. 2 chapter 11 (Pannenberg 1994) for supplementation on pneumatology and soteriology. He does say however that the church is now ruled by the exalted Lord through the Spirit, and lives in the light of the expected final coming of his kingdom. *Jesus God and Man* is corrected by Pannenberg later as to the nature of the rule of the exalted Christ in relation to the church; he says that his presentation in *Jesus God and Man* (Pannenberg 1977b: 219): 'stands in need of correction. We certainly should not treat the church's proclamation of the gospel as a part of the prophetic office of Christ in the sense that its work may be identified with his without distinction' (Pannenberg 1994: 449).

Rather the church's proclamation of the message of Christ serves him when it accurately conveys the gospel, and he is then at work in and by it. The tension between the already and the not yet continues, we live between the times, and that is the reason for the existence of God, who rules all things, being contested and debated, the final end is not yet and the Christian thesis is still therefore provisional, formally speaking.

Pannenberg closes his great work by widening Christology to its fullest scope and elaborates Christ and creation, which he does by way of the doctrine of the election of Jesus, applauding Barth for his ground-breaking work in connecting the doctrine of election with the Father's choice of Jesus for creation and all humanity. This is a move away from an abstract and hidden decree of election to an historical and concrete view of election in and for reality. Whereas Barth speaks of the pre-existing election of Jesus for creation, Pannenberg places this at the eschatological summation of all things; Jesus' election is the summation of humanity and creation from the perspective of the end, thus constituting the meaning of all history and creation in his own eschatological person. Pannenberg disagrees with the idea that all things ultimately tend to Christ by an intrinsic law or entelechy, a view he finds in Rahner, and asserts his own characteristic view of history as coming from the future to draw it forward, thus avoiding a necessesitarian logic of history which makes genuine contingency and freedom in history hard to ground. By orientating the election of the world in Christ from the eschaton he ensures, we can argue, that he avoids the problem of history in effect being of no value in itself since it is occluded by the overwhelming election of Jesus Christ before creation, this is McGrath's criticism of Barth's doctrine of the election of Jesus Christ (McGrath 1986). It is surely a strength of Pannenberg's very unusual ontology of the future perfect that historical freedom and contingency is given a ground in the freedom of God, and that this averts a deterministic historical process.

The eschatological Lordship of Christ, moreover, establishes the unity of the cosmos, which is not in itself a unity but receives its unity through humanity, that is to say the mass multiplicity of the universe is united through human thought and wisdom and is made into the universe for humanity. There is therefore a principle of unity and diversity at the heart of the very structure of the cosmos and this is revealed in the man Jesus and his identity as the eternal Son.

Pannenberg does have a very powerful section on the Spirit's role in creation much earlier in the book (Pannenberg 1977b: 169–78), stressing the eschatological and ontological dimensions of the Spirit, dimensions lacking in much of the western theological tradition in contrast to that of the East. The Spirit glorifies the Father and Son, the exalted Lord of creation and the Spirit brings new life to the dead and is the creative origin of all life, grounding the diversity and unity, union and differentiation, needed for all creation and life. Pannenberg's closes *Jesus God and Man* with a strong affirmation that all created reality has its purpose and unity in the eschatological judgement of Christ, in whose light the totality of reality is given and decided, and in this way the creation of all things is mediated through Jesus as well as towards him. Creation means far more than its temporal beginning, it is an act of God's eternity, and its totality will be unfolded at the eschaton rather than at the beginning.

The shape of this Christological cosmology parallels the resurrection argument: the beginning of creation is an anticipation of the eschaton, only from the end can the beginning be understood, each presupposes the other logically, and the reality of the beginning will be read back retroactively from the end. Meaning, for Pannenberg's ontology, constitutes being at its deepest level. Pannenberg has the reverse of an empiricist philosophy with its acceptance only of 'brute facts' established by detached observation, rather true facts are established by meaning, and in this sense we can say that Pannenberg is influenced by the German objective idealist tradition, although as we shall see in the next chapter on the Trinity, his theology is rooted not in a model of 'mind' incorporating all else, but an authentic trinitarian pattern of mutuality, interdependence and love at the heart of all reality. This is revealed in the strongest sense in the life of Jesus, confirmed and enacted as the very Son of God at the resurrection.

CONCLUSION: THREE LEVELS

Pannenberg's Christology is a *tour de force*, a magnificent argument drawing on a vast wealth of biblical, theological and philosophical resources, without doubt appropriating eschatology as the matrix for the deity of Jesus and restating the doctrine of the Trinity in brilliant fashion. This Christology rejects both the traditional Chalcedonian and the post-Enlightenment humanist Christologies: the former is unable to integrate God into history, the latter similarly fails to unite the man Jesus with God, falling prey to a deist agenda. There is no doubt that in his focus on the resurrection of Jesus Pannenberg touches the very nerve of apostolic Christianity and theology: the New Testament is written in the belief that Jesus was raised after his crucifixion and that his true identity was given thereby. This is the route taken by Christian theology to the affirmation in 451 of the Chalcedonian Christology of the person of the divine Word assuming human nature to himself, and this definition did import a dualism into Christology which removed the eschatological matrix of the crucified and risen Lord. Chalcedon has, since the Enlightenment, been subject to criticism of its dehistoricizing tendency and Platonist dualism, criticism including conservative evangelicals such as James Denney. Jesus the man becomes evaporated in the incarnation of humanity by the divine Logos.

Even so orthodox a theologian as Donald Baillie could argue that Chalcedon's two nature Christology was fundamentally docetic. (Baillie 1948). Chalcedon offers a divine 'person' assuming human nature, leaving the problem of the human person being absent, displaced or overwhelmed by the person of the divine Logos. Baillie's suggestion was to appeal to the analogy of the 'paradox of grace' to supply the dimension of divinity to the man Jesus, who was wholly open to the grace of God, which means to God's very being. All that the man Jesus achieved was prompted by, enabled by, in effect enacted by, divine grace. The answer to the question 'would any person fully open to divine grace thereby be qualified to be the divine Son?', is met by an appeal to divine election: God chose this man, not another, and we are not able to contest the divine decision of prevenience (Baillie 1948: 134). And this prevenience carries back into God and God's choice for this work, which means that in God is a divine Word of predestination of Jesus. Ontologically however we might equate the Jesus presented by Baillie with the Mary, ' full of grace' presented by the Roman Catholic Church's dogma, a holy human being totally obedient and led fully by God's grace. Her identity, however, is not that of the divine. We must also say that Baillie's Christ is not interpreted in terms of eschatology at all, the resurrection being very difficult to integrate, and indeed the suspicion is that he presents in effect a doctrine of inspiration to the highest degree, rather than incarnation. But like Pannenberg, Baillie offers a two-tier Christology: the man Jesus is a man, totally determined by the being of God, by grace.

Panneberg's theology of the future perfect offers a dialectical identity of the man Jesus and his ultimate meaning as the eschatological divine Son, retroactively read back over the history of the human Jesus. In his *Systematic Theology* vol. 2 Pannenberg uses the language of the concealment of the eternal Son in the life of the man Jesus. If we ask 'would any man totally open to God the Father be thereby divine, if raised from the dead?', the ontological question, it is hard to give a negative answer, and like Baillie, Pannenberg would have to appeal not to the prevenient grace of God but to the proleptic eschaton: that is to say, this man always was going to be recognized and constituted the divine Son in the final future, and the future come in advance at Easter. Pannenberg's doctrine of being, that is constituted by final significance, gives Jesus an ontological basis, if one accepts his metaphysics of time and reality. The person of Jesus, moreover, is a relational person, whose relation to the Father is taken up into God's very being, and so always was inherent in his eternal being. Jesus therefore is truly a man, a human person, and yet mapped onto his human identity is his identity as the eternal Son. The two are distinguished, while being united as the one in relation to the Father, for example:

> Whereas we cannot identify the salvation of the world as an aim that Jesus set himself in the historical humanity of his work, we may well describe the atoning function of his death with a view to the world's salvation as the object and goal of the Son of God, who was at work in the history of Jesus. (Pannenberg 1994: 442)

If we work 'from below', from our human historical analysis and interpretation, we reach the point of eschatological 'taking up' of the human Jesus' life and fate into the divine, by his resurrectional significance, in the order of being as well as of knowing: the real is the rational. Pannenberg offers us a profound trinitarian Christology of being arising from eschatological meaning, Jesus is truly a man, who is the eternal Son, instituted and constituted so at the eschaton, arrived at Easter. The very being of God is more complex than we had imagined, revealed as relational and taking up created historical time and space, showing an inclusion of, and embracing of, finite life in eternal life: the trust of the man Jesus for the Father is taken up into, and as, the love of the eternal Son for the Father.

Our journey of seeking the truth from history, historical events and meanings, leads us conceptually and historically 'upwards', from the lower level of knowing and being to the higher, the higher enfolding the lower and indeed flowing from it. There is an elliptical shape to this flow from our interpretation towards the heart of true being, the Christ, whose light works backwards upon our openness to seek after God. History is revelatory of divine being, finite time is taken up into eternity, the resurrection of Jesus translating his humanity to where it always really was, the divine. This is a complex interweaving of levels of knowing and being fusing in meaning, time taken up into eternity, the rhythm of the cosmos proving to be prolepsis itself, reaching ahead and being supported by the divine constantly conveying reality to the created order. Pannenberg's Christology is not simply a matter of human interpretation, rather the future perfect ontology takes this interpretative truth of revelation into the life of the eternal Son and as it were blesses it as the way to worship and faith. Human interpretation finds its way into the ultimate truth, the rational and the finally real are united. We are drawn forward as a human race towards and into this truth about ourselves, and about the threefold God whence we came and to which we return.

Pannenberg speaks of three levels of the Christ event: first, the human historical level of the work and fate of Jesus; second, the same history as the medium of the eternal Son of God, who is at work in it as he became man in the person of Jesus; third, this same history is also the medium of the active presence of the exalted Lord through the apostolic proclamation that explains the saving meaning of this history (Pannenberg 1994: 441). Pannenberg's Christology begins with history and ends with the end of all things, the great consummation of the cosmos, enacted at Easter and the key to the universe's meaning as it moves towards its continually anticipated climax. The language of Christology ends with that of doxology and the gift of the eschatological Spirit, as we are taken to the holy of holies with the man Jesus, who proves to be the divine Son facing the Father in the Spirit.

CHAPTER 4

HISTORICIST TRINITARIAN ONTOLOGY

FOCUSED TEXT: ESSAYS FROM *GRUNDFRAGEN SYSTEMATISCHER THEOLOGIE BAND 2*[1]

THE TRINITARIAN SPIRIT

Considerations of *Revelation as History* and *Jesus God and Man* leave the reader in no doubt that Pannenberg has constructed an economic trinitarianism of a panentheistic kind, the sovereign Father freely mediating history into being which is to return to its source, its self-centred alienation overcome by the obedience of the finite man Jesus in his total trust and openness to the Father. The end-time event discloses the totality of history as having divine meaning and therefore being. The man Jesus, representing all reality before God, is revealed and eschatologized as the eternal Son of the Father. The meaning of history is inherent in its process and open to 'unaided' reason, although the Spirit, for Pannenberg, is the Spirit of all reality and thought and so at work in all human quest and inspiration for truth (McKenzie 1980). God the Father is the God of the open future, bringing creation into being and relating to it as the deep ground of meaning and hope, while being distinguished from it. God the Son is the eternal mode of the man Jesus and his open obedience to the Father, one in being with God and yet continually differentiating himself from God in humble filial dependence. The eschatological Christ event reveals the nature of God as triune, and reveals the structure of reality as proleptic, reaching forward into the future and being confirmed by the onset of the future from the Father. For Pannenberg the very shape of reality is trinitarian, as the final quotation from *Jesus God and Man* shows very clearly: 'Jesus' saying about losing and finding life has universal ontological relevance' (Pannenberg 1977b; 396). Events move forward and are taken up into new configurations of meaning at the arrival of God's new future, they are not fixed and insulated but rather porous and open, open to the future and open to each other in a kind of organism. This is a doctrine of creation as well as of redemption, events are released from the future by the Father into their own free existence and destiny for openness to God. This is an organic, dynamic view of being in relation, orientated to the future hope as the meaning of all things, the future whence all reality comes to us as a gift, the final eschatological point from which truth comes to finitude – as the resurrection meaning comes back into history with the true identity of Jesus.

Here we should fill out this economic trinitarianism somewhat in terms of the doctrine of the Spirit, the mode of the divine who knits the present to the oncoming future and brings about new syntheses of meaning, taking up the past into the future, again a motif very much part of the German idealist intellectual tradition and of Hegel in particular, with due modifications to the future orientation of history. Pannenberg does not define the process of the retroactive vindication and confirmation of Jesus' eschatological identity as the work of the Spirit, but this must be the case since the Spirit is revealed as the Spirit who raised the man Jesus, son of David, to unity with God the Father. The Spirit is at work universally and immanently, correlating the old and the new, usually described in terms of the past going forward into the future, but surely this must also include the role of mediating eschatological meaning and new understanding backwards from the proleptic end into the present, hence into the worship of the church where the true identity of Jesus is realized. The retroactivity, constituting the life of the man Jesus, must be the work of the Spirit through time, through the realm of idea and concept, of meaning transforming, or taking up, the finite being of Jesus into divinity.

In line with the rejection of dualism, the Spirit is the universal Spirit, the Spirit of God who is the 'all determining reality' not merely the reality determining the church and faith. There is no 'God-free zone' in Pannenberg's ontology, dualism of sacred and secular is abolished. Pannenberg is critical of doctrines and practices of the Spirit focused solely on piety and claims to special forms of knowing: rather the Spirit is integral to the Christian doctrine of creation and its structure. Christians know of the Spirit, that their knowledge of God in Christ entails the Spirit's work since God can be known through God: this does not mean that this awareness is closed to anyone who cares to reason towards it.

Pannenberg argues that all life in the universe is ec-centric, oriented to the future and self-transcending in dynamic structure. Humanity has a special awareness of this:

> Perhaps the human mind has a special realization of this ecstatic character of life. Man not only lives beyond himself in having experience of what is going on in his environment and relevant for his own life, but the human mind is characterized by a reflective attitude to himself and is therefore able to take his stand beyond himself and to know that. The human represents an intensified form of self-transcendence, ie: of the ecstatic structure of life . . ..
> This ecstatic element of the life of the mind I call 'Spirit'. (Pannenberg 1970c: 18)

While Pannenberg has rightly criticized pneumatology focused on knowing and mind, this portrayal of the work of the Spirit, indeed Spirit itself, emphasizes consciousness and reflection of the self in time, the transcendental dimension of our capacity to think about ourselves. Humanity represents intensified consciousness of itself as Spirit, the ecstatic life of the mind. As humans we are looking beyond ourselves for something to give meaning and unity to our life experiences, and this self-transcending dynamic exists because of the divine Spirit 'which, being future, is transcendent but as transcendent it is immanent in the human self transcendence' (Pannenberg 1970c: 21). God is free and future while being immanent in creation, sustaining the dynamic of prolepsis and ec-stasis, being open to the next event and to God, as Spirit. Pannenberg has created a close link between human consciousness and the divine Spirit and thinks that the differentiation of the Spirit from the Father and the Son is important in obviating a pantheistic logic to his theology – identifying our consciousness with that of the Spirit of God – since we differentiate ourselves from God, as did Jesus in eschatological joy and worship.

The Spirit is at work universally, albeit unrecognized as such for the most part, synthesizing and enlivening the history of the world as the divine living immanence, keeping events open to the God of the free future, the Father. The Spirit is the *Aufhebung* of historical time, the 'taking up' of the historical flow of events into the infinite or eternal, which itself unfolds into the finite and temporal as revelation, from the eschatologically unified future.[2]

The Spirit, for Pannenberg, glorifies the humiliated, brutalized and executed Jesus by raising him to life as the divine Son, thus resolving the ambiguity of God's appearance in the form of blood, toil, tears and sweat of human sin, injustice and misery; the Spirit is the 'moment' in the life of God and of human history when the meaning of the Christ event is clarified as reversing false judgements and the kingdom of evil. The Spirit is the moment of the bearing of the pain of the negative in history, the pain of remaining open in trust to the Father. And in all this the Spirit is free and not a mere unfolding of a logic determining history, God is 'personal' or rather 'persons' in mutual dependence, unity and self-differentiation, not in a timeless meaningless merri-go-round but in and through a 'life and death' history of development. The identity of the Spirit is an identity found in the Son and Father and their unity and differentiation, and this Spirit is the ec-static consciousness of humanity finalized at the eschaton as having a divine identity in the man Jesus.

THE TRINITARIAN GOD OF HISTORY

Pannenberg teaches that the real life of the God is in play in the history of Jesus, since that actually is the decisive, unique revelation of the divine trinitarian relationship of Son to Father in the Spirit. We are taken into the very being of God through the economy of the trinitarian God. With Barth and Rahner, Pannenberg goes with the theological logic that the economic Trinity cannot be split from the essential, or 'immanent', Trinity, and that the history of Jesus with the Father not merely reflects a higher divine life, but is that divine life of union and humble self-differentiation.

But he logically widens and deepens this theology, since the whole of history is under the Lordship of God and its total meaning is determinative for the being of God – while God freely brings this history into being from the future, another instance at the deepest level of the pattern of the future perfect. He says,

> the linking of the immanent Trinity to the economic Trinity cannot be restricted to the history of Jesus up to his resurrection from the dead. The executing of the world dominion of God by the exalted Lord and his end-time handing back of the kingdom to

the Father are now to be seen from the standpoint of the historical controversy concerning the deity of God, of the heavenly Father whom Jesus proclaimed. (Pannenberg 1991: 330)

Here he applauds the work of Moltmann, who showed that the Spirit's role of glorifying the Son and the Father in history is also real within the very trinitarian life of God, and argued that the consummation of salvation history integrates into the consummation of the trinitarian life of God in itself. When all things are in God and God is all in all, then the economic Trinity is subsumed in the immanent Trinity. Jenson is also cited as agreeing that the immanent Trinity is the eschatologically definitive form of the economic Trinity.

Here we are clearly in danger of dissolving the divine trinitarian life into the totality history, of absorbing the immanent Trinity into the economic Trinity. Pannenberg insists that the two are distinct, but yet the same. The immanent Trinity, he asserts, is to be found in the Trinity of salvation history, 'God is the same in his eternal essence as he reveals himself to be historically' (Pannenberg 1991: 331). History is real and decisive for God, and the end time will both reveal and accomplish this self-definition, the economic trinitarian life. But yet this life is always going to be what it is already, perfected and yet to come into perfection. The order of knowing and the order of being are juxtaposed to enable Pannenberg to have his economic trinitarian cake, and to eat it essentially. Union and distinction, knowing and being, are two of the dialectical movements in play as Pannenberg seeks to elaborate his historicist interpretation of the trinitarian life of God. Pannenberg denies that he is rendering the Trinity into a product of history. 'Refuted herewith is the idea of a divine becoming in history, as though the trinitarian God were the result of history and achieved reality only with the eschatological consummation' (Pannenberg 1991: 331). Quite so, that does seem a possible interpretation of his metaphysics. But he continues by way of rebuttal and defence of God as not being the product of the process:

In our historical experience it might seem as if the deity of the God whom Jesus proclaimed is definitively demonstrated only with the eschatological consummation. It might also seem as if materially the deity of God is inconceivable without the consummation of his kingdom, and that it is thus dependent upon the eschatological coming of the kingdom. (Pannenberg 1991: 331)

That perception, however, is mistaken, the reason being: 'But the eschatological consummation is only the locus of the decision that the trinitarian God is always the true God from eternity to eternity.' (Pannenberg 1991: 331). This confirms the usefulness of our interpretative tool of the future perfect tense for grasping Pannenberg's perplexing metaphysics: the perfection of God is not really at stake in the order of being, salvation history 'always was' going to confirm the identity of God as this trinitarian, free, sovereign, holy God; and yet on the finite way forward, from the past into the future, this was provisional – but only provisionally provisional – until the final confirmation is given, the decision located at the end by the sovereign fiat of the Father. The resurrection of Jesus has, from God's angle, decided the matter.

The eschatological consummation gives the confirmatory decision, the constitutive decision, the ontological decision, that the trinitarian God is – and so always must have been – the Lord of all reality. The meaning of the proleptic arrival of the eschaton bestows the divine and royal status of God's Son on the man Jesus: that is who he always was and that identity runs back to inform the substance of his humanity. Metaphysically there could hardly be a greater reversal of the Platonic 'substances' dualism used by the Chalcedonian Christological tradition: the human Jesus is sublated, inclusively taken up, to the divine status at the eschatological event of Easter, and this ontologically reads backwards in time so that he was always the Son in concealed form. The form of the finite historical is wholly open to divine being, and in its totality is the divine being manifested.

Once more we wrestle with Pannenberg's dialectics of history and logic, with time and eternity, with knowing and being. 'The world as the history of God', is his phrase, confirming the earlier 'revelation as history'. In his mature theology Pannenberg has undoubtedly moved to re-emphasize the eternity of God, the 'perfect' end of the future perfect, to protect himself from the charge of dissolving the divine life into the world process. We can perhaps say that God is genuinely in this process, while not its victim, and while transcending it: just as a person is necessarily a body, and would not be human without this body, and yet transcends the body and is not reducible to it. The body is necessary, but not sufficient, to the person. In the case of Pannenberg's God, the world came into being by his free choice, but once it exists then God's very nature demands that it be subject to divine Lordship. Its eschaton will reveal that this was true all along, and that God was always God, despite the contested nature of this fact in all the ambiguities resulting from the freedom of historical creatures. This kind of model may help clarify how Pannenberg can both reject the idea of divine becoming in history, while insisting that 'today we see that differentiating the eternal Trinity from all temporal change makes trinitarian theology one-sided and detaches it from its biblical basis' (Pannenberg 1991: 333). His theology seeks to hold together the transcendence of the divine being together with his immanence in the world, but also the eternal self-identity of God together with the debateability of his truth in the process of history. He seeks to achieve this through a radically trinitarian theology, which will at the same time be an ontological structure which runs through all reality as the best possible interpretation of how things really are.

Pannenberg's untranslated essay *Der Gott der Geschichte* (Pannenberg 1980: 112–18), specifically treats this area of trinitarian doctrine and God's relation to world history and can help amplify and clarify *Systematic Theology* vol. 1 (Pannenberg 1991) on this topic, which we will do in the following paragraphs. He finds the classical approach to the relationship of the Trinity to history problematic because the immanent, or essential, Trinity was conceived without the historical connection between God and the world, hence theologically detached and external to historical process. 'The God of the classical doctrine of the Trinity is still only secondarily the God of history and of historical revelation' (Pannenberg 1980: 123). Pannenberg argues for the divine identity of Jesus as the Son in revelational unity of being with the Father. God is the Father of this Son and not otherwise. Here we have a doctrine of the Trinity which connects the life of human history with the very being of God. The economic Trinity, the work of the triune God outside of himself, is inseparable from the immanent Trinity, God in himself. There has to be a distinction between immanent Trinity and economic Trinity, according to Pannenberg, because if God's revelation in Jesus Christ involves the trinitarian structure, then there must be a trinitarian structure in the eternal reality of God himself – prior to the existence of creation. On the other hand, the economic Trinity is not merely an image (in the Platonic sense) of the eternal trinitarian structure in the being of God. The immanent or essential Trinity, God in God's very being, is dependent on the process of history, hence on the economic Trinity. This is so not only epistemologically but also ontologically for God, given the actual finite reality of a world. Pannenberg considers the eternal reality of God itself to be dependent on the outcome of history – although such dependence occurs only on the condition that there is a world, rather than being a necessity binding God, who in fact brings creation into being out of freedom. There is a world and therefore, if God exists, he must show himself to be master of that world, since at present this is not beyond dispute; the truth of the proposition concerning the existence of God depends on the eschatological future of his kingdom or rule. Such is Pannenberg's logic.

Pannenberg appreciates the aim of Process theology to achieve an integration of God in the processes of history, but finds that it topples over into rendering God a factor in the universe, rather than maintaining the free and sovereign ruler of the universe (Pannenberg 1980: 119). The fact of the incarnation entails however that God is not simply detached from the universe, that this event affected God and so has consequences for the doctrine of divine relations with history, as Hegel, over against Kierkegaard and Barth, understood (Pannenberg 1980: 119). The last two theologians feared that Hegel was sacrificing the eternity of God in the processes of finite history, but Hegel, argues Pannenberg, developed an interpretation of a history of God which included eternal divine self-identity, and he taught that the successively appearing definitions of the general, the particular and the individual are at the same time already united as logical moments in the unity of the concept of the absolute, the all including. Hegel's notion of the absolute as a concept made it possible for him to think of the three movements of the concept at the same time united as immanent Trinity and unfolded into a succession: creation, reconciliation and redemption. The task of mentally conceiving the divine being as a unity integrated with the history of his activity, entails thinking of God as absolute, as completing the world through himself, and for this the idea of the Trinity is vital.

Pannenberg points out that the doctrine of the Trinity arose from God's acts in history, but then became detached and abstracted from history, and he returns to interpreting the trinitarian persons historically – while avoiding the perils of pantheism and making God a mere product of the historical process. As we saw in the last chapter, Jesus' crucifixion, for Pannenberg, affects the man Jesus but also the very being of God: God would not be this God had the cross and resurrection not happened. History affects the divine being, and the divine being brings history into being from the future. 'The resurrection of Jesus is thus just as constitutive for the Godhead of the Father as it is for the Sonship of Jesus. Without Jesus' resurrection the Father proclaimed by Jesus would not be God' (Pannenberg 1980: 123). The history of the Son concerns the divinity of the Father himself, the history of the Son reveals the divinity of himself to the Father. Jesus is revealed as the Son in his self-distinction from God, his Father, and this revelation of Jesus' divinity as Son in distinction from the Father is the work of the Spirit, who is the reality of God's presence in the world. The dialectics of unity and differentiation suffuse this discussion. The Spirit also has divinity only in the self-differentiation from God, whom he glorifies in the community of the Father and the Son. The truth of unity is difference and vice versa, as Hegel's logic affirms, there is no such thing as difference without the background commonality to hold the difference in tension (Caird 1883).

A major mistake in trinitarian theology has been to accept the controlling model of the subjectivity of God, whereas Pannenberg teaches, 'the model of the self-forming subjectivity has no place in the Trinitarian life of God', since 'this life completes itself in its historical revelation and thus also in God's eternity' (Pannenberg 1980: 124). The subjective model leads to the trinitarian persons being defined as mere modes of the subjectivity, a unitive essence logically prior to the threefold modes. This criticism equates with the Eastern Orthodox criticism of western theology embracing Platonic essence as a precondition to the trinitarian persons. Pannenberg says that his view of the three persons of the Trinity amounts to a widening of the classic doctrine of 'attribution' of characteristics from only the economic Trinity and the activity of God ad extra to the immanent or essential Trinity, the very life of God itself, which is therefore a history. Revelation history is integrated into the Trinity itself. The divinity of each person is conveyed through the other persons, an inner Trinitarian 'attribution' of Godhead. As the Father, with respect to Jesus, is the one God present to him through his Spirit; so for the Spirit the one God is revealed in the community of the Father and the Son; and for the Father the reality of his own Godhead, that is the reality of his kingdom and rule, depends on the Son and Spirit: this is historically revealed and true also for the very being and life of the Trinity. Mutuality and inter-dependence is lived in God, revealed as the totality of history, and lived out in the life of Jesus of

Nazareth. This self-differentiation of the persons, moreover, makes room for the created order to exist, differentiated from God but in union with God. Through his glorification of the Son as well as of the Father himself in the history of the Son, the Spirit grants at the same time to creatures a share in the glory of God manifested in Jesus Christ, without abolishing their distinction from God, their creaturehood.

The economic Trinity is therefore the essential or immanent Trinity in a radically real way, entailing the truth of revelatory history for the very heart of God and as historically real, successively real, for God. So much is this so that the divinity of God is 'at stake', as without the rule or kingdom of God being established in history there is doubt over the Lordship of God himself, not only to us in the created order but in God himself: the future of his kingdom is the matrix of the reality of God as of the truth of history as a history of his activity. And yet, here again the dialectic of the future perfect applies: 'But the future kingdom can only in this way be the kingdom of God that his future already determines the present now, and in the same way that the present has already determined all that is now past' (Pannenberg 1980: 127). So the free and sovereign God is releasing the events and meaning of history from its future, with the Spirit present dynamically maintaining the created order as open to the Father. The verdict on the whole enterprise – for it was not necessary for God to create – hinges on the man Jesus, his faith and trust, whether he is at one with the Father, as representing all creation. The truth of history and the truth of God coincide joyfully at Easter, 'through enduring the pain of the negative' in the Spirit on Good Friday.

If my own way of putting this, 'the future perfect tense', is helpful, this means that God does take a risk in creating the world, and is utterly honest in it so that history really is meaningful and not a show in which actual life decisions do not matter, they are life and death decisions. But God is this God of love and justice, of gentleness and power, and will always be who is he is, and was always going to turn out to be: the Father of the Son, self-defined in the life and fate of Jesus of Nazareth. The meaning of the totality of history is found in Jesus and his relations, to fellow creatures but also to his Father and the Spirit, and this relationality is God's very life. We might even say for Pannenberg that doctrinally the *incarnation of the Logos has been superseded by the life of the Trinity being enacted and revealed in finite space and time.* Pannenberg is far more radical than we may realize. His theology is also a trinitarian theodicy and pastoral agenda. He closes this extraordinarily rich essay by quoting Karl Löwith on the problem of suffering in the twentieth century, saying that only Christianity has anything to engage this problem, on which Pannenberg's trinitarian comment is that,

> In the tension between the power and powerlessness of the Creator in the death of his Son and with the glorification of both through the Spirit, the Trinitarian God takes upon himself the suffering of his creation. In this way he is the God of history and of truth. (Pannenberg 1980: 128)

God truly is the God of history, from 'inside' and 'outside', past and future, uniting creation and creator in his trinitarian life. In this theological reappropriation he has certainly taken Hegel's ideas as a profound resource, but by his keeping open the process of history, formally certainly, he can claim to have avoided Hegel's speculative metaphysics.

TRINITARIAN PERSONHOOD – BEYOND SUBJECTIVITY AND SUBSTANCE

We have seen that Pannenberg takes the doctrine of revelation as history and connects that to the doctrine of the trinitarian God. Like Barth, he bases his doctrine of God on revelation but he understands revelation very differently to Barth. In another untranslated essay *'Die Subjektivität Gottes und die Trinitätslehre'* (Pannenberg 1980: 96–111) he criticizes Barth's famous theological grounding of the doctrine of the Trinity in the unfolding of the phrase 'God reveals himself'. This, as we noted above, is rejected by Pannenberg as modelling a single subjectivity as God, who reveals himself ad extra as himself thus disclosing the structure of a subjectivity in self-projection as the very essence of God. To posit this subjectivity at the heart of God is not adequate, says Pannenberg, as the ground of the doctrine of the Trinity:

> Barth dissociates himself energetically from a speculative doctrine of the Trinity, but if one looks more closely the contrast is less deep than it first appears. For Barth did not develop his doctrine

of the Trinity primarily from the result of exegesis, for example the historical relationship of Jesus to the Father, but he argues from the inner logic of the concept of revelation in which subject, predicate and object, or Revealer, Revelation and Revealedness, have to be differentiated. According to Barth this is a matter of the self objectification of God in his revelation, according to which he already, in eternity does not want to be without the other, but wants only to have himself, in having himself with the other, indeed in the other. (Pannenberg 1980: 101).[3]

Barth's unfolding of subjectivity as the basis for the doctrine of the Trinity leads to a modalist view of the persons, according to Pannenberg's critique, modes of the single subjectivity which is the ultimate being of God, a single unity projecting itself outwards and finding its structure thereby reflected. For Pannenberg this is an error: rather revelation is historical and diverse in nature, showing that God likewise is the God of diversity and unity. Pannenberg likewise rejects classical western trinitarianism with its a priori assumption of divine substance, generally interpreted along Hellenistic lines as incompatible with created substance, thus rendering a doctrine of incarnation very problematic. This too is a ground for the doctrine taken outside the context of Jesus himself and his history, leading to his death and resurrection, to the eschatological climax, and the sending of the Spirit.

The Sonship of Jesus was revealed and established by Jesus' resurrection and union of being with the Father, and within that by his self-distinction from the Father, in the Spirit. This trinitarian relation in distinction is the very being of God, a relational being. God revealed himself as the Father, never without the Son nor the Spirit.[4] For Pannenberg the reality of the Trinity, of the one God, is constituted by the threefold dynamic movement of moments in God. He rejects a prior *una substantia* which is logically shared by three entities, albeit 'modes', 'persons' or 'relations'. Nor does he sympathize with more modern interpretations which presuppose the Trinity as a self-unfolding of a divine subject. Instead, the self-differentiation of God is constitutive for the trinitarian persons and for their own divinity, as we saw above in *Der Gott der Geschichte*. This fact, taken from their historical revelation, must also determine the portrayal of the inner-trinitarian connections: and not merely symbolize them as if simply a pictorial way of illustrating a metaphysical truth. The revelatory occurrence for each of the persons of their own divinity is

conveyed through the others in the process of the unfolding historical drama, and this is not a matter of abstraction from historical
revelation, by the human mind, rather it is the inherent inner meaning of the historical events, the self-description of the inner being of
God played out actually on the canvass of history.

The unity of God is, then, one of self-mediation, not a matter of a
prior essence, which is, shared 'subsequently' in terms of logic. Revelation is, we recall, indirect self-revelation, whereby the indirectness
comes not because of the medium, but because of an indirectness in
content, which after consideration yields its inherent meaning, as the
'stimulus to the reflection derives from the event itself'. The mediation
of divine essence ad extra, or into the created order, would seem to be
congruent with the dynamic of God's eternal being – which is affected
by history. Because of the activity of divine love revealed climactically
in Jesus we can call God the living God who has no unity or being
apart from the activity of his life in which he separates another being
from himself while still keeping it alive by maintaining its relation to
himself (Pannenberg 1969b: 70). In the person of the Son,

> the one God comes forth from his Godhead. He stands over
> against the Godhead in the form of the Father. He does not of
> course lose his relation to the Father in the unity of the divine
> essence, for in coming forth he is obedient to his sending by
> the Father and remains united with him precisely by his self-
> distinction from him. In the Son, therefore, the inner dynamic of
> the divine life finds expression in its concreteness as Spirit and
> love. (Pannenberg 1991: 430)

The economic trinitarian action really is the essence of God, out-
wardly. God's being is a living dynamic, in which the persons do not
exist for themselves but 'in ec-static relation to the overarching field
of deity'. Their relationship to the overarching divine essence,
is mediated by the relations to the other two persons. This self-
mediated deity, as has been pointed out, means that,

> as the Father, with respect to Jesus, is the one God present to him
> through his Spirit; so for the Spirit the one God is revealed in the
> community of the Father and the Son; and so for the Father the
> reality of his own Godhead, that is the reality of kingdom, depends
> on the operation of the Son and the Spirit. (Pannenberg 1980: 125)

This self-mediation, in terms of the 'persons' of the Trinity, as we have seen, is an insight of Hegel:

> Hegel was the first to so elaborate the concept of 'person' in such a way that God's unity becomes understandable precisely from the reciprocity of the divine Persons . . . . 'The character of the person, the subject, is to relinquish its isolation. Morality, love, is just this: to relinquish its particularity, its particular personality, to extend it to universality – friendship is the same . . . .The truth of personality is just this: to win it through immersion, through being immersed in the other'. Through this profound thought that the essence of the person is to exist in self-dedication to another person, Hegel understood the unity in the Trinity as the unity of reciprocal self-dedication . . . precisely by means of the sharpest accentuation of the concept of the personality of Father, Son and Spirit. (Pannenberg 1977b: 181–2)

This Hegelian doctrine is reflected in Pannenberg's teaching of the 'dialectical Sonship' of Jesus, whose particularity and deity were found to be coordinating aspects. The particular man Jesus, has the universal significance of deity, and his characteristic was utter self-abnegation, the losing of himself in the Father: thus he is Son. In the losing of himself, the Son finds himself as the Son of the Father, the utterly free God, this is who he really is. This Son, being aware of his Father is therefore, indirectly or mediately, aware that this state of affairs is God's work, and so is aware of the Spirit. The very fact that the Son worships and serves the Father in the Spirit indicates the self-distinction of the Spirit from Father and Son. This is the character of Pannenberg's mutually self-giving unity of God. This 'process of self-dedication' gives us the insight as to the real, living, intense unity of deity. It may seem paradoxical, but self-differentiation constitutes the divine unity.

Pannenberg has been glad to rehabilitate Hegel's triune self-differentiating, self-integrating deity. But he criticizes Hegel for failing as he sees it, ultimately to overcome the subjectivism of the modern idea of 'person'. This criticism of Hegel, following Pannenberg's adoption of his relational idea, is significant in that it drives Pannenberg's criticism of the Kantian heritage to its farthest point. Pannenberg's momentum towards the 'post-Kantian synthesis' reaches its climax, arguably, with his doctrine of the personal character of

God, as well as humanity. Pannenberg discusses the philosophical and theological debate between Fichte and Hegel over the nature of God as 'Person' in several places (Pannenberg 1957–65; 1972a: 27–8; 1980). The issue between Fichte and Hegel was whether the infinite God could be a Person:

> In the dispute over atheism of 1798 Johann Gottlieb Fichte maintained that God cannot be thought of as a person without contradiction, because the idea of person includes the notion of the finite. As 'person' a being is always thought of in comparison with something else – a world of objects or persons. The idea of the 'I' essentially and inalienably includes a 'Thou' and an 'It'. Consequently no 'I' seems capable of being everything; it always is, as person, limited by other things, and hence finite. (Pannenberg 1972a: 27–8)

We have seen that Hegel's view of person sought to overcome this difficulty.

> According to Hegel, the person does not in every respect have its counterpart outside itself, as limitation of its own being; it is rather the nature of the person to be related to its counterpart even to give itself up to that counterpart and thus to find itself in the other. Moreover, a person finds himself again in the other in the degree to which he has surrendered and given himself up to that other. Thus in the personal life the contrast to the other, the limitation, is abolished or overcome. (Pannenberg 1972a: 28)

Indeed, for Hegel, the truly personal would be infinite: finite personhood is partial, since we only partially overcome the contrast to the other. Pannenberg, however, argues in his article *Person und Subjekt* (Pannenberg 1980: 80–95), that Fichte's criticism of the notion of God as personal is only apparently overcome by Hegel's reconception of the notion of subject (Pannenberg 1980: 86). Fichte himself retracted from his early position of asserting a self-positing ego, and Hegel's concept of the self-positing subject, which is with itself in its 'other', fails finally to escape Fichte's later critique, according to Pannenberg. Either 'the other' is not clearly distinct from the self-positing subject, or else there is genuine, original, distinction, which vitiates the true identity, and the subject then is no longer absolute.

If the subject, by finding itself in its 'other' becomes, through this 'other' an other, then the subject is no longer for Pannenberg the all-embracing absolute, but rather the process of the history of its change, through which his self is granted to him. Pannenberg dislikes Hegel's identity of subject as self-insulated and absolute. He wishes, as it were, to open up Hegel, in a sense to out-Hegel Hegel, to increase the emphasis on openness and relationality by moving away from the central insulated subject as self-positing. Pannenberg's amendment of Hegel runs along the line of the history, the process which comes from the future. The becoming of the subject, the 'history transcending its subjectivity' (Pannenberg 1980: 86), points us in the right direction to the true heritage of Hegel, moving beyond mere subjectivity to the process of being person.

He sets out his key triadic understanding of the ego, the self and the person as follows:

> Instead of being a postulation of the ego, the self represents itself in a process of change in a story or history, in the course of which it is not clear what the self will become. But the ego, far from bringing forth the self for its part needs the self to gain stability and continuity. For this it needs a manifestation, present to the ego of its not yet completed self, and that, as we shall see, is the person. Thus we reach a thought of the person which is different to that of the subject and as shall be seen allows a better solution to the problems of Trinity and Christology which are connected with the concept of person. (Pannenberg 1980: 88)

Such a move will overcome the contemporary absolutizing of subjectivity, Cartesian or Romanticist, against which Pannenberg's whole agenda operates. Pannenberg wishes to elucidate a doctrine of person which retains the modern experience of creative subjectivity, includes it, but does not absolutize it. As he says in the concluding paragraph of *Person und Subjekt*,

> The point of the doctrine of the Trinity lies precisely in the fact that the one God per se, apart from the three persons, is not person but only in the form of the Father and of the Son – and then also person in the form of the Spirit. The countenance of the one God is threefold, and not only for us but also for the trinitarian persons themselves, their relationship to the divine

being is mediated or made possible or communicated only through the other two persons. Thus person is only countenance or face, the form or appearance of the one divine being, and the peculiarity of the divine being lies precisely in the fact that it can be conceived in definitively ineffable identity, although this is still susceptible of description, only in the threeness of the persons. . . . The one God can be conceived neither through a concept of being (as substance), nor through the concept of absolute subject. (Pannenberg 1980: 95)

This overarching category, a descriptive, phenomenological one, embraces the 'I', the experiential ego, and the 'self'. Pannenberg rejects the 'ego' as the integrative factor: it is the 'self' which, as the stable pre-figuration of the overall 'person', integrates our ego experiences. As we proceed in the protean experiences of life,

in our self-consciousness we identity ourselves with our self, which gathers together the totality of our self-experience and which is therefore constant, this self, and through this in each moment we let our ego be integrated through our self. (Pannenberg 1980: 91)

Pannenberg radically destroys Kantian subjective idealism. 'It is not the "I" which postulates itself . . . but the self integrates the "I", and only through this gives it identity' (Pannenberg 1980: 91). This means that Pannenberg is advocating a triadic definition of person. The 'I' or 'ego' is the subjectivity which experiences the protean events of life. The 'self' is an objective reality which integrates these experiences of the 'ego' and which is the proleptic being of the 'person', and his identity given to the 'ego'. The 'person' is the overarching reality, which subsumes the 'ego' and 'self' in their dialectical relation through the temporal process. The 'person' really exists at the end of a life, because, as is the case for all Pannenberg's ontology, the end is determinative, retroactively, for what went before. The 'self' is the 'person' proleptically prior to the finally decisive end point of the fulfilled 'person'. Pannenberg intends to break clear of the definition of person as the conscious centre, the core ego, which he sees as dominating philosophy and theology since the Enlightenment, and which represents the hidden anthropocentric metaphysic of modern thought. It seems hard to over-emphasize the 'Copernican revolution' he attempts here.

Pannenberg's doctrine of the Spirit in relation to the dynamic of natural occurrence should be included in any account of his trinitarianism, since it emphasizes his move away from the models of subjectivity and of Platonic substance in favour of relationality and interweaving as being. Pannenberg toys with the idea from physics of 'field theory' as a way of talking of the Spirit's role in the natural order. This model breaks clearly from that of subjectivity or mind and expresses the biblical theme of the Spirit of God as dynamic breath or power suffusing all things and knitting them together. This dynamic field model resonates with the trinitarian structure of interrelation between the Father, Son and Spirit. The person of the Holy Spirit is not himself to be understood as the field but as the unique manifestation (singularity) of the field of the divine essentiality. But because the personal being of the Holy Spirit is manifest only in distinction from the Son (and therefore from the Father), his working in creation has more of the character of dynamic field operations (Pannenberg 1994: 83). The Spirit's work of linking what is distinct is characteristic, and this has a dynamic associated with it, in God's life and in creation, overcoming the rifts and conflicts in the latter realm. Here is the ontological role of the Spirit, a role encompassing human reason and bringing out the meaning of things to human understanding in the light of the totality of all being and time enacted by the trinitarian God in history. The notion of some kind of social personality, on the analogy of St Paul's 'Body of Christ', especially when we recall Pannenberg's strong identification of human consciousness with Spirit, does seem an apt way of describing the Spirit in his theological system.

THE TRINITARIAN LIFE OF THE FUTURE PERFECT

Pannenberg has crafted a wonderfully subtle and interesting trinitarian ontology, recasting the doctrine of the Trinity and developing it after Barth had placed it once more at the centre of Christian theology. John Milbank's view is that Pannenberg, along with Moltmann and Jüngel, work with Hegel's ideas in fashioning trinitarian theology:

In recent Protestant writings on the Trinity, a Hegelian solution to the problem of the Spirit's identity is much in evidence: the Trinity itself is seen in terms of God's involvement in historical becoming, and the Spirit as God's eschatological arrival in the Kingdom (or *as* the Kingdom), already anticipated in the Church. (Milbank 1997: 180)

For Milbank, Pannenberg is the theologian of these with most consistency and insight on the logic of substantial relations with respect to historical becoming.

Pannenberg develops easily the most sophisticated account of the personal relations, by insisting . . . both that God can only be personal if he is personally related, *and* (contrast Kasper) that personhood can only acquire a substantial content in the course of relational *development*. Thus becoming rather than *Monarchia* here gives a Trinitarian account of divine substance. (Milbank 1997: 181)

Substance for Pannenberg is not reducible, however, to subjectivity and becoming is not a matter of necessary development as with Hegel. Milbank's comment picks out the key aims and achievements of Pannenberg's radically trinitarian theology. Pannenberg has overcome 'ontotheology' of classical theism whereby God stands over against the world so dominating it as to freeze out real human freedom and creativity, certainly unable to exist in the processes of time and space, since the 'being' of God is inherently immutable and unable to live historically. The Trinity, for such a theological framework, is a reality existing in total contrast to that of creation and history, and can only image itself at a lower level onto the finite level after a correspondence theory of image and reality. Pannenberg is suggesting an end to this neo-Platonic model of divine correspondence in favour a thoroughgoing historicist model of God and the world, a coherence view of truth and reality rather than the correspondence model. He eschews Process theology as surrendering the sovereignty of the creator into the processes of space and time, and gives up the notion of *creation ex nihilo*, the divine being a factor in the universe, rather than the free Lord of all things, the 'all determining reality'. Neither Process theology nor Platonic 'ontotheology' resonate with the thrust of the faith found in the texts of the biblical tradition which point to events in history as sent by God to achieve his will and reveal himself; the God of the prophets is holy but living and active, never to be predicted or domesticated by humanity, and yet faithful rather than capricious or quixotic. God's ways in creation are not some kind of law, not a kind of Aristotelian DNA woven into the scheme of things which we are urged to obey. Nor is the creator a monad who has predetermined the course of history from its inception, rather like a computer programme booted up and running, the course of events flowing logically from that point to its end.

The prophets pointed forward, in the light of the past, seeking a fresh Word of the Lord to take the people ahead on the right way, accompanied by God travelling with them in good times and bad. The apocalyptic tradition looked even further ahead to the end of days for the deliverance of the faithful people so sorely oppressed here and now, since God is faithful and will vindicate the just in the face of the persecutors. The purposes of God and the finality of his truth will be manifested at this long-awaited end. The coming of God is historical in effect although God's self is no mere product of history but rather its future. Pannenberg develops a doctrine of the free and sovereign Lord of all things coming, a perpetual Advent, from the open future to invite us into that future. God the Father is this free Lord, the giver of the grace of creation seeking to elicit responsive faith and openness to the divine purposes. God's future dominates all history and reality, including that which is to us past and gone since it is not gone from God's presence, which remains future to that past. The power of God's future is love, the future offering itself to us for cooperation and participation in God, which is salvation. God's love from the future grants new events to creation and events pregnant with freedom for participation and response, not dominating and coercive. 'The trinitarian distinctions are based on the difference between future and present . . . future and present – and consequently the 'persons' of the Trinity are comprehended in the unity of God' (Pannenberg 1969b: 71).

In this way God is God the Father to his freely originated creation, and as the Son he is God differentiating himself from the Father, a differentiation inseparable by definition from unity. The Son is Jesus the man from the perspective of eternity, eternity which embraces time rather than contradicting it as in the Platonic understanding. We could say that the Son is the revelation of God's being in the historical finite form, in relation to and distinction from the freedom of the person of God who is the Father of history and of the Godness of God. Jesus lived in openness to his Father, as for the eternal life of the Trinity the Son's humble self-differentiation from the Father indirectly yields his own divine identity. So too the Father's identity as the ruler of all things is yielded by the responsive love of the Son and his kingdom, implemented over sin and death by the Spirit. Thus the trinitarian life of God threads through the time line of history and creation, to the eschaton of total meaning and truth of all being, the eschaton bestowing the identity of the Son and Father and Spirit through their various roles and interactions in historical development. To quote Jüngel, God's being is in becoming, but for Pannenberg this becoming is a development through history, freely enacted out of love for the created order thereby brought into being. What is constitutive for God is so for history, from God.

God's trinitarian presence suffuses history in his revealing presence manifested decisively in Jesus and his fate, it entwines human seeking after God and God's gracious coming to history with ever new events sustaining and renewing all things. This is a moment for God's very life and for history:

> But in the moment in which God's self is definitively found, as is possibly the truth in the history of Jesus, this entwining is taken up in the identity of the divine being as trinitarian self-reference of God in the differentiation of the Father and the Son by the Spirit who connects them, who is just as much a Spirit of self-differentiation as of fellowship or commonality. The self-realisation of God cannot be thought of as a punctiliar event, but if indeed it is a matter of the self-realisation of 'God' the all determining reality, rather all happening is drawn into this process so that all things are constituted creatively by him and defined by him. (Pannenberg 1980: 143)

This self-realization of God in and through history, the same process as 'revelation as history' from another angle, presents a radical integration of the God and the world, and yet God is freely bringing the world and history into being, with the cooperation of the world indwelt by the Spirit and the Son, and so is not merely a factor in the universal process. The totality of this process is technically still open, even after Easter's proleptic eschaton, but in fact it will become what it always was going to be, the future of this God in interelational reality and personhood. This will be realized and perfected in covenant partnership with creation, not apart from it. The final end point therefore is the eternity of God as it has included and embraced history and humanity in its own relational love, love putting itself at risk in the world process – and still sovereign. To ask whether this was necessary for God, whether God needed to reveal himself to himself through finitude, the Hegelian journey of *Geist*, is a question that cannot be asked, since God chose this world and to create it in this way, after his own life of relationality, becoming and development. T. S. Eliot is grasping at this same point in his poem 'East Coker' which he starts with: 'In my beginning is my end', and finishes with 'In my end is my beginning' (Eliot 1944).

Perhaps Pannenberg might in fact appeal to the medium of poetry to help the perplexed unfold to the imagination what his theology articulates rationally, the medium of literature, the writing and rewriting of texts and of experience, is a suggestive analogy indeed. Our identity is our narrative of life as it is lived, not an isolated spiritual mind encased in matter whose activities and configurations are without significance. Pannenberg's trinitarian theological ontology is surely expressing this point in its portrayal of the historical self-description of God in Christ taken through the whole micro and macro contexts of meaning. We are ourselves in time, we are a story with an end giving the real significance to that story, and that constitutes who we really are, and so must have been all along, in Pannenberg's thought. And yet there is also development. In God's life this pattern of mutual relations is not frozen, nor a structural repetition without real significance, but does embrace temporal successiveness and becoming. For Pannenberg,

Self-realisation is an extremely difficult category, it presupposes on the one hand the self as the subject of the realisation, but with that it has to conceive of a self without reality for the beginning of the process of self-realisation. On the other hand the self is supposed to be the object of the realisation but can therefore be real only as its result, so that the question is raised as to which reality it is that carries on the process which helps the self to reality. Thus self-realisation cannot be ascribed to the actions of a finite subject which as presupposed is bound to the successiveness of time, so that the moment of action and the moment of the realisation of the goal of the action fall apart. (Pannenberg 1980: 142)

He acutely points up the conceptual difficulty of an initial and ready constituted self, unrealized, then reaching the state of self-realization while remaining the same self, there is an added development, a becoming of who we really are, and somehow the start and the fulfilment hold together through the narrative of being and becoming, the narrative or history is the realized self and the self which realizes itself. In particular a view of the ego, or subjectivity, as the core of self is rejected since the self really does develop. And for Pannenberg we are most aware of who we are when we are open to God, when we find God and God finds us and these two movements intertwine. Human self-discovery coincides with the discovery of God as the source and fulfilment of our being in relation to him and to our neighbour – we are not insulated bubbles of ego but are relational holistic beings. Pannenberg takes this with utmost seriousness ontologically and not just epistemologically: human discovery of divine self-revelation is at the same time God's self-realization in history, and this divine self-realization through the history of humanity, culminating in the Christ event, is the work of God, the all-determining reality.

Pannenberg sees the Son as having his deity in relationship with the Father, the God of the open future. Father and Son are not each divine in themselves, 'but only through the community of the Spirit which unites them. The unity of the divine being is not absorbed in personal relationships but is mediated for each of the persons through their relations to the other persons' (Pannenberg 1980: 92–5). The Son is the proleptic objectivity of the Father oriented towards the Father whom he experiences in the Spirit. For the Father the Son is the realization of his divinity. Pannenberg disclaims any attempt to distinguish in God the ego and the self-being because such distinctions belong to finitude. Nevertheless the triadic model of person remains meaningful in understanding the Trinity.

To sum up, Pannenberg seeks to avoid the Scylla of substance and the Charybdis of subjectivity, and aims instead to define divine being as his history of dialectical threefoldness.

The persons are referred to the other persons but always inseparably from human history since the economic Trinity is affected by creaturely history as well as deciding it. They achieve their selfhood ec-statically outside themselves. Only thus to they exist as personal selves, and only thus do they have unity in and through mutual activity. (Pannenberg 1991: 430)

He stresses that the trinitarian life is more personally relational than the human, which is not so exclusively constituted by the relation to one or two other persons as it is in the trinitarian life of God. The mutual relations of the trinitarian persons are such that the existence as persons is wholly for and from the others. The identity of the Son is wholly given in relation to the Father, and vice versa. This is divine love and divine dynamic being. It is actual love, not an abstract idea of love. Divine love constitutes the concrete unity of the divine life in the distinction of its personal manifestations and relations:

> we may know them only in the historical revelation of God in Jesus Christ. But on this basis they and their unity in the divine essence make sense as the concrete reality of divine love which pulses through all things and which consummates the monarchy of the Father through the Son in the Holy Spirit. (Pannenberg 1991: 432)

The centre of reality, the all-determining reality, for Pannenberg, is no cosmic mind but rather the life of divine self-giving and responsive love. The relational historical Trinity sums up Pannenberg's onto-logical vision of reality. This gives us the unity of God, which is not to be pre-supposed as a prior reality or idea so much as concretely constituted in and through this life act of self-mediation and identity-in-the-other. This is the essence and existence of God. The biblical view of the unity of God focuses on the divine self-identity, 'I will be who I will be', as he translates God's words to Moses (Exod. 3.14). This is not a timeless concept, but the faithful God whose action and purposes express his character of holiness, wisdom and patience. Divine unity finds its deepest identity in concrete love, the unity of the true infinite, which transcends that which stands over against it in love. Here is the key to eternity and time, since they coincide at the eschatological consummation of history, the point at which,

> there is room for becoming in God himself, namely, in the relation of the immanent and the economic Trinity, and in this frame it is possible to say of God that he himself became something that he previously was not when he became man in his Son. (Pannenberg 1991: 438)

Here is the profoundest suggestion in Pannenberg's theology, that God becomes, and yet that in this he becomes – himself, more deeply what he always was, and was always going to be.

It is worth noting here that Pannenberg does not accept the feminist criticism of the language of the Fatherhood of God. Starting as he does from the Jesus of history, his life and work, he stresses the fact of Jesus' prayer to God as Father being a Jewish tradition. It is therefore related to the patriarchal constitution of the Israelite family, with the father as the head of the clan and responsible for their care.

> The aspect of fatherly care in particular is taken over in what the OT has to say about God's fatherly concern for Israel. The sexual definition of the father's role plays no part. A mark of Israel's faith from the very outset is that the God who elected the patriarchs . . . has no female partner. To bring sexual differentiation into the understanding of God would mean polytheism: it was thus ruled out for the God of Israel. (Pannenberg 1991: 261)

Pannenberg argues that the fact that God's fatherly care can be expressed in terms of motherly terms 'shows clearly enough how little there is any sense of sexual distinction in the understanding of God as Father' (Pannenberg 1991: 261). He does not agree that because Israelite culture was time bound and patriarchal, that the term Father is also relativized, such a demand would only be valid if our language for God were a human projection only, reflecting prevailing social mores. He argues that the Hebrew understanding of God was prior to, and a presupposition for, their singling out of terms from their culture as appropriate, and not just a product of that culture. Hence the term Father is still valid today, despite the breakdown of forms of family and society and much disreputable human fatherhood. Jesus' use of the term is decisive, and indeed this self-distinction from God finds its clearest expression in the prayer of Jesus to the Father. The whole life of Jesus, the way he fulfilled his vocation in loving obedience, cohered with his teaching and praying, and it was suffused with the presence of the Spirit.

Here we see the creative love of God in all its faithfulness, a term preferred to 'immutability', which is too static to do justice to the movements of divine life and richness. If God wills the independence of his created order, the success of his creative love depends on the faithfulness of his creative love, on the outpouring of his eternity in time. God's creative love 'makes space' for his creature, and his patience waits for their response, in which their destiny and so their true being is fulfilled, and given.

The issue of divine transcendence and immanence likewise finds its most hopeful resolution in the trinitarian way of love, uniting the God's transcendence as Father and his immanence in and with his creatures through the Son and Spirit. This upholds the permanent distinction between the divine and the creaturely. The omnipotence or power of God likewise is no oppressive force, but works most deeply through the Son and Spirit, with creation free to be itself to fulfil its destiny. The 'all-determining reality', Pannenberg's description of God, actually has the connotation of the all shaping or orientating reality, giving the world its destiny and seeking to bring that to fulfilment.

Creation's fulfilment is understood incarnationally, that is to say both freely attained and divinely shaped. The incarnation of the Son, read back from the resurrection of Jesus, overcomes the dualism between eternity and time, as the divine present of the Father and his kingdom is present to creation through the Son. 'The present not only contains all the past within it, as the idea of Christ's descent into Hades shows, but it also invades our present in such a way that this becomes the past and needs to be made present and glorified by the work of the Spirit' (Pannenberg 1991: 446). The pattern of the resurrection of Jesus, confirming the past and made present by the Spirit, a pattern we have characterized as that of the future perfect, explains the divine relation to created time. Pannenberg believes that this overcoming of dualities, such as time and eternity, finite and infinite, results from the love of God.

This trinitarian love embraces the tension of the infinite and finite without setting aside their distinction. This is not a matter of synthesising opposites through the logic of an idea or concept, as with Hegel. The dynamic of love alone can leap over the frontiers of logic: the Holy Spirit of the divine Trinity is not Hegel's Absolute Spirit, or *Geist*, pure mind or thought. Pannenberg here makes a determined effort to demarcate his theological system from that of Hegel, quite rightly pointing to the Trinity of active love as superior to that of thought, at the heart of being and knowing. The Trinity is a concrete, rather than ideal, life and action. The common life of love of God constitutes itself by way of self-distinction, of mutual acknowledgement and indwelling. The self-differentiation among the persons is not a centripetal flight, but a harmony of union in distinction. Hegel's concept of the ultimate union of opposites is taken up, not into thought but into love and mutuality, notwithstanding that we are convinced of the credibility of revelation as history by our reason and the Spirit. History advances suffused by the divine presence to meet and accept the free grace of the divine Father, that is divine freedom who is in relation to the Son, united by the Spirit. The created world is not an accidental epiphenomenon of this divine history but integrated into it so deeply that God decides to realize his identity through the historical process – which yet is what it always was going to be, love in action, which is eternity. The start of the historical time line and the end are joined by the totality of historical meaning, but also, it seems to me for Pannenberg the two 'ends' join up, if we add the third dimension of depth to the straight line, in eternity forming an elliptical loop rather than just a time line with two ends. For Pannenberg the economic Trinity relates to the essential Trinity in this elliptical pattern of the future perfect tense, not in the correspondence structure of the classical tradition. The perfected future is the future perfect and the eternal being of God, which encloses and creates the totality of history – a history on which God has freely made himself dependent, bringing into being a true covenant partner. This doctrine of the Trinity does not take the final Hegelian step of sublimating diversity into the unity of the absolute.

CHAPTER 5

CREATION AND HUMAN BECOMINGS

FOCUSED TEXT: *WHAT IS MAN?*

OPEN TEXTURED CREATION

The very structure of reality is disclosed by the Christ event as anticipatory, each event or cluster of events pointing forwards to their development, taken up as new meaning arrives. All events are transparent to the next event: 'Jesus saying about losing and finding life has universal ontological relevance' (Pannenberg 1977b: 396). Just as Jesus gives himself for the ultimate eschatological purpose of God, so this is exemplary for the structure of every individual event. 'Everything is what it is only in transition to something other than itself; nothing exists for itself' (Pannenberg 1977b: 395). Not only does our knowledge move forward in the way described so neatly by E. H. Carr, the future becoming the criterion of truth in history as it arrives and corrects the past, but this is so ontologically: events move forward towards the eschaton, the eschaton that is in fact present from the future moment by moment. Pannenberg continues,

Every particularity possesses its truth in its limit, through which it is not only independent but is also taken up into the greater whole. Through giving up its particularity, everything is mediated with the whole and, transcending its finitude, with God, who neverthe-less wanted this particularity to exist within the whole of his creation. That which lives . . . finds its existence outside itself. At the highest level the same is true of human subjectivity, namely it must empty itself to the world and the 'Thou' in order to win itself in the other. (Pannenberg 1977b: 396)

The whole of creation hums with the proleptic orientation epistemologically and ontologically, summed up in human relationality as it gives itself away to the other in order to gain itself, as Jesus discloses most clearly. Pannenberg's canvass of reality is theological through and through, there is no dualism between sacred and profane, spiritual and material, noumenal and phenomenal: all events gain their being from divine creative acts of grace. Jesus not only reveals God as the trinitarian God of all reality, of past, present and future, but discloses the structure of how all things are: open to the sovereign free Father and open textured to all else, an organic vision of reality. God is creating by differentiating reality from himself and his desire is for trust and openness from the created order towards himself: Jesus exemplifies this perfectly, he is the fulfilled and perfected creature as well the divine Son.

Christian theology, in its doctrine of creation, has come to lay massive emphasis on its beginning and origin, at the expense of the ongoing sustaining of the world, and indeed of its final cosmic destiny beyond the human. The Eastern Orthodox are less guilty of this imbalance than the Western traditions. Pannenberg is keen to reinforce the theology of God's continual creative activity. The continuing preservation of the world by God is an essential part of Christian doctrine, without it a kind of deism would develop, removing God from the process of the world. Creation does not exist of itself, and Pannenberg teaches that the conception of creation out of nothing applies to continuous creation as much as to the protology of creation.

Indeed the great stress on the idea of divine creation as the establishment of all reality as finished and finalized in form has real problems. The ancient view of divine preservation is focused on the conservation of the originally given order of things. The species of plants and animals were assumed to have been fixed at the outset of creation. Everything was thought to have been established at the same time and for ever, as if by the copying of a divine template. But the modern theory of evolution is clearly very different indeed from the ancient view.

Pannenberg turns a necessity into a virtue by pointing out that continuous creative activity by God seems to be required, over against a fixed and finished model of creation. This, however, he argues is a biblical way of looking at things. As well as the divine originative event, the Bible speaks of divine upholding and supervising of the world, in the prophetic writings, the Wisdom literature, even on the lips of Jesus in the Gospels. In the Bible we get a picture of both a divine initiation and the history of divine activity: not the idea of the divine watchmaker letting the creation simply tick by itself. God is deeply involved in the world process. Pannenberg points to the scientific understanding of new forms of existence in nature, consonant with a theology of a continuous creativity, and with the prophetic understanding of God bringing about the new and unexpected event.

This connects to the contingency and freedom of creation, distinctively emphasized by Pannenberg. Contingency means that the process is open to new and enduring forms of life. And of course for the Christian, God alone explains the possibility of all this richness and potential of the universe, as it reaches forwards into what is new, while being sustained by the order of the structures and patterns of reality. This activity of the eternal God conveys freedom and contingency, not a fixed programme which is to unfold by a law of necessity inherent in the process. It must not, on the other hand, be seen as resulting from a whim on the part of God, a capricious act of freedom. Both the eternal and the free aspects of God must be seen as invested into the created order, so as to constitute a covenant partner of God, autonomous and free, while most truly so in the orientation to the divine destiny.

The best hypothesis to account for this synthesis of divine being and free act in his core doctrine, is that of the Trinity, truly the centre around which all other doctrines revolve. Pannenberg rejects the model of God as a monad with a will which implements ideas in the divine mind to enact the created order. This is overly anthropomorphic and individualistic. With all Eastern Orthodoxy in heaven and on earth applauding, Pannenberg says that the Trinity provides the best way into the doctrine of creation, a better model than that of the individual mind. The trinitarian approach is coherent with the biblical idea that the Son was constantly cooperating with the Father in creating the world. The theme of the divine self-differentiation of the Son from the Father becomes central again. This dynamic life of God is in fact also the raison d'être of the creative act, uniting the act of God with the being of God, divine relativity reaching out in love to bring another into being.

This fresh emphasis in the doctrine of creation is made plain in core doctrinal statements prior to the *Systematic Theology*:

> Through the self-differentiation of the Father from the Son and Spirit, without which the one God does not have his full reality, God as Father gives, at the same time, a particular existence to the creatures, an existence which has not lost from the very beginning any chance of autonomy through its dependence on a continuously working omnipotence of the Father God and creator; but rather with the designation to partnership with God receives a personal worth vis-à-vis God himself. (Pannenberg 1980: 126)

The Son's humble, eternal self-differentiation from the Father is worked out in history as the self-subordination to the kingdom of God in the ministry of Jesus; and here we see the creative origin of all that is distinct from God, the reason that there can be something which is not divine. The eternal act of self-differentiation is the possibility in God for the existence of a creation not of the divine being.

This is a very stimulating notion addressing a real theological problem: what in God can make non-divine being possible, apart from the naked will of God? The answer is not a Platonic form in the divine, reflected outwards, but a living relationality in God. This is the originative principle of creation's space and time. In the freedom of the divine love and self-differentiation we see the freedom of God enacting creation to convey and bestow contingency into the universe. The Son is the generative principle responsible for the otherness of the creation, the autonomy of created beings. In generating ever new creatures, a network of relationships emerges in the world, with the creative dynamic formed to interweave, unite and differentiate.

This is why creation can issue from the hand of God, and yet be free and independent – but in dependence on God, as human implicit religious sense testifies. The resolution of unity and diversity stems from divine Wisdom, the Logos:

> If the Logos is the generative principle of all finite reality that involves the difference of one thing from another – a principle grounded in the self-distinction of the eternal Son from the Father – then with the advent of ever new forms differing from

what has gone before there comes a system of relations between finite phenomena and also between these phenomena and their origin in the infinity of God. (Pannenberg 1994: 62)

This Logos or creative word is not simply transcendent and external to the creaturely forms being brought into being, he is also at work in them as he 'constitutes for each its own specific existence in its own identity' (Pannenberg 1994: 62). The transcendent immanently shapes reality, for transcendence itself is also relational, mutually indwelling at the core of life. All reality is open textured and porous, relational, and this fact stems from the Trinity at the centre of the universe, whose creative act brings particulars into being with an order and a life, and a propensity to complexity and future orientation. This is not by a correspondence structure from God to history but a coherence structure of the life of God flowing out in the Spirit as history, as free and self-creative history in relation and distinction with God.

WHAT IS MAN? OPENNESS AND CLOSEDNESS

Pannenberg's early text *What Is Man?* (Pannenberg 1970a), is an accessible statement of his view of humanity, its destiny and definition, and provides us with his attempt at describing human experience, bringing to life the way reality is for us in this future-oriented world. Running through the 11 chapters is the theme, now familiar to us, that human existence is open textured, open to the world as it comes to us from the future with all the particularity, contingency and freedom that we experience. Anthropology is a crucial discipline for theology to engage with, it is a field that cannot be left to the atheist critics as their exclusive territory. Religion is in a precarious position over against atheist criticism if the atheist analysis of the human condition holds sway, since atheism reduces religion to anthropological data and theology needs to respond to this, and will not be able to do so without its own anthropological position. And this theological analysis is very possible, according to Pannenberg.

He discusses the human condition in relation to that of animals and their contextual environments. Animals relate to their environment as fixed and adapt to that surrounding environment. Man is able to transcend his own situation and instincts, and he constructs his environment in all sorts of ways, culturally and technologically. Mankind presses beyond all current pictures of his environment, striving to open up what is there already. We have a sense and taste for the infinite, as Schleiermacher put it, we are restless and feel dependent on the beyond although we cannot grasp it, and in this way we presuppose God as the source of our freedom over nature, our instincts and environment. Pannenberg quotes Herder's description of man as the 'first emancipated creature of the creation' (Pannenberg 1970a: 12). Our sense of openness to and beyond the world, this incessant questing, comes from our destiny beyond the world. It is not enough to describe this facet of humanity as the push to construct culture, since we are pressed to question our culture and reach beyond every cultural form as well as beyond nature. This is a very interesting point for consideration today with its massive stress on cultural relativism as a kind of absolute. Our true relativity is to the beyond, to God our goal and giver of life. We master the world by our cultural constructs and in particular by the development of language and our imagination by which we detach from the immediacy of the world and creatively reflect on our place in the scheme of things. Human creativity and construction of the world raises the question of God and how we produce language and culture. We can argue that God accounts for our experiences of inspiration as it stimulates our creative aspiration.

Trust is an anthropological phenomenon crucial to us in life, we trust others in personal relationships and in doing so we trust their goodness and virtue, we trust their faithfulness and constancy. We are open to others in relationships and honour the trust placed in us. If we seek to control the other person then we are using that person as an object, not trusting and being open as is our true orientation. Religion likewise often falls in trying to control the deity, not trusting, and this leads to a distorted religion. When we fall into desire to control and manipulate, to want total security, we cease true relationships and true faith, we become the ultimate concern ourselves (Pannenberg 1970a: 38). The power of the future is the antidote to this idolization of the self in the now, the turning inwards rather than being open: the future is never mastered and always bringing the surprising and new to us. Our hope is to be directed to this future horizon, and 'only the person who is certain of his future can calmly turn to the present day' (Pannenberg 1970a: 44). We all think about our death, and the question of God, therefore, is raised. The notion of the immortal inner soul was a key issue in this future hope, but now anthropology has shown that we are holistic beings, that our physical being is inseparable from our 'inner' feeling: to separate them is to create two abstractions from our behaviour. Language arises from our surroundings, from recognizing and being recognized, and is inherently integrated to our physical being, for example. The future hope beyond death must involve our whole personal experience, and our communal existence together: our being and our history, our life narrative, are taken up together. The resurrection of the dead, the metaphor of rising from sleep, takes up the destiny that characterizes each person's human existence as openness beyond death (Pannenberg 1970a: 53).

We seek, in our questing into the future, as wide a horizon of meaning and reality as possible, of universal and not merely culture relative scope. Provisional answers drive us onward, and ultimately this has to be towards God who is beyond all things. 'Man's very nature is this movement through the world toward God.' (Pannenberg 1970a: 54). This movement, however, is interrupted and blocked by our own self-centredness, our egocentricity which shuts down our openness towards God and his future. Our life is in fact lived in the tension of openness, or exocentricity, and egocentric self-assertion which imprisons us and blinds us to our destiny; and we are incapable of resolving the tension ourselves. The Romantic movement unconvincingly envisaged the ego as absorbing its surroundings. We long for a resolution to resolve this tension, to integrate our outgoing and our egocentric tendencies, and God provides this unity to our experience of life. Faith in God beyond death but also present in the Spirit brings the resolution to the believer.

The question of time and eternity relates to our condition in this regard, we are located in time and only a point beyond the flow of time would give us the truth of time. Eternity is the beyond in the midst, the truth of time is the concurrence of all events in an eternal present, not standing against time and not creating 'any different content than time', (Pannenberg 1970a: 74). It is the truth of time hidden in the flux of time, yet larger than time. The analogy of the life in the body might, again, be another way of trying to state Pannenberg's meaning, the greater includes the lesser while each is dependent on the other, indeed are mutually inconceivable without each other; yet the life orders the body while being integrated into it. God is present to every time, nothing passes from his presence.

Sin is the claiming by the ego of each new moment for itself rather than receiving it as a gift and a trust from the eternal, so the now of the ego can become an idol of focus and ultimate concern, an insulating inward movement of hardness, cynicism and fear rather than faith and open trust. Judgement, says Pannenberg, lies beyond death and amounts to the egocentric meeting with the eternal, and the person who has not remained faithful to his destiny to be open will be destroyed in the judgement before God in the face of his infinite destiny. That person has closed off his destiny.

Only from a standpoint within the stream of events itself is time divided into past, future and present. Seen from beyond the flow of time, all events coincide in an eternal present. We already experience that in an initial way in our own consciousness of the present. The unity of our life in the eternal concurrence of all events can, however, enter into our life only after death, with the resurrection of the dead. However, eternity means judgement, because in the eternal concurrence our life must perish because of its contradictions and especially because of the basic contradiction between the self and its infinite destiny. Only for the person who is in community with Jesus does the resurrection mean eternal life as well as judgement. (Pannenberg 1970a: 81)

The destruction of judgement seems to come from a disunity for the ego and its subjectivity, a shrill dissonance between our true destiny and our experiential ego, since it has closed itself off from God, the final end point to unite and heal the fragmentary diversification of the series of 'nows': our rootless chaotic ego has made itself into that finalizing, totalizing, point, or series of points, with no healing fulfilment, death bringing only a final end. It is strange at this point in his exposition that Pannenberg does not mention the death of Christ as overcoming egocentricity. God alone warrants the unity of the diverse creation and the unity of human existence in its tension between openness to the world and self-centredness.

Pannenberg works out his theological anthropology, in terms of the dialectics of openness and closedness, individual and social, particular and universal, part and whole, diversity and unity; they move through the process of time en route to the meaning of all things in their 'concurrence'. This is a doctrine of human becomings rather than simply of human beings, we are 'a work in progress', we are becoming who we are or who we really should be, and we turn out to be what our lives have shown us to be. Yet this task of living life and becoming our selves is also a gift of divine creation, as moment by moment we receive life from the God of the open future. This God hypothesis is the most credible we have as rational humans to account for our experience of meaning and life in the widest perspective, it is no mere leap of faith. His treatment of the subject in *What Is Man?* broadens out from the individual to relations with others, to construction of cultures, and ultimately to the universal perspective which is his epistemological, hermeneutical and ontological goal. He argues that we are pushed logically onwards to the universal thence to the beyond, the divine. The Hegelian style of logic is clear.

The individual in society works out in terms of the I – Thou relation described by Buber and Ebner, and before them Hegel with his doctrine of finding oneself in the other, pointing to the act of recognition as the basic act of all human community, the subject moving out of itself to find, and empathize with, the other person (Pannenberg 1970a: 85). Our lives only succeed when we help others, and failing to respect others damages ourselves in the light of our divine orientation and destiny. Self-consciousness exists from the fact of our being recognized as a person by others, we are inherently social beings, and human love shows the passionate interest one has in the other, helping us experience our destinies as common. Pannenberg argues that interpersonal relations are rooted in God, revealed in Jesus' relationship of open trust with his Father: the power of this God and this relation are at work in humanity. Social justice flows from recognition of persons, and so from love for persons, in institutional form; legal forms will change but this reality of love for neighbour and personal recognition remains their root. Law becomes corrupt when this root is ignored and it is used for selfish or tribal purposes against the universal good, and to abandon the vision of a legal system for all quickly leads to fragmentation of society into competing tribes.

Pannenberg understands the social process in the modern world as one of human construction rather than accepting a fixed social environment. He has some sympathy with Marx's economic analysis of human alienation from what he makes: the worker in effect becomes a victim of the system of exchange of products. Marx however failed to see that humans are not only dependent on products produced but also on culture and traditions, on their fellows, and finally of course on God. Modern secularized society is in danger of fragmentation, of pure diversity, because it has lost its sense of orientation to the universal future, the divine source of our unity as people, as of our diversity. Western technology is now accepted globally, but non-western nations reject the concomitant western cultural traditions out of which science and technology grew. Only a common universal horizon can heal widening cultural rifts, and avoid 'the clash of civilizations' now so feared. Marx himself, as Pannenberg points out, used a kind of Hebrew eschatology as his concept of a goal and purpose to history, a final utopia of mutual love to which we should all strive and hope. But only the Christian tradition,

> opens a free view for the future of the world in the light of God's future, yet does not rob men of an orientation to the richness of the forms of life in earlier times. Rather the spirit of Christianity has accepted all the traditions it has encountered . . . it has transformed these traditions, but it has also preserved them in modified form. (Pannenberg 1970a: 135)

Without Christianity we would not have preserved contact with Greek antiquity, for example. At the same time Christianity brings with it the critical attitude in the light of the change mediated by God's newly arriving future. We are fundamentally historical creatures in our experience of life and history should be the key category in analysing who we are, since this discipline treats of concrete events and not merely abstract structures as sociology so often does. Our individuality arises from our history, what happens to us and how we react to that in the course of life, and this entails our openness to the world, events, and our attitude of trust for the future:

> It is just in this openness that a person's own decisions and the concrete things that happen are accepted as the concretization of his own striving and as God's guidance. Thus man's historicity is based on his inherent openness to God. It opens him up for the experience of the world and lets his life attain its individuality in the history of his particular path through life. (Pannenberg 1970a: 141)

Particularity and universality are key poles in Pannenberg's anthropology, the intermediate category of cultural meaning he seeks to place under the overarching horizon of universal history and its eschatological point of meaning for all humanity and their interdependency. The whole history of religions is an important phenomenon for Pannenberg, showing the human orientation towards the beyond, entwining with the giving from God of insight to trust and take forward, and indeed critical insights by which past religious practice can be reformed. The history of Israelite religion has proved the crucial tradition in opening up the understanding of the historical nature of God's revelation, and the purposive goal of all history for all creation.

IMAGO DEI

As we recall from the last chapter, Pannenberg develops an anticipatory view of the person, who will be who she truly is at the end of her life in its totality, when God will decide who and what that person was, as he decided in the case of Jesus. Pannenberg broke away from subjectivity as the core definition of a person and opened it up to the narrative of a whole life course. We remind ourselves from his article *Person und Subjekt* that,

> The 'person' includes the 'ego' and 'self' and is ultimately constituted by their temporal course as a whole. 'The person, can neither be identical with the I in its difference to self nor even with the self on distinction to the I. The person cannot be identical with the mere fact of the I consciousness; in the word person we mean more than the punctiliarly appearing I. The word person is related to the whole life of an individual. We are already an I. We still become a person although we are already one. Person refers to the mystery which goes beyond the presence of the I, the mystery of the as yet incomplete totality of his unique life history, the totality on the way to its particular definition, Person, then, is neither the I nor the self each taken for itself. A person is the presence of the self in the moment of the I, in the claim of the I through our true self and in our proleptic consciousness of our identity. Person is the I as 'countenance' through which the mystery of the as yet unfinished history of an individual is on the way to his destiny. (Pannenberg 1980: 91–2)

A person is therefore a process or a becoming, oriented to the future and continually anticipating and sketching her own objective 'self' which provides the identity for the subjective 'ego' or 'I'. Pannenberg refers his use of the anticipatory category to apocalyptic thought and to its empirical fit with the realities of history and our experience of it, our sense of historicity of life. Our overarching 'person' is not immediately accessible to us as we journey on through life, but it is proleptically and provisionally manifested to our 'ego' by our 'self', the objective integrating entity which provides our self-identity in its historical provisionality, to our individual consciousness. We are hermeneutical beings. In his article 'Person', we read:

> In the individual's life-history person achieves the form of personality. Every human being is a person from birth by virtue of his orientation. Personality, however, must first be achieved by each person through the attitude which he takes in the light of his human orientation in life, through the answer which he gives with his life to the question of his orientation. (Pannenberg 1957–1965: 233)

An individual human being is constituted by his life history and personhood goes beyond the presence of the ego, a human becoming as much as a human being. A human is a question about himself referred to God and on the way to God (Pannenberg 1980: 92), a history of meaning involving tensions of egocentricity and openness, individuality and society, a history answered at the end of this narrative as its totality comes to final view. Our life history, the content of human becoming on its way to ultimate identity and being, is implicitly directed to God. The Bible has described this as 'being in the image of God'. We receive our being, in all its provisionality, a hermeneutical developing entity, from the open future and we respond to that gift as we move forward, dialectically taking our past forward, the Spirit enabling us to change and make new syntheses of our lives as the possibility of newness comes to us from the Father. We are oriented to the future in our given freedom and the Spirit will gather us into the great final symphony of the eschatological finale. Our freedom is entailed in our being 'in the image of God', fulfilled of course in the freedom and trust of the man Jesus.

Pannenberg draws on Herder in fleshing out his doctrine of the *imago dei* as a formative, dynamic concept describing the human propensity for education, reason and religion. The *imago dei* does not mean a fixed state of perfection but a progress of formation of the unfinished completion of human life, gained by divine providential gift. Pannenberg relates this theory to human perception, arguing that this implies a background of universal awareness presupposed in all acts of perception, a background or assumption that must be located beyond the world. We implicitly presuppose this divine background in our thinking: 'That which can become the explicit object of religious consciousness is implicitly present in every turning to a particular object of our experience' (Pannenberg 1985: 72). Our being in the image of God is accessible to human reasoning, as is revelation as history of which our reasoning and openness are part. For Pannenberg we are indeed human becomings, awaiting the verdict on our identity as to who we really are – again Jesus is the model already set for us.

THE SPIRIT OF HUMANITY

The individual experiences of the ego are integrated and ordered by the 'self', the provisional overall 'person', the final unity of the diversity of human experience. The person is the presence of the self in the instant of the ego and personality is a special instance of the working of the spirit, a special instance of the anticipatory presence of the final truth of things. Living beings relate actively to their perdurance, identity and truth, transcending what is now manifested in them, so

> to that extent, the spirit is more intensely present in the ecstatic movement of love and is, in addition, present in a special way in human consciousness as the medium of the presence of the person's own identity, as distinct from, though united with, the truth of things. Thus in the medium of the human soul and in the place that is the ensouled body, the presence of the spirit constitutes the identity of the person as a presence of the self in the instant of the ego. (Pannenberg 1985: 528)

Pannenberg here does not use 'soul' in the traditional dualist sense but is simply, as in the biblical tradition, 'the bodily being as living' (Pannenberg 1985: 523) and Spirit is the divine life source and not here simply defined in terms of consciousness. Human action comes from the life-giving spirit enabling such action, ultimately from God.

This entails the ecstatic or exocentric pattern of life, a pattern that humans understand in their consciousness of time, a consciousness and awareness of the Spirit.

As the human reaches out ecstatically, or exocentrically, to the other it shares in the life of the Spirit so that the spirit is at the very heart of the creaturely life. The Spirit in this way forms community, uniting people together for the good, transcending individuality. Reason and love show the operation of the Spirit, overcoming disharmonies and conflicts. 'Perhaps it is along this line', says Pannenberg at the conclusion of his magnum opus on humanity, 'that we should conceive the destiny of human beings to be images of God and as such to exercise rule over creation' (Pannenberg 1985: 531) although the completion and salvation of history lies only with God's action, coming from the future. And this destiny participates in the life of Christ as the fulfilment of the image.

ALIENATION

The problem of evil arises not primarily from our finitude but from revolt against the limit of finitude, the refusal to accept our boundaries, the desire to be as God. The source of evil and suffering, says Pannenberg, lies in the transition from God-given independence to self-independence (Pannenberg 1994: 172). Physical evil Pannenberg links to entropy, the tending to chaos of things without new energy. 'Those that cannot take on new energy and thus transcend themselves come under the neutralizing sway of entropy' (Pannenberg 1994: 172). Basically, we cut ourselves off from the Spirit by turning inwards, by ceasing to trust in the goodness of things, by shutting ourselves off from the divine life. Christ, the new man, reverses this with his filial union with his Father, and his humble self-differentiation from God. He fulfils creation, and at the same time discloses and establishes the identity of God. The consequences of our ego-worship can spiral to enormity.

Human estrangement from God blocks our orientation for God and makes our own egos as God; it is our failure to differentiate ourselves from God:

It is the sin of Adam to live out the designation of man to community with God in the manner of wanting to be like God. Precisely the denial of the difference of the personal creatureliness

148

from God contained therein has led to the division of man from God which is established in sin and executed through the power of death. (Pannenberg 1980: 126)

Human beings are 'exocentric', having a centre in what is other than ourselves, being open to these others and so finding ourselves, we transcend ourselves in being present to the other in this structure of going out to what is distinct from us. When our ego seeks to impose itself on others, then our constitution from the other is perverted. This is quite a traditional view, fundamentally about egocentric lust or desire for oneself alone, and God becomes a means to an end, centred in myself. We might add to Pannenberg's picture that we can and do 'open' ourselves to what is destructive and negative, that we affect each other for the worse in our idolatry and build cultures – 'field forces' even – of evil negativity, black holes sucking us and our fellows down. This Christian view of life as a battle with sin and evil is lightly played in Pannenberg, for whom the real dialectic is that of the past and the future, not holiness and sin.

Here we may ask whether the tension between openness and egocentric life is inherent to human nature, we have always been thus, and since this comes from the hand of God, with no doctrine of a decisive fall to act as a break so as to exculpate God from creating us in this way, is our sinful nature somehow necessary? We might put this question another way and ask whether if all humans had, like Jesus, lived in full open trust towards God, giving their identity into his hands and not freezing it in their own egocentric present decisions, differentiating themselves from God as did Jesus, would the race thereby be divine also? In other words is the reality of sin, of egocentric selfishness, not needed in order to ground our status as creatures in contrast to the divine? Is fall equated with creation in this theological anthropology? Pannenberg seeks to resolve this by claiming that our natural conditions lead us into sin, but that our human created nature is not inherently sinful, because we are essentially, as will be seen in our final destiny, images of God (Pannenberg 1985: 107). We are in the process of forming our own beings and identities, despite our alienation from God: 'And through such knowledge about our identity as a human, even in alienation, we are already referred to the revelation of the image of God in the resurrected Christ as the new man' (Pannenberg 1980: 220).

HUMAN CONSTRUCTION OF REALITY – FROM THE FUTURE

Pannenberg's vision of humanity in the image of God, include a strong element of human creaturely construction and change of the world, our environment, and human probing of its structures as new insights arrive from the future. 'Man's knowledge of himself is always mediated through his knowledge of the world through the process of acquiring the world for man' (Pannenberg 1980: 220). This capacity of humankind is not to dominate the world but to represent the rule of God in creation, his *imago dei* (Pannenberg 1980: 221). Seeking out the structures of the world also enables us to discover ourselves more deeply, this is part and parcel of our openness to the world and to God. Understanding the world as a whole presupposes an horizon taking in all reality, thus we make sketch plans of how things are, and we all need some such assumption to live life reasonably and not collapse into chaos. We make such projected horizons, and yet they also are given to us from the future. The Christian projected sketch entails God as the most reasonable plan, provisional of course and open to new evidence. New syntheses arise in this pattern of negative mediation, the future will tell which interpretations are true as we move on in time.

This triadic dialectical movement of reason in time projects hypotheses to account for the data from the past as we move into the future. In this way humanity exercises dominion over the world with the ability to rise above the present situation and make powerful hypotheses which in turn will be tested by events. Theology and science are as inseparable as revelation and history: 'As a science of God its subject matter is reality as a whole, even though as yet uncompleted whole, of the semantic network of human experience' (Pannenberg 1976: 165). Just as 'revelation as history' is indirect, so too with a theological appraisal of the scientific enterprise, which should be no God free zone. The concerns of hermeneutics, of meaning generally, connect with science notably in the semantic network of meaning presupposed for all reasoning. The anticipatory nature of human knowledge is very much the shape of scientific discovery: hypotheses are developed taking account of the relevant extant data, and then tested repeatedly until a new theory is demanded by the facts (Pannenberg 1976: 42).

Our knowledge is no mere arbitrary construction of the world but is stimulated by the meaning of events and God invests himself in the models of reality we correctly project in time: there is a 'co-givenness' of God with human experience of the world. This entails the self-conditioning of God in his indirect self-mediation to humanity in our horizons of meaning. God is present in these projected horizons:

The reality of God is always present only in subjective anticipation of the totality of reality, in models of the totality of meaning presupposed in all particular experience. These models however are historic, which means that they are subject to confirmation or refutation by subsequent experience. (Pannenberg 1976: 310)

Truth and meaning, with the human endeavour at gaining knowledge of the universe, are shot through with divine presence, the spirit in the world sustaining the humming dialectic to ever deeper theories of truth. Pannenberg sees science as simply an aspect of this process, and so is very glad to use science and debate with scientists over the question of truth and reality. He argues, consistently with his ontology and epistemology, that theological statements are in theory verifiable but not until the eschaton – as is the case for science. 'God is the all-determining reality, and so not at our disposal, assertions about God and his actions or revelation cannot be directly verified against their object', but it is possible to test assertions by their implications. In many cases, both with hypothetical laws of the natural sciences and with historical assertions, this is the only way in which the factual status of what is asserted can be verified. 'Even Popper's procedure for critical verification is based on the testing of a theory by means of the conclusions derivable from it' (Pannenberg 1976: 332). The power of a particular theory to have a deep ongoing explanatory power for the finite order of things is the key test – and the Christian thesis claims just this, as for example does the theory of evolution.

This point brings us to Pannenberg's acceptance of scientific advances and their relevance to theological claims. We have mentioned his use of 'field theory' in an attempt to help explain the Spirit in the world, and this was debated by natural scientists as mistaken if taken non-metaphorically. The theory of relativity likewise is interesting to Pannenberg with his emphasis on time and the final concurrence of events to give the meaning of all things. Evolution is a view of the development of reality very congenial to Pannenberg's ontology coming from the future and building up from the past into the future, with the Spirit synthesizing the new from the past and the failures falling away. Pannenberg is of course committed to an open field of knowledge with all critical questions and theories on the table, and he finds science a helpful dialogue partner for theology, sharing in fact its conceptual practice of developing hypotheses to account for the evidence.

In his article 'Human Life: Creation versus Evolution?' he tells believers that the creative self-organization of life in the process of evolution, since the transition from inorganic matter to the first organisms, corresponds to the blowing of the divine wind of the Spirit, bringing about ever new forms of life – 'thus blowing through the evolution of life until it overcomes all perishableness in the resurrection of Jesus Christ' (Pannenberg 2000: 120). As Pannenberg says, evolution is a modern concept and cannot be derived from biblical conceptions, but is compatible with the biblical concern to assert the divinely given origins of all life and its connectness. He affirms evolution as long as it includes the divine activity throughout the process. He corrects modern 'creationists' over the biblical understanding of the soul: living soul is analogous to animal life in the biblical creation stories, and there is no need to see evolution as contradicting what they are saying about divine activity in creation, a continual activity.

Pannenberg believes that theology must acknowledge that something new happens in every single event, if the concept of evolution is to be compatible with a biblical theology of God and nature. Newness occurs in the emergence of new forms of life in the evolutionary process. He is advocating a future-oriented version of emergent evolution, made possible by the Spirit at work in all things, especially in the bridging role of bringing forward higher qualitative being from lower. Evolution by way of mechanistic process is not compatible with Christian theology, but when geared to the future, to the free God who invests his being into the process to convey newness and freedom, then evolution is a very helpful understanding of how creation proceeds (Pannenberg 1994: 115f). Organisms depend on their contexts for life, but they also develop the capacity of self-organization in the swarm of complexity. Human beings developed likewise, not as a matter of chance, and they reached the highest stage of independence and self-organization. Humans gained the capacity to discern between objects and to discern the objects themselves as self-centred entities. In this way they learned to discern themselves in the swarming world of complexity all around. They came to understand the world around, and themselves, to be limited, and therefore inherently religious, since limit or finitude presupposes transcendence of that limit. This marks us out from animals.

Newness occurs in the emergence of new forms of life in the process of evolution, and this element of newness or contingency, over determinism, was not the focus of the early mechanistic interpretation of Darwinism. This has however been acknowledged and emphasized in the conception of epigenesis, the emergence of something new. 'Contingent newness belongs in the concept of emergent evolution' (Pannenberg 1994: 116). This is now credible science and important for the doctrine of creation which sees God's relationship to the world in terms of free creative acts from the start of the world and throughout its course. God gives freedom to events, gives self-creativity and not necessity, indeed only because of this gift from the free and open future can creaturely freedom exist at all rather than grim determinism. The interdependence of all events, their capacity to be taken up and forward in the process described by temporal succession, all this comes from the divine gift of newness and freedom. The resulting spontaneous creativity of life is the form of God's creative activity, and this is incompatible with a mechanistic interpretation of emergence as entailed in most secular views of evolution. God creates superabundance in creation and natural selection does not exclude the activity of the creator. Self-organization is characteristic of life at all levels of evolution, accounting for their spontaneity, and this spontaneity is key to human consciousness and freedom. 'Self organization is the principle of freedom and of superabundance in the creative advance of the evolutionary process' (Pannenberg 1994: 119), in which the divine spirit is continually acting in all life at all levels.

Pannenberg's treatment of evolution theologically is a powerful and interesting rebuttal of purely reductionist and determinist accounts. He also argues that religion played a key part in human development, indeed a constitutive one. The idea of God projects a transcendent point stimulating concepts about humanity beyond the immediate present, a kind of satellite dish for the mind to gain a wider perspective, an historical perspective among others. The development of religion is crucial to the evolution of humanity from prehuman animal life: 'religion is constitutive for the beginnings of humankind' (Pannenberg 1994: 122).

A very stimulating symposium of dialogue between Pannenberg and scientific thinkers can be found in *Beginning with the End* (Albright and Haugen 1997) where Pannenberg sets out his vision for the interface of science and theology and responds to responses. There he explains why to took up the notion of 'field' in speaking of the Spirit and its activity in creation: it avoids the focus on mind and intellect so dominant in the West, and the field concept relates the whole to the parts in a way giving priority to the whole (Albright and Haugen 1997: 429). He does not think it 'physicalises' God, rather if anything it helps spiritualize physics. Animals and plants are sustained by this life, likewise humans who are also souls or creatures, which are alive and yet consciously dependent on God's Spirit as the transcendent source of life. Pannenberg makes the interesting point that the old Stoic view of Spirit, with its material connotation, is closer to the biblical notion than the intellectualized view taken by some important theologians such as Origen, and their legacy was a detachment of Spirit from the non-mental order of being. To help overcome this narrow mentalistic emphasis, Pannenberg looks to a new and adventurous model, that of fields of force, taken from physics.

The biblical idea of Spirit is closer to this view of a dynamic force, which shapes the realities within its field of influence (Pannenberg 1994: 79f). This also can, once again, resemble the Hegelian idea of the particulars of the physical body being in the life of that body, and the life suffusing the body and bestowing life and coherence on its constituent parts. The difference again is that the field force idea seems to want more sovereignty accorded to the field over the items in its influence, items needed if the field is to have force over any particular thing. Pannenberg intended his language of field force to function in a way that is more than merely metaphorical, since the Spirit really is the life or dynamic coursing through the universe in patterns, but he is committed to the provisionality of theories and so may need to adjust or drop his field theory application to the doctrine of the Spirit.

It must be pointed out that eminent scientists who are also Christian theologians disagree strongly with Pannenberg on his use of this scientific concept. John Polkinghorne, for example, says that the field theory used by Pannenberg is now out of date among physicists, the theory in which particles were to be considered as 'singularities of the cosmic field'. Polkinghorne tells us that fields are carriers of energy and momentum, 'and this is the basis of my criticism of regarding field theories as if they were immaterial or even, in some sense, "spiritual"'. Polkinghorne rejects Pannenberg's defence that matter is not a strictly physical concept but a philosophical one, because 'all the physical entities of the universe are excitations in fields', and fields must participate in the material (Polkinghorne 2001: 795–7). Pannenberg thinks that it is the independence of the field concept of force from the notion of body that makes its theological application possible, so as to describe all actions of God in nature and history as field effects. But this independence has been powerfully rebutted by Polkinghorne. Pannenberg's model of the force field, it seems, will lead him back to something more like Hegel's integrated life and body logic.

Whatever the objections of physicists, the interesting point is that Spirit for Pannenberg bursts open the notion of mind and enables the theologian to recapture a sense of mystery in talking about God instead of the facile anthropomorphism that often accompanies the image of God as mind. The priority of the whole contextual field of meaning, in contrast to the model of an individual mind, is important to Pannenberg: the field model prevents a reduction of the concept of meaning to that of action by emphasizing the hermeneutical contexts given by the whole:

> if meaning is dependent on human action, then there cannot be any superindividual whole of meaning that constitutes the meaning of individual existence and action . . . . Meaning is not dependent on and created by human (purposive) action, but human action shares in the spiritual reality of meaning that is based on the priority of wholes over parts. (Albright and Haugen 1997: 432)

This dynamic life was seen by the Hebrews as a breath of life, which we today would regard as a metaphor, but Pannenberg thinks it more than an arbitrary image:

> because it indicates the dependence of life upon a flow of energy
> that enters our body from the outside and passes through our-
> selves. Like a flame our life is a process of exploiting a flow of
> energy by degrading the high level potential energy of our food
> and the oxygen we breathe into a state of increased entropy. Life
> is an autocatalytic process of self organisation that exploits the
> gradient of energy in our environment, like the flame does by
> keeping its equilibrium at the price of slowly consuming a candle.
> (Pannenberg 2000: 120)

Pannenberg can use scientific explanation as more than illustrative
metaphor in this way, bringing together the facts told by science with
the fact of God from theology, seeking to show harmony and mutual
enlightenment. His clear-eyed rejection of dualism, epistemologically and ontologically, is never more clearly evident. Conceptual
hypotheses derived from data test themselves in relation to the events
and happenings, concept and history act in dialectic together
(Pannenberg 1976: 421) – ultimately the resurrection of Jesus confirming his life and hermeneutical context, but also in science and
other disciplines. Science of course desperately *tries* to break down
hypotheses, theology tries responsibly to show the power its 'hypothesis' to explain reality as a whole, being open to disproof should that
happen.

Pannenberg accepts Philip Hefner's systematic structure of his
theological project as 'a research programme', and we could well see
this as a useful description even from *Revelation as History* and its
idea of indirect self-revelation and his oft-stated commitment to
provisionality as new events including new mental events and insights
come to us to break down and modify current theses. But Pannenberg's theology ends in worship and love of God, at the end of his
Systematic Theology, and he is primarily a theologian rather than a
philosopher, and certainly a historian of ideas detecting the Spirit
working through this history of fact and theory synthesising and
reconfiguring meaning.

Pannenberg ends his chapter 'Theology as the Science of God' by
giving his criteria for falsifying theological hypotheses. They are to be
judged not substantiated if and only if first, as intended hypotheses
about the implication of the Israelite-Christian faith they cannot

demonstrate that they are express implications of biblical traditions (even when changes in experience are allowed for); second, they have no connection with reality as a whole which is cashable in terms of present experience and shown so by current philosophy (in this case theological statements are transferred to the critical categories of mythical, legendary and ideological); third, they are incapable of being integrated with the appropriate area of experience or no attempt is made to integrate them (e.g. in the doctrine of the church as it relates to the church's role in society); and fourth, their explanatory force is inadequate to the stage reached in theological discussion, that is, when it does not equal the interpretive force of existing hypotheses and does not overcome limitations of these which emerge in discussion (Pannenberg 1976: 344–5). And of course for Pannenberg the science of God is also the science of the field of energy as this indirectly may, by its inherent meaning, stimulate thought bringing insight on, for example, the Spirit in the world. His theological falsification criteria do connect with scientific progress, hypothesizing and reaching for truth as it arrives in our sketching and reflecting the structures of the world.

CONCLUSION – ANTI-POSTMODERN?

For Pannenberg God is the 'all determining reality' who is therefore God of all dimensions of reality and can be found at work in all human endeavour, which endeavour will thrive the more it does not shut itself off from new concepts and theories, from new discoveries and possibilities. This is the case for 'secular' disciplines as for theology, in fact there is no really 'secular' realm, epistemologically and ontologically all is a gift of the Father enacted in the Son and made alive in the Spirit – even though most people may not realize this divine dimension and mystery to life, in the West anyway.

Pannenberg on the one hand is continually probing behind phenomena conceptually, seeking to unfold the implications of concepts to test their power to explain how things are in the universe, as his fourth falsification criterion just described above shows. On the other hand he looks to history, to concrete events, to test and prove concepts, and to move them along and develop them: concepts are events from God as are 'events' whose meaning has to be thought out indirectly by human reason, with the Spirit's enabling. The universal scope of concepts and religious claims is vital for Pannenberg, and this is why he attracts criticism from some of the postmodern philosophical community. Jacqui A. Stewart, for example, in her book *Reconstructing Science and Theology in Postmodernity*, takes him to task for lacking in cultural appreciation and failing to probe the human in terms of the emotional and affective life, and failing to take account of feminist perspectives (Stewart 2000). Pannenberg certainly does seek to get behind movements and phenomena to locate their core ideas, even ideas seeking to undermine universal reason as decisive, such as his treatment of Nietzsche (Pannenberg 1985: 151–2), and his deep probing of Heidegger's thought, (Pannenberg 1985: 209, 237). But he always wishes to appraise and assess in the light of overall human universal experience, and the postmodern critic precisely rejects this possibility of universalizing human experience. Not all postmodern thinkers take offence at Pannenberg, as we saw with the highly appreciative remarks made by John Milbank on his doctrine of the Spirit and its move away from the dominating, ontotheological, model of mind to its movement and self-discovery in the other.[1] In fact theology must point to God as the way of looking at reality in order to balance the mathematical and technological dominion of our horizons. The idea of God is comprehensive in scope, God is by definition all encompassing, involved with all that is.

Pannenberg develops a thoroughly trinitarian view of reality, its structure and content leading all creation to the love of God in Christ and his resurrection, God immersing himself in creation to discover his own depths of being and meaning, while fulfilling the destiny of the world. Here indeed is a view owing a great debt to Hegel's logic and procedures, and yet not arriving at Hegel's 'Absolute' of an all-including mind encompassing all reality and thought. Pannenberg's Trinity affirms diversity, self-humbling in the face of the other, the very reverse of the domination model of God, the hostile stare, which postmodern theology rightly rejects in favour of a plural, integrationist view of God. As with Hegel, Pannenberg builds his case for God carefully and dialectically, finding Spirit at work at the heart of things and finding reductionist accounts of reality unconvincing. The heart of reality is however love, not mind, for Pannenberg. His tendency to appeal to the universal and the whole as his way of testing concepts may ultimately come at the logical price of individuality being endangered by the final end and the reign of the whole, the defining context for meaning, including individuals whose meaning, hence being, is given by ultimate meaning. Might there be a danger of the individual self finding its personhood and identity absorbed in that of the Son? This is far from Pannenberg's intention, but his system tends in that direction. Whether his eschatology protects against this is an interesting issue. It is to his 'final end' we now turn to end this treatment of Pannenberg's thought.

CONCLUDING WITH THE END

THE CREATIVE END

The final end of history will constitute the whole of history as God's self-disclosure, the decisive truth of all things will be revealed, which is the God of Jesus Christ, his love for his creation and his deity as Father, Son and Spirit making space for creaturely reality. Freedom and contingency of creation will be disclosed as rooted in the life of God, the inseparability of the particular and the universal, of persons in relation and not otherwise. Jesus' saying about finding and losing oneself has ontological significance, as Pannenberg says at the end of *Jesus God and Man,* all things are interrelated, indeed related so deeply as to be porous one to another as we grow and develop towards, and from, God the Father. This end is of course present already, proleptically, and so Pannenberg offers us thoroughgoing eschatology realized provisionally now, and this yields the anticipatory structure of all reality and personhood, on its way to becoming what it really is. Thoroughgoing eschatology gains its content from its preceding history, guided and given by God, who will confirm the Lordship of Jesus.

Until that day this Lordship will continue to be contested, such is the integration between the order of knowing, the order of being and the order of created being with divine being: God has freely chosen to allow himself, his truth, and his divine rule to be really historical and to divest himself of power until the eschaton. The meaning of the totality of – divinely inspired – history will decide who God most truly is, having freely allowed himself to be dependent on the outcome of history in Christ and the Spirit. The Father entrusts his deity to the Son. The end is vital to Pannenberg's whole theological vision, which is the same as his 'secular' vision, since the retroactive constitution of being from the end, back over the life lived towards that end, requires a specific eschatological end point as the basis for all meaning.

This retroactivity confirms that this was always going to have been the case, so the end is really the beginning, a loop linked with the beginning of God's purposes, revealed in the Christ event. In the drama of this looped history, God makes space for creation and allows it freely to pursue its destiny to the worship of the Father. This is not a doctrine of predestination from the past, but giving of freedom from the future. On this claim of eschatology over protology hangs Pannenberg's whole metaphysical structure. God is open to God, the economic Trinity to the essential Trinity, Jesus to the Father, all hangs in the balance until the glory and victory of Jesus at the resurrection, and then God's fullness, his true identity, his self-determination and sovereignty are established and confirmed. This confirmation comes through human interpretation of meaning as the events of Easter unfolded in their religious context, and this is not an inference from history (Robinson and Cobb 1967). Rather God is present in our experience and our subjective anticipations, 'history does not subsist independently over against God' (Robinson and Cobb 1967: 253), any more than humanity subsists over against history. We do not have a spectator standpoint from which to infer truths out of a constantly changing flow of temporal reality in all its provisionality: the finite is not independent over against God's action, and every insight is but a stage to a new insight (Pannenberg 1971a: 60).

This structure of world history is the same structure as that of human life with its provisional self providing stability through time to the experiencing ego as the human life moves forward to its destiny, at the same time receiving this destiny from the future. The eschaton will reveal who we really are, and this event will coincide with, perhaps be taken up into, the great act of revelation of total meaning and of the very being of the trinitarian God which has taken creation up into itself. Pannenberg has radically parted company with the Kantian tradition of the subject defining all things, the very being of a person can be constituted after death, as was that of Jesus, through the determination of that person's meaning – 'meaning' not in the existential subjectivist sense but in the historicist objective sense of meaning in context: as persons we are objective entities, ultimately defined by God as to our meaning and being. We interpret and are interpreted, provisionally then finally.

Individual identity

We have seen that Pannenberg argues for a real judgement at the end of things, that those who have grounded their lives on their self suffi-cient ego, closed off from concern with their true destiny, openness to God and the world, will suffer a final end. Totally egocentric, they have insulated themselves from God. Here Pannenberg seems theo-logically to underplay the Christian doctrine of the atonement as God's act for sinners, illustrated by the story of the thief on the cross next to Jesus, who is forgiven as he dies, notwithstanding his life of ego centric self-assertion. Pannenberg's doctrine of human becoming, its pattern of ego, provisional self and final person, overrides the sheer grace of God in Christ's death for us. But, on the other hand, he also offers a vision of human unification and cosmic unification at the eschaton. God has 'endured the pain of the negative' (Pannenberg 1971a: 249) and reconciled the finite present into his own free future.

Pannenberg stresses the immanence of the eternal in the flow of time: this participation will work the other way, and the temporal creature will find participation in the life of the eternal. God makes space for his creatures in the fulfilment of their destiny, a destiny gained by the Son. Christians, he says, 'expect a future in which all their temporal life will be permeated by praise of God and will be glorified as incorruptible fellowship with this eternal God' (Pannen-berg 1998: 602). Implied in this destiny of worship is an opening up of richness and wonder beyond what the totality of our lives have known. Here we see in a glass darkly. Pannenberg teaches that death for us is death, not the escape of a soul which survives, in neo-platonic fashion. When we die, we entrust ourselves, our persons, our very existence to God. We lay ourselves down in death with Jesus, in baptismal pattern. We are held by God in death: 'Herein the identity of creatures needs no continuity of their being on the time line, but is ensured by the fact that their existence is not lost in God's eternal present' (Pannenberg 1998: 606). The eschaton is very much the resurrection, beyond death, so that our death is part of our life destiny and meaning, a wider view of who we are than our conscious ego or soul. According to this very objective view of personhood, the self integrates all the experiences of the ego and holds them through time. It is itself held in God transformatively, and inte-grated into participation with the life of worship in the trinitarian life of glorification of the Father. Here our real self is revealed to us and implemented as we enter into the full rule of God, a kingdom of self-giving love and praise. If we have no open self at all, if our ego is turned in itself, it cannot receive participation in God's life and Spirit and so perishes: Pannenberg is not a universalist and seems resigned to the loss of those who fail to use their gift of freedom to humble themselves in trust before God.

Pannenberg finds Heidegger a very fruitful dialogue partner in the understanding of human beings facing up to the ultimate future, facing death as their final completedness, and living in the light of that. This is partly reflected in Pannenberg's view of our moving into the future with total trust. For Heidegger human life, *Dasein*, gains its meaning in the light of the completion of death. Pannenberg as a Christian regards death as not the final end. Death itself cannot give us our ultimate meaning and being, but God can (Pannenberg 1990: 84f.). The completedness of the human self, *Dasein*, is at the resurrection from the dead with Christ, not alone in death. God comes to us from the future with promise and love, we are not bravely left to be stirred from our complacency by the thought of death facing us moment by moment in Stoic fashion. Death does not itself, for Pannenberg, complete the ripening of our life, a final satisfying wholeness, it is a stage we pass through. We really do die and our identity is held in God and then given a new transfigured way of being at our rising to new life with Christ. God the Father really is the end: like Jesus we trust in his vindication and kindness as we die, and give ourselves, our whole lives, to him. Like Jesus, we distinguish ourselves from God, humble ourselves, and find ourselves as we truly are, our identities given and confirmed, read back over our lives, the mystery of the Spirit hiddenly present all along.

Corporate identity

Pannenberg's doctrine of the open-textured nature of all things, their openness to the future, their capacity to immerse themselves in the other and be taken up and forward in the process of history, this doctrine means that 'no man is an island unto himself', that we are all destined and orientated to personal society and social personality, to inner community with each other in God.

The essential future of the individual, on which depends the ultimate decision concerning the meaning of his life and the signification of individual elements in this life, cannot therefore be separated from the essential future of mankind as a whole. (Pannenberg 1971b: 202)

There is to be reconciliation and unity at the eschaton, when the Christ event will be fully realized for all reality. 'The prospect of a united human race emerges as an area of intersection and coincidence of the divine reality on the one hand and of the extrapolated tendencies of human history and even of the entire evolution of organic life on the other' (Pannenberg 1972c: 65). The Omega point of the eschaton, to use Theilhard de Chardin's term, will be the unity of humanity with God, the climax of human self-transcendence and mastery of the world in human freedom. The eschaton will consummate man's freedom and God's all-determining free reign. God will discover himself as this God, the Father in the Son and Spirit.

Here we may ask again whether Pannenberg's move against the ego as constitutive may lead to the danger of the human self being absorbed in a greater whole, whose identity flows from God, the source of self-differentiating unity. But the doctrine of Trinity saves Pannenberg from the question of whether human individuality is swamped by divine mind at this point, since the Trinity is itself a relational being and we are to be in Christ, who is in distinction from and union with the Father. Here Pannenberg's stress on particularity in relation to universality is maintained. If humanity is 'taken up' in Hegelian style into the Son then we are in danger of losing individual eschatology in all its diversity in favour of a unification of humans into a single differentiated entity: the sets of differentiations from the Father to the Son and the created order might sublimate 'upwards', and the Trinity is the way Pannenberg tries to hold the line here. The eschaton for a Christian theology needs to preserve and transfigure human identities as partners with God: this is clearly Pannenberg's aim, but there is a strong tide towards the universal eclipsing the particular, of this dialectic fusing, of unity synthesizing diversity.

BEING, ETERNITY AND TIME

God's eternity and future

Time and eternity figure constantly in Pannenberg's theological discussions, and while he reckons with the problems of simultaneity,[1] he believes that this phenomenon, so close to the idea of the eternal in his view, can embrace duration, and does not lead to a 'freezing of the frame'. He has used Augustine's famous treatment of hearing a melody to illustrate the wholeness and completeness of reality shaping and defining the course of history (Pannenberg 1990). Duration is real but is also bridged, diversity is held together by unity, the unity of the future wholeness which we anticipate. As we hear the melody, we are in the midst of its flow, and yet the overall shape of it gives it a structure and wholeness, and yet that will in fact be given to us at the end: the future whole suffuses the present and past. For Augustine our soul achieves a kind of enduring presence through the flux of time, remembering the past and anticipating the future, and this perception is faintly analogous to divine eternity where nothing fades away and the future is already present. Eternity is timeless for Augustine.

Pannenberg understands that the unity of temporal duration in fact arises because of the eternal participating in the flow of the multiplicity of time. Here he draws on the thought of Plotinus. He believes 'that the flow of temporal moments cannot be conceived at all without presupposing, with Plotinus, the eternal simultaneity of all that is separated within time' (Pannenberg 1990: 90). For Plotinus eternity is the whole of life in simultaneous presence; whereas life in time is successive, eternity is the totality of these events but now in simultaneity. Eternity for Plotinus, and Pannenberg, is the simultaneous whole of life, and this is constitutive of time itself, the cohesiveness of the succession of temporal processes. The eternal is present in the flow of time, as we saw in *What Is Man?* Pannenberg teaches that 'eternity is the truth of time, which remains hidden in the flux of time. Eternity is the unity of all time, but as such it simultaneously is something that exceeds our experience of time' (Pannenberg 1970a: 74). There is no conflict between eternity and time therefore, the latter is 'taken up' by the former, and we can view this again in an Hegelian light also:

The thought of eternity that is not simply opposed to time but positively related to it, embracing it in its totality, offers a paradigmatic illustration and actualization of the structure of the true Infinite which not just opposed to the infinite but also embraces its antithesis. (Pannenberg 1991: 408)

Eternity is constitutive of the totality of time that is differentiated from it, and we recall that the pain of the negative has been absorbed in the process of time by the Son, overcoming the antithesis to the Infinite. There is a positive relation of eternity to time, and the former suffuses the latter, to be revealed at the end of time as eternity which has included all time.

Pannenberg, however, finds no real eschatology in Plotinus, for whom humans are not striving in history to find their identity as they live towards the future of God's kingdom. Further Pannenberg wishes to assert that the future is real for God also, and there will be something new for God's future, albeit from God's future also. Likewise God's kingdom is still to come, while being proleptically here. Temporal events are to affect God's identity, as we have seen, for Pannenberg, and the eschaton will mean the actualization and self-realization of the Father, Son and Spirit, an event which will include the meaning of all history and disclosure of all identities. Divine eternity participates in time, while creating time: the Sonship of God faces the Fatherhood of the free God of the future, with the Spirit bringing forward events into their self-transcendence and movement towards their promised destinies. Pannenberg has so emphasized the inseparability of the economic and essential Trinity, insisting that the historical process really does affect the 'inner' being of God, the essential Trinity, that it seems difficult to introduce a notion of eternity that can transcend this integration of economy and essence. Yet eternity is distinct from time in its simultaneity of temporal succession – while being united with it out of his freedom not out of necessity, perhaps the key point he wishes to assert. God chooses to be this God and to create by way of self-investment into time, structured after his own personal-relational structure and through that structure as it runs through history in its dialectical synthesis.

God's eternity is complete, our time incomplete and so has an open future, God the Father. God however is the only future of God, he has no future other than himself. Aquinas spoke of God as the act of being itself, *esse subsistens*, so that God is nothing but the actuality of being, and Pannenberg compares this to his own view of the essence of God, having no future apart from his pure divinity itself. God is Lord of time whose future constitutes his present. Pannenberg does not accept Jenson's criticism of this claim that God's future is not distinct from his presence because that seems to lead back to the old idea of eternity as timeless presence: rather Pannenberg argues that the presence of God is different since it is his future, which means his total freedom. God, unlike us, has no future outside his own being. Here we must wonder at the limits of our language and experience in speaking of God, but Pannenberg has set the whole ontology of Trinity and creation up in this way that depends on tensed facts, the future particularly, as more than analogies. Is it really meaningful to speak of God's own future, which is not future to God? This question opens up deep and complex philosophical problems about time and in what sense time is a reality.[2] Pannenberg needs to address such problems, since his theology is utterly dependent on the concept of the future as a reality and on the end time as the point of meaning which will work retroactively to constitute the present.

At the eschaton the kingdom of God enters time, eternity being the future perfection of everything. Everything that occurs and perishes in time is preserved in God's eternity, which embraces all temporal events and identities and brings them to their final destiny, that of praising the Father with the Son in the Spirit. It seems that the economic Trinity includes the creation, overcoming death and giving it participation in the great symphony that is the very life of the essential Trinity. Here we do well to emphasize that since his early writings Pannenberg has stressed love as the basis of creation: 'God in his powerful future separates something new from himself and affirms it as a separate entity, thus, at the same time, relating it forward to himself' (Pannenberg 1969b: 70). And it is a great act of reconciling love, enacted in time at Easter, that completes this created order.

The doctrine of the Trinity is utterly crucial to this whole theological project of history, since it gives a living God as the essential Trinity, having eternal life and history in himself. The trinitarian distinctions are even 'based on the difference between future and present', ontologically not just for our human knowing. The Trinity is congruous with our history, and ascribes unity to the relational life of the persons, rather than a static monotheism of 'the dead or static unity of a supreme being as an existing entity indistinguishable within itself' (Pannenberg 1969b: 71). Pannenberg develops a whole ontology centred on this living Trinity which we find revealed in history and in the person of Jesus, a living God of a narrative kind who bestows the life of creatures and includes that life with his own, without dissolving the finite into the infinite. Pannenberg gives us a supremely living God so generous as to wish to confirm his own identity by his act of overflowing love in creation. For God the history of creation will run out, and thereby gain its meaning in eternity: but God in his essential Trinity will still have his own future, of which he is the Lord. God is this life, with relation and succession in his eternity, known however in simultaneity to God. Pannenberg teaches that unlike finite beings, God is the supreme observer so that God's eternity is 'simultaneous with all events in the strict sense' (Pannenberg 1994: 93). All events, past, present or future of whatever time frame are present to God, and embraced in a divine eternal present.

Static eternity for humanity?

When Pannenberg comes to consider what it means for a person to participate in God's wholeness, he understands it as the re-experiencing of one's past life from God's point of view. What was once experienced in the successiveness of time is now viewed from a new perspective, set in the context of the whole of history and comprehended in the eternal present of God, in which there is no distinction between past, present and future. We saw in *What is Man?* that 'eternity is the truth of time, which remains hidden in the flux of time' (Pannenberg 1970a: 74). In his recent work Pannenberg maintains this doctrine, speaking of the unifying of all individual moments of our life's history into the simultaneity of 'God's eternal present, to be seen from the standpoint of the divine ordaining' (Pannenberg 1998: 610).

John Hick describes this view as one of recapitulation (Hick 1976: 221–6) but Pannenberg thinks he is being misinterpreted, and writes of 'an element of compensation' within the transfiguration of newness of eschatological life' (Pannenberg 1998: 639). He argues that the eschatological concurrence of events and their meaning will in effect be a judgement, negative and positive, a purging away of what is negative and a promoting of what is good, in this crisis of transition and transfiguration. Reviewing one's life from God's perspective would open up possibilities and depths of experience that had been unknown before. It would not be a mere repetitive recapitulation. Pannenberg does not address Hick's demand that those whose lives were ones of terrible suffering should be given, in their new transfigured lives, new experiences which would entail, as creatures, successiveness and temporal life of some kind – the 'element of compensation' must be capable of being lived.

Hick is concerned about the lack of any really new experience after the eschaton for creaturely reality. This question relates to the issue of final meaning decisively constituting being and identity. Paul Fiddes criticizes Pannenberg here over whether it is doctrinally satisfactory that the end of time closes this wholeness into its final form, thus foreclosing on new experiences in the life of God after death. Meaning has reached 'closure', to use the postmodern concept, rather than opening up new possibilities for the redeemed human being in God. The future is not future any more to us, once we have arrived at our future perfect end (Fiddes 2000: 214–15). The self has found its fulfilment in personhood finally. Identity is reached. But why should this be frozen, rather than expanded, deepened, actualized in the Sonship of God, asks Fiddes. Pannenberg seems to have become imprisoned by his extremely strong view of divine simultaneity over against creaturely history and experience, God becomes the onlooker rather than the participatory creative life of the Trinity: Pannenberg's strongly relational view of the Trinity should be able to suggest ways of human experience being taken up, in unity but differentiation, into the life of God.

Pannenberg can certainly point to his constantly emphasized concept of the meaning of a person gaining in depth after individual death: the resurrection of Jesus shows that the meaning of the man Jesus did not close at his execution, rather its potential remained open to divine vindication. His understanding of the ego, the self and the person as a dynamic becoming into and from the future of God, *could* be developed after death because God's being does not freeze in a stasis, and therefore our life meaning is related to the relational life of the Trinity of love. Pannenberg has options open to develop, ironically some possibly along the lines of the healing process for the individual that are found in the redemptive act of writing, as portrayed in bell hooks' discovery of first person and third person remaking of personal identity, from future to past and back. Pannenberg with Jüngel (Jüngel 1975: 121–2), as Fiddes points out, has a vision of eternal destiny which fails to balance 'closure' with 'openness' because he conceives the whole as a simultaneity of time in which there can be no real development, adventure or progress. He also assumes that the whole as possessed and known by God is a sort of fixed maximum. God has perfect freedom in having no future outside himself, and no future that is different from his present.

But, with Fiddes, we can understand the wholeness of time as a healing in which there is not a total loss of successiveness, and the wholeness of life as a perfection which is ever expanding. Such a wholeness can still be the source of successive time as we know it in history; it can still transcend it and be retroactive upon it. We can think of examples of human life when a person is fraught with fear, paralysing her life, then she is assured and loved, liberated, and this changes everything, not only her future but her whole life and self is somehow exorcised and made whole. Karl Barth used the term 'the healing of time' (Barth 1957: 617–18), he has used the language of simultaneity while insisting that this is not a total absence of time but is 'God's time for us' which knits up our fallen time, in Christ.

Here it might be suggested that Pannenberg's idea of personhood, retroactively working back to create and recreate us, rather than only 'recapitulating us', might be paralleled, paradoxically perhaps, with a black feminist writer, bell hooks (sic).[3] She develops a theory of writing, in order best to portray personhood, by way of bring together narrative in the first person, then revisiting the same events but in third-person narrative. The meaning of her life gains richness, her self-understanding is more than merely the immediate experience of the present moment: she writes both forwards, then backwards in reflection, reading back a richer fuller being into who she already was, and is becoming. Vital to her story is her baptism in her black Baptist church in America (hooks 1997). An irony in this parallel is that Pannenberg attracts criticism from the 'post-modern' school as being an Enlightenment thinker, rationalistic and lacking in the sensitivities to the human condition, now being disclosed by feminist authors! hooks finds her true self, freedom and vindication, as she reads and writes her life story backwards and gains a true wholeness and 'real' self.

For Pannenberg baptism is our way of participating in Jesus as disciples, and the human experience of Jesus surely is to be shared and united to that of his own friends, not observed individually in simultaneity from the angle of the Father. Is there scope for the humanity of Jesus to allow Pannenberg to create space for human experience after the eschaton? The Spirit holds us after death, with Jesus, surrendered to the Father's love and care. This movement of love distinguishes itself from the Father and the Son, always opening up the Father–Son relationship in new ways to new depths and to a new future. God arguably continually becomes what he is.

Part of this future will be the inclusion of created beings within the divine life. The Spirit holds God open for a future which will be retroactive in God's self, making God what God already is.

Pannenberg can certainly point to his constantly emphasized concept of the meaning of a person – not meaning 'in' a person we note – gaining in depth after individual death: the resurrection of Jesus shows that the meaning of the man Jesus did not close at his execution, rather its potential remained open to divine vindication. Pannenberg's understanding of the ego, the self and the person as a dynamic becoming into and from the future of God, could be developed after death, because God's being does not freeze in a stasis, and our life's meaning is related to the relational life of the Trinity of love who in history embraced our humanity in his Son. Ultimately we face not the end, but the Father, and with Jesus in the Spirit. Frank J. Tippler rejects Hick's criticism of Pannenberg as unfair (Albright and Haugen 1997: 160). A philosopher of science and scientist, Tipler agrees with Pannenberg's eschatological ontology and theology, it makes perfect sense in his eyes to affirm the Omega Point as divinely raising the dead. For Tipler,

> the type of life enjoyed by the resurrected individuals is entirely at the discretion of the Omega Point, as is their resurrection in the first place; the human soul is not naturally immortal, for modern physics has shown that it dies with the brain. Thus, except for the conscious future act of the Omega Point, we would die never to rise again. The life of the resurrected dead could be as pointless as the scenario ridiculed by Hick, merely a replay of the original life, or it could be a life of continued individual becoming, an exploration into the inexhaustible reality which is the Omega Point (or even into purely sensual delights, such as pictured in the Garden of the Koran.) It is even possible for the Omega Point to guide each resurrected person, by means of consultation with each, into 'the perfection of the personal creature as a whole. (Albright and Haugen 1997: 160–1)

Tipler writes as a secular scientist, not a believer, but he finds Pannenberg's statements on reality and eschatology coherent with his own physics of the cosmos, one that involves the rise of the computer as to surpass the human mind and one that sees the end of homo sapiens, 'the heirs of our civilization must be another species' and so for that civilization ad infinitum into the Omega Point. 'We shall, so to speak, live again in the mind of God.' The Omega Point could retrieve our data and simulate us perfectly – Tipler's eschatology is wholly secular but he finds Pannenberg's claims entirely coherent and reasonable.

But ultimately, for Pannenberg, we participate in a life, not a closure of being as we discover and are given our true identity by the Father. We share in the Sonship of Jesus, and so we share in the worship of the Father in the Spirit, a doxological destiny of praise. Pannenberg in fact concludes his *Systematic Theology* on this very note, speaking of earthly praise of God by his creatures as anticipating 'the praise of the heavenly community of the perfected' (Pannenberg 1998: 646). Pannenberg's view of religious language has consistently been that it is primarily doxological, glorifying God (Pannenberg 1970b: 237). Pannenberg can surely argue that this heavenly praise does not indicate a foreclosure of experience, and in this way he might mitigate Fiddes' criticism. Pannenberg looks forward to 'the revelation of his love in the consummating of creation for participation in God's own eternal life' (Pannenberg 1998: 645). The meaning of our lives is given to us as individuals integrated with the human family, the body of Christ, a new personality of a corporate kind, transposed into a new experience of love and life, a way caught up in worship of the Father. Here surely is the full enrichment of human experience including succession, but perhaps akin to the epiphanic moment of hearing a wonderful piece of music and losing our sense of time, although 'it' still continues and in fact successiveness is essential to the music (Fiddes 2000: 139).

Therefore Pannenberg may need to consider developing a theology of the new way of being in and with God, or of being rather less agnostic about this. He says that the life of the future world is not the resumption and endless prolongation of this life, along the same temporal time line; it will unfold its dynamic through growth in the vertical dimension of our present life (Pannenberg 1972a: 175). Yet, as Fiddes argues, some form of duration and experience seems necessary in the new life within the eternity of God. It might even be suggested, perhaps provocatively, that 'closure' of life to new experience, as it reaches its future wholeness, equates more with Nietzsche's doctrine of the eternal recurrence, than to Christian worship! Pannenberg has not yet explained a way to integrate, or 'take up', ongoing openness into his eschatology, and suggest an openness which is enriched after the whole of earthly life gains its 'final' meaning, so that the sons and daughters of God can indeed be lost in wonder, love and praise, as he expects. He certainly intends no static idea of the afterlife, 'The transformation of our mortal life', he says in an early work, 'does not mean a frozen rigidity, as would be the case if eternity were to be viewed as timelessness' (Pannenberg: 1972a: 175); and he stresses the common resurrection of the dead rather than simply that of individuals – for the divine intention is the kingdom of God over all humanity. Our ultimate identity, constituted by the meaning of our lives, is given by the God of the future, and in context of our relationships with others. The problem is that our true identities are finally given, after their anticipatory becoming, at the eschaton, but then are formally at least given closure and the structure of openness and relationality finishes. Our eschatological life is a status conferred on us, rather than a new life given to us with God in covenant.

CONCLUSION – THE FUTURE PERFECTED

Here we reach the promised, or rather anticipated, end of our consideration of Pannenberg's magisterial work of theology, and the end is both his strength and it seems something of a problem, since when it is attained, having been anticipated, openness and creativity for the transfigured created order closes under the simultaneity of the divine observer. The eternal God has eternal life himself, and has his own future of which he is Lord, as was the case when he freely invested himself into human history and its unknown future, of which he was always Lord as Easter showed in temporal form. The whole theological structure, epistemologically and ontologically is one of meaning coming from the future, of openness to God's future, and the future is a tensed fact: when the future is no longer the future, which by definition has to be so, then the theological framework depends on Pannenberg's theology of eternity, which itself includes a future tense, but God's future and so under the divine Lordship. The life of the Trinity is a life of mutuality and love, the created order is given space in this life when eschatologized, but with a form of life which is no longer open for new and deeper experiences of the multi-dimensional God who is holding them in existence. This seems problematic as Fiddes points out, and not necessary. If indeed Pannenberg's doctrine of eschatologized humanity is not conceptually powerful, then it fails his own test as a falsifiable theological assertion. And of course Pannenberg stresses the provisionality of theological, as all other, theories, should new arguments or evidence arise to question the status quo, and it would be possible to adjust his view of simultaneity.

We could suggest that the doctrine of simultaneity reflects an Hegelian strand of logic which Pannenberg very deliberately uses throughout his theological exposition, and which in fact conflicts with his trinitarian ontology. Divine trinitarian life is not, Pannenberg emphatically stresses, a mind model, not the Hegelian absolute subjective substance rising above mutuality and love. The doctrine of simultaneity suggests not the participation and integration of the economic and essential Trinity set out by Pannenberg so much as a detached observer's all inclusive mind. Pannenberg's brilliant reappropriation of Hegel must run the risk of failing to control Hegel's logic at least in places, and this may have emerged with his doctrine of simultaneity.

Another facet of this problem of the actual eschaton and nature of redeemed humanity is the fact that a closed mode of being for eschatologized humanity conflicts surely with the ontological vision stated at the close of *Jesus God and Man* about the porous nature of things including us as we change and develop, as we immerse ourselves in 'the other' thus discovering ourselves and serving others simultaneously, the ontological application of Jesus teaching to 'die to live':

> Through giving up its particularity, everything is mediated with the whole and, transcending its finitude, with God, who nevertheless wanted this finitude to exist within the whole of his creation. That which lives must go outside itself to maintain itself; it finds its existence outside itself. At the highest level the same is true of human subjectivity, namely, it must empty itself to the world and the 'Thou' in order to win itself in the other . . . Jesus has made room for other men and forms of life in the uniqueness of their situations instead of making his particularity a universal law. (Pannenberg 1977b: 396)

Here is a vision of humanity reconciled to the Father through the life, death and resurrection of Jesus, affirming individuality and resisting the final Hegelian logic of universalizing the individual into the Absolute.

That is critically important for Pannenberg, he has deployed Hegelian ways of analysing our knowing and being, and his future orientation is his great bulwark against the evaporation of human individual minds into the inclusive embrace of the Absolute. Jesus, and his Hebraic eschatological context, reshape the Hegelian dialectics to avoid ultimate synthesis and *Aufhebung*, sublimation beyond personality, relationality, love in the trinitarian life Pannenberg affirms so strongly. Creaturely life therefore should be enriched by a deepening form of new life experience, a more corporate kind, but not dissolving individuality and not freezing life through a final given meaning. The justifying verdict will have been given, but new sanctified life needs to be developed, 'taken up' into communion with the God of communion and ever deeper richer self-openness and love. Worship must mean life and fullness, creaturely participation in the trinitarian life has to entail 'experiences' beyond those of purely finite existence.

Pannenberg's theology is articulated in terms of time and tense. It is a theology of the future perfect tense. History moves forward towards the anticipated end time, the point of meaning and truth, which are however present proleptically already and revealed to be so at Easter in the resurrection of Jesus, the event in context giving forth its inherent meaning. E. H. Carr's dictum about truth emerging, as the future reveals what is convincing and what falls away, shows that this is a plausible world view, although for him the Judaeo-Christian eschatology of the Last Judgement is precisely a myth to illustrate this structure. Pannenberg's theology seeks to convince such cultured despisers of religion that the structure of reason in time is rooted in God, not pure chance, and that the proleptic structure of history and meaning is a revelation of the divine itself. History, for Pannenberg is open and yet when it arrives at its destination, is seen always as never having a different outcome since God is Lord of the history he freely created, and freely entered. This reveals the eternity of God also: God has eternity, with its future, but is Lord of that future, thus stepping outside of tense at the ultimate point. God is self-defining as having a future which is free and fixed.

This shape of history, with the Father as its future and yet Lord of that future, can contrast with Moltmann's theology in seeming less powerful as a statement of divine protest or empathy or judgement on sin and suffering in the world. Milbank makes this contrast:

> For Pannenberg also, the Spirit represents the moment of resolution after the ambiguous appearance of God under the form of sin, suffering and death. With more consistency and insight than

Moltmann, he retains the logic of substantial relations with respect to historical becoming, such that the Son and the Spirit are 'always already' present as an anticipation of the future which alone finally defines their subsistent content . . .. This however tends to entail a weakening of Moltmann's tragic, staurological perspective, in favour of a developmental immanence of the final, peaceful outcome. (Milbank 1997: 180–1)

Pannenberg's historicist economic trinitarianism of the future perfect may lack the genuine shock and trauma of the death of Christ, the actual experiencing by God of human suffering in the person of the Son. For Pannenberg the 'meaning of the event' and its concept is to the fore rather than the act of the Son in relation to the Father in the Spirit, and the cosmic impact of this, theologized in Colossians as the very centre of divine redemption: 'making peace by the blood of his cross' (Col. 1.15–20 RSV). The holy *act* of the holy loving God against sin and evil, at the shocking cost of Calvary in the midst of the sin of history, passing judgement upon it – that Evangelical, and indeed Catholic, not to say Lutheran, stress at the heart of the Gospel, seems faintly heard. The synthesis of the past moving into the future seems to eclipse the act of the trinitarian God in time for his creation, a different eschatology breaking into a world of chaos and misery and disobedience by the Lord of vineyard.

If my understanding of Pannenberg's ontology is correct, and meaning does constitute being, as it constituted Jesus the divine Son, then this tendency to read history as yielding meaning in context rather than as the personal journeys of people through the 'blood, toil, tears and sweat' of life, will tend to evaporate personal passion in favour of structure, in this case proleptic structure, rolling forwards with its energy from and to the giving future.

Jacqui Stewart (Stewart 2000: 152) cites Gillian Rose's criticism of Pannenberg along such lines, saying that Pannenberg attempts to escape from the omnipresence and determinism of the Hegelian system. This he fails to do so because in his attempt to locate the possibility of the truly novel in God, as grounding the unity of contingency and continuity, he postulates an unfolding of history and truth in which everything becomes congruent. The ground of this congruence is also the source of all action, so that no real contradiction can ever occur, 'development does not presuppose aporia but excludes it'.[4] The theological historicism of the future perfect disguises a smooth development of synthesis, without sufficient clashes, as a Christian view of history taking evil totally seriously would give – notably of Calvary. Nevertheless, Jacqui Stewart cites Anthony Thiselton as holding that Pannenberg does succeed (Stewart 2000: 152), but thinks that he stresses structure and system over 'life world', the real world of social life and its toils which break structural analysis open so often. This line of questioning, the lack of the genuinely tragic passion and agony at the heart of the theology of history, must again relate to the Hegelian logic taken up by Pannenberg and its emphasis on structure and pattern through real history of real people.

Pannenberg's work to theology is an immense gift and resource, a patient and meticulously argued case of total consistency, taking up New Testament eschatology in the most interesting way and developing all the major doctrines of the Christian faith in an indisputably intriguing and often convincing way. Pannenberg's future orientation of reality has been a stimulus of the strongest kind, shaking up conventional theology and offering interpretations of apocalyptic which are much needed. His constant way of thinking has been to assert a hypothesis and then formally allow the challenges of secular thought to have their say and to become dialogue partners. Theology is therefore provisional, new evidence may arise to bring down the theological house, and Pannenberg would have to evacuate. This is the great defence he has to those who accuse him of being an Enlightenment thinker, modern, but not postmodern, not sufficiently pluralistic, still under the illusion that the grand narrative is available.

Shults is surely correct to defend him as 'post foundationalist' (Shults 1999) rather than 'foundationalist': God is the centre of his theology, the relational and ultimately mysterious God whose being is Father, Son and Spirit, in subsistent relationality. Being is relational, is love and self-giving. This is no rationalistic foundation, but an invitation to participate in life and in love. Epistemologically, as we have seen, he is close to non-foundational and non-relativist historical thinkers such as E. H. Carr with his understanding of reason in time confirming or rejecting current interpretations of reality. Pannenberg's theology takes us ultimately to praise and worship: to be part of the divine relationality of mutual serving and self-humbling. Self-differentiation means that this is no oppressive grand narrative being imposed on the world, rather a humble act of divine generosity and sustaining. It may even be possible to take the postmodernist critics at their word and point to the divine life of differentiation as difference, continual pointing away from person to person, to the other, to the new. 'Not in himself, but in the other, the Spirit is with himself'. History and meaning is provisional, in his theology, is indeed 'deferred' and so in strict accordance with the strict criteriological canons of Derridean orthodoxy: Derrida's theory of multiplicity, of course, is a unified theory itself. For Pannenberg the ultimate unity of the diversity of the world is the diversity in unity of the Trinity. The Father entrusts the created order to the Son in the Spirit, indeed entrusts his very deity to them.

Pannenberg offers us a subtle Christian trinitarian theological ontology working off an Hegelian base and seeking to revise it through a profound engagement with the figure of Jesus in his thought context, particularly apocalyptic, in continual dialogue with the secular world, since this is God's world. Perplexing at times he certainly is, and any thinker treating time and eternity probes the most difficult of subjects, but he opens up problems and offers new horizons of understanding – offering them in a spirit of provisionality.

NOTES

INTRODUCTION

[1] 'It is in fact hard to imagine a more emphatically intellectual path to Christian affirmation than the one travelled by Pannenberg' (Pannenberg 1969b: 15).

[2] Representative examples of Hegelian influence on British theology at that time can be seen in William Sanday's *Christologies Ancient and Modern* (Sanday 1910: 59–109), and Edward Caird 's *Hegel* (Caird 1883). See also J. B. Baillie's article 'Hegel' (Baillie 1913: 568–87). Helpful treatments of Hegelian influence on theology include Claude Welch in his *Protestant Theology in the Nineteenth Century* vol. 1 (Welch 1972), John Baillie in his *The Idea of Revelation in Recent Thought* (Baillie 1956). Karl Barth in his *Protestant Theology in the Nineteenth Century* (1972: 384–421) and Paul Tillich in his *Perspectives on Nineteenth and Twentieth Century Protestant Theology* (Tillich 1967: 71–207) give their own contrasting analyses of Hegelian thought. See also Jörg Splett 'Relation' (Splett 1970: 240–2), Alois Halder 'Idealism' (Halder 1969: 86–91), and Walter Kern 'Identity-Philosophy' (Kern 1969: 91–4). Hans Küng is a superb expositor of Hegelian thought in relation to Christian theology; see, *Does God Exist?* (Küng 1980: 129–69) and also his monograph *The Incarnation of God* (Küng 1987).

CHAPTER 3

[1] This Hegelian move of 'taking up', '*Aufhebung*', suffuses Pannenberg's thought, notwithstanding his robust defence against speculative Hegelianism, a defence resting on appeal to actual historical occurrence coupled with divine freedom and futurity coming to finite history 'from before'.

[2] Quoting Hegel: *Lectures on the Philosophy of Religion* vol. III pp. 24f. This was also quoted earlier on p. 182, with 'submerged' translated as 'immersed' – probably a better translation.

CHAPTER 4

[1] W. Pannenberg *Grundfragen Systematischer Theologie Geammelt Aufsätze Band 2, Göttingen:* 1980. This collection of essays is as yet not translated

for publication in English, and is not to be confused with *Basic Questions in Theology* vols 1–2 discussed above. These essays include: '*Der Gott der Geschichte*' (1980: 112–28); '*Die Subjektivität Gottes und die Trinitätslehre*' (1980: 101); '*Person und Subjekt*'; '*Christologie und Theologie*'.

2 Graham J. Watts has produced a fine study of Pannenberg's doctrine of the Spirit, noting the influence of Hegel's philosophical idea of the infinite on Pannenberg at this point (Watts 2005: 123–63).

3 Pannenberg detects the influence of the nineteenth-century theologian August Isaac Dorner in Barth at this point (Pannenberg 1980: 98–9).

4 Here the full import of Pannenberg's foundational work is seen: 'One can think of revelation in the strict sense only if the special means by which God becomes manifest, or the particular act by which he proves himself, is not seen as distinct from his own essence.' (Pannenberg 1969a: 7).

CHAPTER 5

1 See Chapter 4 above.

CONCLUDING WITH THE END

1 'The concept of absolute simultaneity has run into difficulties from the standpoint of relativity theory. For many observers there can be no strict simultaneity in many reference systems because determining time depends on light. Yet this does wholly eliminate simultaneity.' (Pannenberg 1994: 91).

2 See 'The Unreality of Tense' by Hugh Mellor (Mellor 1997: 47–59).

3 Bell hooks spells her name in lower case very deliberately.

4 Quoted by Jacqui A. Stewart op cit, from Gillian Rose *The Broken Middle* (Rose 1992: 7).

BIBLIOGRAPHY

Albright, C. R. and Haugen, J. (eds) (1997) *Beginning with the End: God, Science, and Pannenberg.* Chicago: Open Court.

Aulen, G. (1931) *Christus Victor.* London: SPCK.

Baillie, D. M. (1948) *God was in Christ.* London: Faber.

Baillie, J. (1956) *The Idea of Revelation in Recent Thought.* London: Oxford University Press.

Baillie, J. B. (1913) 'Hegel', in (ed. Hastings, J.) *Hastings Encyclopaedia of Religion and Ethics* vol. 6. Edinburgh: T&T Clark, pp. 568–87.

Barrett, C. K. (1973) *A Commentary on the First Epistle to the Corinthians* (2nd edn). London: A&C Black.

Barth, K. (1956) *Church Dogmatics* vol. 4/1 (eds Bromiley, G. W. and Torrance, T. F.). Edinburgh: T&T Clark.

Barth, K. (1957) *Church Dogmatics* vol. 2/1 (eds Bromiley, G. W. and Torrance, T. F.). Edinburgh: T&T Clark.

Barth, K. (1975) *Church Dogmatics* vol. 1/1 (2nd edn Bromiley, G. W. and Torrance, T. F.). Edinburgh: T&T Clark.

Barth, K. (1972) *Protestant Theology in the Nineteenth Century.* London: SCM Press.

Burhenn, H. (1972) 'Pannenberg's Argument for the Historicity of the Resurrection', *Journal of the American Academy of Religion* 40: 375.

Caird, E. (1883) *Hegel.* Edinburgh and London: William Blackwood and Sons.

Carr, E. H. (1961) *What is History?* Harmondsworth: Penguin.

D'Costa, G. (ed.) (1990) *Christian Uniqueness Reconsidered.* Maryknoll, NY: Orbis books.

Eliot, T. S. (1944) 'East Coker', in *The Four Quartets.* London: Faber.

Fiddes, P. S. (2000) *The Promised End.* Oxford: Blackwell Publishers.

Forsyth, P. T. (1938) *The Work of Christ.* London: Independent Press.

Galloway, A. D. (1973) *Wolfhart Pannenberg.* London: Allen & Unwin.

Grenz, S. (2005) *Reason for Hope: The Systematic Theology of Wolfhart Pannenberg* (2nd edn). Grand Rapids: Eerdmans.

Halder, A. (1969) 'Idealism', in (ed. Rahner, K.) Sacramentum Mundi vol. 3. London: Burns & Oates.

Hegel, G. W. F. (1977) *Hegel's Phenomenology of Spirit.* Oxford: Oxford University Press [German edn 1807].

Hegel, G. W. F. (1988) *Lectures on the Philosophy of Religion* (ed. Hodgson, P. C.) Berkeley: University of California Press [German edn 1827].

Hegel, G. W. F (1998) *Lectures on the Philosophy of Religion* vol. III. (ed. Hodgson, P. C.). Berkeley: University of California Press.

Heidegger, M. (1962) *Being and Time.* London: SCM Press.

Hick, J. (1976) *Death and Eternal Life.* London: Collins.

hooks, b. (1997) *Wounds of Passion.* New York: Owl Books.

Hunsinger, G. (2004) 'The Daybreak of the New Creation: Christ's Resurrection in Recent Theology', *Scottish Journal of Theology* 57: 2, 163–81.

Jüngel, E. (1975) *Death: The Riddle and The Mystery.* Edinburgh: St Andrew Press.

Kern, W. (1969) 'Identity-Philosophy', in (ed. Rahner, K.) *Sacramentum Mundi* vol. 3. London: Burns & Oates.

Küng, H. (1980) *Does God Exist?* London: Collins.

Küng, H. (1987) *The Incarnation of God.* Edinburgh: T&T Clark.

Lapide, P. (1984) *The Resurrection of Jesus – A Jewish Perspective.* London: SPCK.

Macquarrie, J. (1981) *Twentieth Century Religious Thought* (revised edn). London: SCM Press.

McGrath, A. E. (1986) *The Making of Modern German Christology: From the Enlightenment to Pannenberg.* Oxford: Blackwell.

McKenzie, D. (1980) *Wolfhart Pannenberg & Religious Philosophy.* Washington DC: University Press of America.

Mellor, D. H. (1997) 'The Unreality of Tense', in (eds Le Poidevin, R. and MacBeath, M.) *The Philosophy of Time.* Oxford: Oxford University Press.

Milbank, J. (1997) *The World Made Strange.* Oxford: Blackwell Publishing.

Mostert, C. (2002) *God and the Future: Wolfhart Pannenberg's Eschatological Doctrine of God.* London: T&T Clark.

Newman, J. H. (1845) *An Essay on the Development of Doctrine: An Hypothesis to Account for a Difficulty.* London: James Toovey.

Pannenberg, W. (1957–65) 'Person', in (ed. Galling, K.) *Die Religion in Geschichte und Gegenwart. dritte Auflage,* V, Tübingen: J. C. B. Mohr, pp. 230–5.

Pannenberg, W. (1969a) *Revelation as History* [with Rolf Rendtorff, Trutz Rendtorff, and Ulrich Wilckens] (2nd edn). Transl. David Granskow. New York: Macmillan.

Pannenberg, W. (1969b) *Theology and the Kingdom of God* (ed. Neuhaus, R. J.). Philadelphia: Westminister Press.

Pannenberg, W. (1970a) *What Is Man?* Philadelphia: Fortress Press.

Pannenberg, W. (1970b) *Basic Questions in Theology* vol.1. London: SCM Press.

Pannenberg, W., Braaten Carl E. and Dulles Avery (1970c) *Spirit, Faith and the Church.* Philadelphia: Westminster Press.

Pannenberg, W. (1971a) *Basic Questions in Theology* vol. 2. London: SCM Press.

Pannenberg, W. (1971b) *The Idea of God and Human Freedom: Basic Questions in Theology.* London: SCM Press.

Pannenberg, W. (1972a) *The Apostles' Creed.* London: SCM Press.
Pannenberg, W. (1972b) 'The Doctrine of the Spirit and the Task of a Theology of Nature', *Theology*, 75: 8–21.
Pannenberg, W. (1972c) 'Future and Unity', in (ed. Cousins, E. H.) *Hope and the Future of Man.* Philadelphia: Fortress.
Pannenberg, W. (1972d) 'A Theological Conversation with W Pannenberg', in *Dialog*, xi, 286–95.
Pannenberg, W. (1976) *Theology and the Philosophy of Science.* London: Darton, Longman and Todd.
Pannenberg, W. (1977a) *Faith and Reality.* London: Search Press, 1977. Philadelphia: Westminster Press.
Pannenberg, W. (1977b) *Jesus God and Man* (2nd edn). London: SCM Press.
Pannenberg, W. (1977c) *Human Nature, Election and History.* Philadelphia: Westminster Press.
Pannenberg, W. (1980) *Grundfragen Systematischer Theologie,* Gesammelte Aufsätze Band 2, Göttingen: Vandenhoeck und Ruprecht.
Pannenberg, W. (1981) *Ethics.* Philadelphia: Westminster Press.
Pannenberg, W. (1985) *Anthropology in Theological Perspective.* Edinburgh: T&T Clark.
Pannenberg, W. (1988) 'Revelation in Early Christianity', in (ed. Evans, G. R.) *Christian Authority: Essays in Honour of Henry Chadwick.* Oxford: Clarendon Press, pp. 76–85.
Pannenberg, W. (1990) *Metaphysics and the Idea of God.* Edinburgh: T&T Clark.
Pannenberg, W. (1991) *Systematic Theology* vol. 1. Edinburgh: T&T Clark.
Pannenberg, W. (1994) *Systematic Theology* vol. 2. Edinburgh: T&T Clark.
Pannenberg, W. (1998) *Systematic Theology* vol. 3. Edinburgh: T&T Clark.
Pannenberg, W. (2000) *Natur und Mensch – und die Zukunft der Schöpfung. Beitrage zur Systematischen Theologie Band 2.* Göttingen: Vandenhoeck & Ruprecht.
Polkinghorne, J. (2001) 'Fields and Theology: A Response to Wolfhart Pannenberg', in *Zygon* 36: 4.
Robinson, J. M. and Cobb, J. B. (eds) (1967) *Theology as History.* New York: Harper and Row.
Rose, G. (1992) *The Broken Middle: Out of Our Ancient Society.* Oxford: Blackwell.
Rumscheidt, M. H. (ed.) (1972) *Revelation and Theology: An Analysis of the Barth-Harnack Correspondence.* Cambridge: Cambridge University Press.
Sanday, W. (1910) *Christologies Ancient and Modern.* Oxford: Oxford University Press, pp. 59–109.
Schleiermacher, F. (1928) *The Christian Faith.* Edinburgh: T&T Clark § 89 [German edn 1830].
Schwöbel, C. (2006) 'Wolfhart Pannenberg', in (eds Ford, D. and Muers, R.) *The Modern Theologians* (3rd edn). Oxford: Blackwell, pp. 129–46.
Shults, F. L. (1999) *The Postfoundationalist Task of Theology.* Eerdmans: Grand Rapids.

Splett, J, (1970) 'Relation', in (ed. Rahner, K.) *Sacramentum Mundi* vol. 5. London: Burns & Oates.

Stewart, J. A. (2000) 'Reconstructing Science and Theology', in *Postmodernity: Pannenberg, Ethics and the Human Sciences.* Aldershot: Ashgate.

Tillich, P. (1967) *Perspectives on Nineteenth and Twentieth Century Protestant Theology* (ed. Carl, E. B.). London: SCM Press, pp. 71–207.

Tipler, F. J. (1997) '*The Omega Point as Eschaton*', in (eds Albright, C. R. and Haugen, J.) *Beginning with the End: God, Science, and W. Pannenberg.* Chicago: Open Court.

Vermes, G. (1993) *The Religion of Jesus the Jew.* London: SCM Press.

Watts. G. (2005) *Revelation and the Spirit.* Milton Keynes: Paternoster Press.

Welch, C. (1972) *Protestant Theology in the Nineteenth Century* vol. 1. New Haven and London: Yale University Press, chs 4, 7 and 13.

Young, F. (1991) *The Making of the Creeds.* London: SCM Press.

Zizioulas, J. D. (1985) *Being as Communion.* Crestwood, NY: St. Vladimir's Seminary Press.

INDEX

creation 12, 33, 58, 61, 80, 87, 88,
90, 95, 98, 102–10, 114–18,
125–9, 133, 135–59, 160, 161,
167, 168, 172–6

Dasein 163
death 13, 15, 17, 29, 39–49, 69–79,
84–101, 106, 111–19, 128,
141–3, 149, 161–3, 167, 169,
170–6
destiny 14, 58, 61, 64, 65, 72, 87,
88, 89, 109, 132–7, 139,
140–8, 150, 158, 161, 162,
167, 169, 172
determinism 26, 29, 153, 176
dialectic 1, 4, 5, 15, 24, 26, 42, 46,
47, 60, 62, 63, 67, 70, 75, 79,
81, 82, 85, 99, 100, 101, 106,
112–17, 121, 124, 130,
143–50, 151, 156, 158, 164,
166, 175
Dilthey, W. 17
Dorner, I. 180
doxology 107, 172
dualism 3, 5, 11, 31, 37, 45, 63, 72,
105, 109, 113, 133, 136, 156

eccentricity/exocentricity 27, 110,
141, 148, 149
economic Trinity 62, 63, 86, 87,
100, 108, 109, 111, 112, 114,
116, 117, 120, 130, 131, 161,
166, 167, 174, 176
ego 122, 123, 124, 130, 141, 142,
143, 145, 146, 147, 148, 149,
161, 162, 163, 164, 169, 171
election 38, 92, 103, 105
Enhypostasia 100, 101
Enlightenment 5, 8, 22, 31, 51, 69,
96, 105, 124, 170, 177
entropy 148, 156
epistemology 1, 3, 5, 29, 31, 35, 42,
43, 46, 52, 53, 63, 64, 82, 114,

130, 136, 143, 151, 156, 157,
173, 177
eschaton/eschatology 1, 13–17,
20–3, 33, 36–40, 45, 47, 49,
50–65, 71–9, 82–9, 95, 98,
101–19, 126, 128, 131, 135,
144, 145, 147, 151, 159,
160–4, 166–77
essence 10, 11, 12, 32, 34, 38, 45,
47, 49, 66, 71, 75, 77, 78, 79,
80, 81, 82, 83, 84, 85, 86, 87,
89, 91, 93, 97, 98, 99, 100,
101, 112, 116, 118, 120, 121,
125, 131, 150, 166, 172, 180
essential or immanent, Trinity 111,
112, 114, 116, 117, 161, 166,
167, 168, 174
estrangement 149
eternity/eternal 10, 16, 26, 68, 77,
80, 82, 83–94, 97–101, 106–8,
110–16, 119–20, 127–34,
137–9, 141–77
evil 69, 94, 111, 148, 149, 176, 177
evolution 137, 152, 153, 153, 164
existential 21, 31, 161

fall/fallen 149, 150, 170
feminist 132, 158, 170
Feuerbach, L. 55
Fichte, J. G. 121, 122
Fiddes, P. S. 169, 170, 172, 173, 181
field 1, 22, 42, 44, 56, 96, 120, 125,
139, 149, 152, 154, 155, 156,
157, 183
Forsyth, P. T. 95, 181
freedom 3, 4, 11, 14, 21, 26, 28, 29,
36, 55, 63, 71, 85, 95, 98, 99,
103, 114, 115, 126, 127, 134,
136, 137, 138, 139, 140, 147,
153, 160, 161, 163, 164, 166,
169, 170, 179
future 1, 11, 13–18, 22, 26–30, 36,
39–49, 50–6, 60–7, 70–7, 78,